How the Aid Industry Works

How the Aid Industry Works

*An Introduction
to International Development*

Arjan de Haan

Kumarian Press
An Imprint of Stylus Publishing

How the Aid Industry Works
Published in 2009 in the United States of America by Kumarian Press, 22883 Quicksilver Drive, Sterling, VA 20166 USA.

The text of this book is set in 10.5/13 Janson Text.

Editing and book design by Joan Weber Laflamme, jml ediset.
Proofread by Beth Richards.
Index by Robert Swanson.

Printed in the United States of America by Maple-Vail. Text printed with vegetable oil-based ink.

∞ The paper used in this publication meets the minimum requirements of the American National Standard for Information Sciences—Permanence of Paper for printed Library Materials, ANSI Z39.48–1984

Library of Congress Cataloging-in-Publication Data

Haan, Arjan de.
    How the aid industry works: an introduction to international development / By Arjan de Haan.
        p. cm.
    Includes bibliographical references and index.
    ISBN 978-1-56549-287-5 (pbk. : alk. paper) — ISBN 978-1-56549-288-2 (cloth : alk. paper)
1. International economic relations. 2. Economic assistance—Developing countries. 3. Economic assistance—International cooperation. 4. Development economics. 5. Developing countries—Foreign economic relations. I. Title.
    HF1411.H217 2009
    3389109172'4—dc22.

                                                                    2009017483

Contents

Boxes, Figures, and Tables

Preface

There is no lack of writings on international development. Recent publications such as Jeffrey Sachs's on how the end of poverty can be achieved, former World Bank economist Bill Easterly's criticism of the optimism about what aid can accomplish, and the increased openness of international financial institutions (IFIs) that NGOs successfully advocated for have all contributed to the enormous amount of information that has become available. A growing number of think tanks are regularly producing technical material on a range of aid issues, trends, and modalities, and the number of acronyms used in the day-to-day language of practitioners is overwhelming and ever expanding.

How the Aid Industry Works is an introductory text that provides an overview of the practices of the "industry" of international development. It thus intends to fill a gap in the literature on international development. It focuses on a basic description of aid practices: how they evolved, what they are, experiences, and debates around them. The book tries to cover a wide range of aid agencies, including those sharing the "European consensus," those of the United States, and those of the newcomers, particularly China. Throughout the text, descriptions of practices and debates are illustrated with real-life examples from projects and programs in specific contexts. Many of the examples are from India and China, because of my personal experience, though these are by no means typical developing countries. As an introductory text *How the Aid Industry Works* will guide the reader to further readings, both academic development studies texts and materials produced by development agencies themselves.

The fascinating experience of teaching a course on the practices of international development to third-year undergraduate students at the University of Guelph, Ontario, has provided the main motivation for and the concept of the book. I experienced an acute lack of basic texts for the purpose of introducing students to the practices of international development. Students, while usually committed to the cause of international development, are generally aware of the critique of international development but have an insufficient basis to assess that critique. A desire to learn more about the practices and to gain insight into the many different approaches was expressed consistently by students.

The material herein is thus aimed at students in advanced undergraduate and graduate courses on international development. As Lawrence Haddad's summary note of the IDS Sussex roundtables in 2006, for example, demonstrates, this is an ever-growing field, and the number of courses in Europe and North America is increasing. Development practitioners, administrators, and managers may also find this book helpful as an orientation to the complex aid industry.

The text is as "neutral" as possible; that is, it provides the arguments of proponents and opponents. But it is also analytical, helping the reader to understand the practices from different perspectives. The book is neither a defense nor a critique of development aid; it is neither optimistic nor pessimistic. Given the enormous diversity of development practices, it may be impossible to assess whether aid "works." I have much sympathy with many of the critiques of international development. More important, I strongly believe there needs to be more systematic and well-informed commentary in order to make aid more accountable.

But the industry has well-documented successes, even if always incomplete. Aid has contributed to the Green Revolution and to combating diseases such as smallpox and polio. UN agencies have provided enormous support to refugees. Private companies have contributed to eradicating river blindness. I believe that aid programs in China have helped improve poor people's lives faster than they would have been improved without the presence of aid agencies. I have worked with many people in the aid industry, many of whom are extremely committed and have provided significant contributions that are recognized by partners in poor parts of the world. International organizations have contributed a great deal—though perhaps not enough, or not quickly enough—to tackling the HIV/AIDS crisis, which is often confronted with resistance in the North as well as among governments in the South. While the World Bank has provided misguided advice at times, and there is little doubt that it needs serious reforms, for example, in the selection of its president, it is not responsible for poverty in the countries to which it lends. I believe Sebastian Mallaby's observation that "most Bank staffers had joined the institution because they wanted to fight poverty" (2005, 47). I do not think that NGOs are generally better, or worse, in providing aid. This book tries not to take sides but rather to help readers form their own opinion.

Finally, a few words about the choice of the title, particularly the reference to the aid industry. The world of development or international aid, in my experience, is indeed—and should be—an industry, that is, a branch of economic activity. Although it uses public (tax payers' and voluntarily donated) money, it disburses this in a professional way, with generally strict procedures, reporting, and professional administrators, many of whom have a long-running career in international development. While many of these officials are well paid, and indeed often fly business class, most of the people in the industry are extremely committed and indeed "industrious."

Second, I use the word *aid* rather than *development* because while the desired outcome of the industry is development, the focus of this book is how the industry contributes to this, and this is mostly through providing financial assistance. Many argue that the word *aid* suggests an imbalance in power relations. I agree, and I strongly feel that the relationships need to become much more equal, a process that I am fortunate to be witnessing in China at the moment. But as I try to show, the way this industry works is still primarily by disbursing aid, and many of its advocates continue to express paternalistic attitudes. There is still some way to go for the industry to become one of *development*. In any case, merely changing the language will not change the practices.

Acknowledgments

Students of the international development program at the University of Guelph, Ontario, motivated me to write this book. During my short period there I continued to be amazed by their interest in and commitment to international development issues. Graham Kendra was one of them, and she provided excellent help in preparing a reference list that helped to prepare the text of this book.

When I left Guelph, I moved to China, where I found the emergence of a new world of international aid, with a South-South emphasis, and a historically unique transition from being an aid recipient to being an aid donor. Much inspiration for my continued writing came from colleagues and friends like Qiao Jianrong, Sun Xuebing, Sarah Cook, James Keeley, Li Xiaoyun, and Huang Chengwei. I presented the introductory chapter at the International Poverty Reduction Centre, China, and benefited from the many questions and comments. Adrian Davis and John Warburton, both at the Department for International Development (DFID) China, commented on the introductory chapter, and Ellen Wratten as my head of profession at DFID provided moral support for the continued writing of the book. My venture into writing may appear slightly outside the organization's corporate priorities, but I have found inspiration for continued writing about development within DFID.

Shahin Yaqub provided detailed and extremely useful comments on material I sent him, and he symbolizes much of what I appreciate about the global lives we lead. Rosalind Eyben, my mentor in the aid industry and great advocate of social development concerns, provided detailed comments on chapters and very generously shared her written work. Paul Shaffer provided very useful comments particularly on the chapter on monitoring, and over the years I have learned much from his work on promoting combined methods of poverty analysis. In this book I draw freely on the joint work with and ideas of DFID colleague Max Everest-Phillips on the politics of aid. I presented part of this book's text at the Institute of Social Studies in The Hague and learned much about the importance of acknowledging the position from which one writes; this book is indeed written from the narrow perspective of an insider.

It is important also to acknowledge the many sources on which I have drawn freely and hence my debt to the many people who work to enable access to the material that informs writings like this, and more important, the knowledge of practitioners around the world. In particular, without information sources like ELDIS, which provides summarized documents from over seventy-five-hundred development organizations, and that of GSDRC (Governance and Social Development Resource Centre), I would not have been able to produce this text.

I have greatly benefited from the encouragement of Jim Lance, editor, and the patient work and support of Erica Flock, production editor, at Kumarian. I owe a similar kind of gratitude to Vanda Morgan for her coaching and teaching me to focus on the essentials.

Finally, as always, my family has had to put up with yet another writing project. Nanaki and Sohail got less time to cycle around the house and play baseball from me than they deserve. My partner, Paramjit, may never get used to the constant banging on computer key boards, and rightly so.

Acronyms

AfDB	African Development Bank
ADB	Asian Development Bank
CDD	Community Driven Development
CDF	Comprehensive Development Framework
CEDAW	Convention on Elimination of All Forms of Discrimination against Women
CERF	Central Emergency Response Fund (UN)
CGD	Center for Global Development
CGI	Clinton Global Initiative
CGIAR	Consultative Group on International Agricultural Research
CIDA	Canadian International Development Agency
CRC	Convention on the Rights of the Child
DAC	Development Assistance Committee
Danida	Danish International Aid Agency
DFID	Department for International Development
EC	European Commission
ESAF	Enhanced Structural Adjustment Facility
ESF	Emergency Social Fund (Bolivia)
Eurodad	European Network on Debt and Development
FAO	Food and Agricultural Organization
GAD	gender and development
GDI	Gender-related Development Index
GEM	gender empowerment measure
GNI	gross national income
GTZ	Gesellschaft für Technische Zusammenarbeit
HDI	Human Development Index
HDR	*Human Development Report*

HIPC	heavily indebted poor countries
IADB	Inter-American Development Bank
IBRD	International Bank for Reconstruction and Development
ICRC	International Committee of the Red Cross
ICSID	International Centre for Settlement of Investment Disputes
IDA	International Development Association
IDRC	International Development Research Centre
IDS	Institute for Development Studies
IFAD	International Fund for Agricultural Development
IFC	international finance corporation
IFI	International Financial Institutions
IFPRI	International Food Policy Research Institute
IIED	International Institute for Environment and Development
IILS	International Institute for Labour Studies
ILO	International Labour Organization
IMF	International Monetary Fund
IMFC	International Monetary and Finance Committee
IOM	International Organization for Migration
IPCC	Intergovernmental Panel on Climate Change
IPEC	International Programme on the Elimination of Child Labour
IRD	Integrated Rural Development
ISS	Institute of Social Sciences
MCC	Millennium Challenge Corporation
MDG	Millennium Development Goal
MIGA	Multilateral Investment Guarantee Agency
NGO	nongovernmental organization
ODA	Official Development Assistance
ODI	Overseas Development Institute
OECD	Organisation for Economic Co-operation and Development
PAMSCAD	Program of Action to Mitigate the Social Cost of Adjustment (Ghana)

PEPFAR	President's Emergency Plan for AIDS Relief
PPA	participatory poverty analysis
PPP	purchasing power parity
PRA	participatory rural appraisal
PRSP	poverty reduction strategy paper
PSIA	poverty and social impact analysis
SAP	Structural Adjustment Program
SARS	severe acute respiratory syndrome
SEWA	Self-Employed Women's Association (India)
Sida	Swedish International Development Cooperation Agency
SL	sustainable livelihoods
SWAp	sector-wide approach
TC	technical cooperation
UK	United Kingdom
UN	United Nations
UNDAF	United Nations Development Assistance Framework
UNDP	United National Development Programme
UNEP	United Nations Environment Programme
UNESCO	United Nations Educational, Scientific and Cultural Organization
UNHCR	United Nations High Commissioner for Refugees
UNICEF	United Nations Children's Fund
UNIDO	United Nations Industrial Development Organization
UNRISD	United Nations Research Institute for Social Development
USAID	United States Agency for International Development
WBI	World Bank Institute
WEP	World Employment Programme
WFP	World Food Programme
WHO	World Health Organization
WID	Women in Development
WIDER	World Institute for Development Economics Research

Why Is Aid Contested?

International development is big business. Total global official aid flows from North to South are well over $150 billion annually, one-third of which goes to Africa. China and India are rapidly enhancing their role as aid providers. And international private philanthropies have become significant in terms of ideas as well as money, with the resources of the Gates Foundation, for example, outstripping the annual budget of major official donors like the World Health Organization. Donations by private medical companies add significantly to overall aid flows.

The number of organizations can be "baffling," according to the Development Assistance Committee (DAC), the body that brings together dispersed aid statistics and has worked hard to coordinate donors. According to its count, there are no fewer than two hundred bilateral and multilateral organizations (including only the "official" agencies) channeling official development assistance (ODA), all with their own strategies and principles. Many forms of public-private partnerships have added to the complexity particularly in the last twenty years or so. In some developing countries forty donors are operating, financing hundreds of projects. Dutch aid, for example, despite efforts to concentrate efforts, can be found in no fewer than 125 countries. Donors like the United States have multiple agencies within the government responsible for various aid activities. The policies of agencies tend to be inaccessible to outsiders and apparently always changing; procedures for project approval, for example, can be extraordinarily long. The language of the aid industry is often intractable, and it uses an incredibly large number of acronyms.

Recently, interest in development aid has seen a big surge, and to a large extent this has been sustained throughout the 2008–9 financial crisis, as the G20 meeting in London in April 2009 suggested. Large disasters like the Gujarat earthquake and the Asian tsunami mobilized governments and large constituencies of civil society, including diaspora communities. The 2008 cyclone in Myanmar and earthquake in China again highlighted the role of an international community, which found a previously unknown open reception in China and advocated continuously for access in Myanmar. The global Jubilee 2000 campaign advocated successfully for debt relief to the poorest and most heavily indebted countries, and the Make Poverty History campaign of 2005 advocated for substantially increased aid commitments. These raised awareness of and interest in the aid industry well beyond the earlier popular advocacy for relief such as that during the Sahel emergency of the late 1970s. Anti-globalization and other protests frequently bring the World Bank and International Monetary Fund (IMF) into the global public eye. Global civil society and protests against international institutions—which in 2007, for example, contributed to the resignation of the World Bank president—have become an inextricable part of globalization.

Alongside renewed concerns to alleviate deprivation in the South, global security concerns have brought renewed attention to global aid efforts. In the United States after 9/11, development was elevated after a decade of relative neglect and became seen as one of the pillars of national security alongside defense and diplomacy (Brainard 2007a; Natsios 2006). In other countries security concerns have been less overt in influencing aid programs, but the war in Iraq did become important for the aid programs, and Afghanistan became an important recipient of many countries' aid.

The practices, achievements, and failures of international development efforts are the main themes of this book. It focuses on the period following the Second World War, when the modern aid industry was built, often in the wake of independence of former colonial countries, supporting the new modernization projects, and accompanied by the new science of "development" economics and studies.

From the outset it is important to highlight the hugely differing perspectives on aid.[1] At one extreme are the many who claim that not enough aid is given, for example, those in the Jubilee 2000 campaign who advocated for debt relief, reversing the net transfer from poor to rich countries. In Canada, Stephen Lewis criticized in nationally broadcast lectures most of the rich countries for failing to live up to their commitments and failing to deal with the global HIV/AIDS pandemic (Stephen Lewis 2005). Jeffrey Sachs, having started his career in international development by advising governments how to reduce inflation, joined the camp of those forcefully advocating for more aid, including his time serving as adviser to Kofi Annan (Sachs 2005). At the other extreme are those who believe too much aid is given. This group includes those in the general public who suffered from the "aid fatigue" that was common in the 1980s and 1990s and those like William Easterly, among others, who does not like the aid practices of ambitious planning and believes development needs to be "home-grown" (Easterly 2006).[2] In the middle are those who focus on the ways in which aid is provided and the need for better assessment (Roger Riddell 2007), as well as those who argue that aid really isn't all that important and that other rich countries' policies—for example, on trade or migration—are much more significant.

For many agencies progress toward the Millennium Development Goals (MDGs) that were agreed upon after a summit in 2000 now provides a unified framework for the goals and measurement of success of the international community. But there are still large differences in the objectives of various countries aid programs (described in Chapter 2), and measurements and indicators of success also are radically different. Thus, individual agencies approach these goals differently, and the way contributions are assessed is not at all clear or agreed. Where donors' national interests are seen as key to the development programs, measurements of success, of course, differ as well.

Moreover, aid has been studied from different theoretical angles (described in Chapter 3). These differences can be summarized under a number of opposites. For example, much of the literature cited in this book has a strong emphasis on the management of aid; this literature has been criticized by authors that emphasize the importance of personal relationships in aid. Realist and Marxist perspectives focus on the role that aid plays in maintaining global power relations; scholars in a liberal tradition emphasize aid as a reflection of collaboration between states. Social-democratic theories highlight that foreign aid is an expression of norms and ideas to assist in the improvement of quality of life; post-modernist approaches focus on aid practices as discourse and ways of exerting power. The entrance of new donors, like China, is likely to bring yet other perspectives that cannot be predicted. I agree with Carol Lancaster (2007) that none of these theories adequately explains the complexities of aid; its principles always reflect a combination of motives, and aid practices tend to create their own dynamics, as do all policies, through the institutions responsible for their implementation.

At the end of the book, and following a discussion about how the impact of aid is measured, readers should be able to make their own judgments about these views. The rest of this introductory chapter highlights some of the main debates about international development: whether aid should increase, about the way aid is given, and whether aid is becoming irrelevant in the face of increasing private financial flows through trade and remittances. This does not cover all the arguments about aid. Notably, it does not cover the question of whether aid *can* reduce poverty. This is a question that runs throughout the book, and the book hopes to help readers to form their own opinion. This introductory chapter finishes with a brief introduction to the chapters in this book.

Argument 1: Aid Flows Should Increase

Commitments to international development are frequently subject to international debates among activists as much as government leaders. According to John Isbister, "Foreign aid has declined so much in both quantity and quality as to be almost irrelevant to the economic development of the third world" (2003, 221). In 2007 civil society organizations like Oxfam and ActionAid were quick to criticize the Organisation for Economic Co-operation and Development (OECD) countries' failure to increase aid to Africa, as promised during 2005.[3]

Calls for increased aid have been common at least since the Second World War, and there have been various waves of attention since. The immediate postwar period witnessed large-scale funding through the Marshall Plan, which provided infrastructure support to Europe. Aid to developing countries focused on technical assistance and cooperation. In 1951 a commission set up by the UN secretary general recommended an increase of aid, to about $5 billion a year, to help countries increase economic growth to 2 percent (Roger Riddell 2007, 27). Voluntary agencies started to expand work in developing countries. The early 1950s also were the period of the classic development theories, which identified both technical assistance and finance gaps as main obstacles for development.

The 1969 *Partners in Development* was one of the first and subsequently most commonly quoted official reports arguing for an increase in aid. The report was written by a commission set up by Robert McNamara, the newly appointed World Bank president, and chaired by Lester Pearson, Canada's prime minister. It called for rich countries to devote 0.7 percent of their gross national income (GNI) to international development, and to reach this level of funding in 1975. It also argued for a simultaneous increase in the efficiency of aid. Its focus was development, with less explicit attention to poverty. The target was adopted formally by the United Nations in 1970 and has featured in international debates ever since. Aid levels did rise during the 1970s, but average spending never came close to the target except in a few countries.

The optimism of 1970 was not to last long. It was quickly followed by emphasis on structural adjustment and stabilization of economies (discussed in some detail in Chapter 3) and aid fatigue based on perceptions that aid had failed to deliver results. Nevertheless, even throughout the 1980s there were calls for increasing aid, including World Bank reports on Africa, for example, in response to the droughts and famines in Sahel and Ethiopia, and because of increasing involvement of NGOs. Levels of aid continued to increase.

The 1990s—with the end of the Cold War, and economic and budgetary problems in donor countries like the United States and Japan—witnessed sharp reductions in ODA. The fall in aid to the poorest countries may have been even larger than the overall decline.[4] The amounts of aid to allied countries, including corrupt and repressive regimes, declined, but simultaneously the donors may have reduced their attention to conflicts and violence in developing countries. With the transition toward market economies, more attention started to be paid to the use of aid for governance reforms in the former USSR and for processes toward democratization in Africa.

From the late 1990s onward calls for increasing aid again became stronger, accompanied by a sharpened focus on poverty reduction as the overarching goal for development. An important OECD report in 1996 signaled a turnaround of the pessimism. The change of government in the UK in 1997 led to the formation of a new and separate ministry, and contributed to greater political interest, for example, among stars like Sir Bob Geldof and Bono.[5] Around the turn of the century the United Nations and the World Bank produced a range of publications highlighting the importance of and their commitment to poverty reduction and the MDGs. In March 2002 a large number of countries once again came together, in Monterrey, Mexico, pledging significant increases in aid flows (UN 2002), which was followed up during the General Assembly meeting in Doha in December 2008. The Monterrey conference was followed by the 2005 Gleneagles Summit under the leadership of the UK government as G-8 chair, and commitments were reaffirmed later when Germany took over the chairmanship of the G-8.

Showing a great deal of trust in the impact of aid, the UN Millennium Development Project calculated the amount of aid that would be required to achieve the MDGs.[6] The United Nations stressed the lack of funding particularly in social sectors; according to the 2005 *Human Development Report*, for example, average health spending in Sub-Saharan Africa was $3–$10 per capita, while the cost of providing basic health care was estimated at $30 per capita (UNDP 2005, 79). The desirability for increased aid was highlighted by analyses like that of Howard White, who entitled an article "The Case for Doubling Aid" (2005).[7]

However, commitments have never been binding, and more often than not simply have not been honored. In donor countries political pressure apparently is not heavy enough, and aid probably not sufficiently significant in national politics, for the commitments to be honored consistently. The commitments by national leaders usually do not have direct legal or administrative implications. Exceptions to this include the UK's International Development (Reporting and Transparency) Act 2006, which commits the secretary of state to report annually on various areas, including expenditure on international aid and progress toward the UN ODA target for such aid to make up 0.7 percent of GNI. But in this case the commitment to increased aid is combined with commitments to enhance effectiveness and transparency, making the increase in allocation far from automatic.

Argument 2: Too Much Money Goes to International Development

The idea that too much money is spent on international development aid is very common. Public opinion often holds that too much money goes to foreign aid, and that very few positive effects are achieved, often because of corruption on the part of the rulers of poor countries. It appears that little of this is based on actual information. For example, in the United States the public often greatly overestimates the amount given to aid.[8] However, some OECD countries' governments are consciously trying to enhance understanding of development and campaigns like the MDGs, though perhaps too little is known about public attitudes toward aid.[9]

In 1989 Graham Hancock argued in a widely read book that the aid business should be abolished and that the highly paid aid bureaucrats, or "lords of poverty," should depart. In his view the industry's history has been littered with failures, and it has escaped public scrutiny. Riding

---

**Box 1–1. Four Decades of Reports on Increasing Funding
for International Development**

Pearson Commission: Lester Pearson, 1969. *Partners in Development: Report of the Commission on International Development.* New York: Praeger Publishers. Called for ODA
commitment of 0.7 percent of GNI.

Brandt Commission: Willy Brandt, 1980. *North-South: A
Programme for Survival.* London: Pan Books. Called for doubling ODA by 1985.

World Bank, 1989. *Sub-Saharan Africa: From Crisis to Sustainable Growth.* World Bank. Proposed doubling aid to Africa.

DAC, 1996, *Shaping the Twenty-first Century: The Contribution
of Development Co-operation.* Paris: OECD. Called for increasing aid, but without quantification, and focusing on enhancing
the effectiveness of aid.

UN, *Monterrey Consensus on Financing for Development* (UN
2002). Urged developed countries to make concrete effort toward the 0.7 percent target (and 0.15–0.20 percent to the least
developed countries), while stressing the need for a "new partnership." The Monterrey commitments were affirmed during
negotiations at Doha in 2008.

UN Millennium Development Project. 2005. *Investing in Development: Millennium Development Goals.*

The Commission for Africa (set up by UK Prime Minister Tony
Blair). *Our Common Interest.* 2005. London: Penguin Books.
Called for an additional $25 billion in aid to Africa.

---

on the wave of interest in aid as highlighted above, former World Bank
economist William Easterly published his view on international development. Based on his practical experience he highlights the "tragedy in
which the West spent $2.3 trillion on foreign aid over the last five de-
cades and still had not managed to get twelve-cent medicines to prevent
half of all malaria deaths" (Easterly 2006, 4). According to Easterly, the
main problem of aid has been the emphasis on grand plans and the domination of "planners," and limited ability to motivate people to carry out
such plans. He suspects that the increased commitments will again be

subject to a dominance of these planners, including those who think they can plan a market but fail to learn from past mistakes.

Calls for reducing aid are substantiated by different arguments, often interrelated. First, there is a common perception that aid has failed—as the quote from Easterly indicates. An article in the conservative US journal *The National Review* in 2002 argued that "a strong case can be made that foreign aid has been the problem for many developing countries, rather than the solution." Linking this to welfare debates in the United States, it continues: "Negative policies were perpetuated in the same way that welfare perpetuated dependency" (quoted in Lancaster 2007, 96). An article in *The Wall Street Journal* stated: "Despite star power, aid doesn't work" (Subramanian 2007), highlighting the potential damaging long-run effects on governance and economic competitiveness.[10] In an "ethnography of aid and agencies," David Lewis and David Mosse state that development policy is characterized by a striking incongruence between a seductive mix of "development buzzwords" and a "striking lack of progress in relation to a wide range of development indicators" (2006, 8).[11] Also, Hancock points out—not without basis—that countries who have not received aid have done well, while those that have received aid have not developed. It is often argued that many of the aid recipients are not committed to development and poverty reduction, and that aid may not manage to help improve governance.

Second, a strand of academic literature, often inspired by post-modernism, has challenged the nature of the aid industry altogether. Authors like Escobar, Ferguson, and Ignacy Sachs "argue that the entire development discourse is Western created and imbued with the usual dichotomies of Western superiority... [and] ... justifies the existence of an interventionist and disempowering bureaucracy. . . . This critique argues that the entire development edifice—the concepts, the language, the institutions built up around it—*causes* the problems it supposedly seeks to solve" (Uvin 2004, 32).[12] Much of the popular critique, particularly against the World Bank or globalization and in support of the agendas of subalterns and social groups in the South, uses these forms of expression, emphasizing continued inequalities in power as root causes of deprivation. Even programs run by UN organizations like the International Fund for Agricultural Development (IFAD) do not escape the criticism that aid institutions cause development problems. While I do not share these criticisms, they no doubt contain much truth, and any practitioner ought to be aware of them.

Third, there are common concerns about aid dependency. In quite a few countries, particularly in Africa, donor funding can form half of the government budget, often for extended periods of time. New funding often leads to setting up of new agencies, and this may not contribute to solving problems and indeed may even worsen problems of existing public policy institutions. Equally, new loans are often thought not to help countries get out of debt traps. Critiques of structural adjustment, which we discuss in some detail in Chapter 3, often argue along these lines, pointing out—as the campaigns for debt relief have done—that poor countries over the years have paid back far more in loans than they have received.

A fourth argument against increasing aid refers to what is commonly called absorptive capacity. It is argued that recipient governments do not have the administrative or policy capacity to use increased aid flows effectively, particularly when these are disbursed in a short period of time. Economists warn of the implications of large financial inflows on the economy, and the possibility that this may cause "Dutch disease," that is, an appreciation of the exchange rate and resulting decline in competitiveness of national industries. However, there is some agreement among economists that for most aid-dependent countries, a foreign aid contribution of about 20 percent to the national budget does not lead to such negative effects and that the economic impact remains positive. And Jeffrey Sachs has strongly asserted against arguments around absorptive capacity that, for example, at current levels of funding it is impossible for health ministries in Africa to maintain a health-care system.

A fifth argument against increasing aid relates to the behavior of donors. While the history of the aid industry has been full of commitments to focus on recipients' priorities, the motives and structures of donors continue to drive the way aid is given; for example, aid is influenced by foreign-policy motives, which partly explain the great attention to aid during the Cold War and after 9/11. Commercial motives have been equally important in the way aid is provided. Much aid is "tied aid," where the money given must be spent on goods and services of the donor country. Donors' procedures also tend to be cumbersome, occupying valuable and often scarce government and administrative capacity. Donor projects and programs often create parallel reporting structures, which is particularly problematic when large numbers of donors are present in countries with low administrative capacity. Finally, donor funding can undermine local accountability (Uvin 2004); donors' role in relation to the accountability of national policies are discussed at different points in this book.

Argument 3: Amounts of Aid Matter Less Than How It Is Given

The arguments about absorptive capacity and donor behavior move us into a different set of arguments about aid, those focusing on how aid is given rather than whether there should be more or less aid. As already noted, advocacy for more aid often goes together with calls for improving the quality of the aid system; for example, the Jubilee 2000 campaign argued that new resources should focus on poverty reduction, the Pearson Commission argued for improvements in efficiency, and the Monterrey Consensus emphasized governance issues as central to delivering increased resources. The prestigious 2005 *Human Development Report* argued:

> International aid is one of the most powerful weapons in the war against poverty. Today, that weapon is underused and badly targeted. There is too little aid and too much of what is provided is weakly linked to human development. Fixing the international aid system is one of the most urgent priorities facing governments at the start of the 10-year countdown to 2015.

Many of the difficult questions about the delivery of aid are central to this book. Some of the more pertinent ones in discussions about increasing aid are discussed below (see Manor 2005).

A first argument emphasizes that aid is not well targeted, that too much money is spent in countries that are not the poorest. There are powerful historical, political, and strategic reasons determining that much aid is given to countries that are not poor. Many bilateral organizations have tried to focus their aid on the poorest countries. The UK with its public focus on Africa has official targets for increasing the share of the total aid budget to the poorest countries. But the pull of other political considerations remains large, and following 9/11 security concerns have led to an increasing—and often competing—focus on states that are thought to be threats to the North. The US aid program is openly tied to foreign policy concerns; in fact, in 2006 a former USAID administrator criticized the European aid programs for failure to align their aid to foreign-policy concerns (Natsios 2006). Similarly, Kurlantzick describes the recent Chinese aid program as a core element of China's global "charm offensive" (2007, 202).

A second and related argument has stressed that much aid—even if it does go the poorest countries—does not reach the poorest people. As we describe in the next chapter, since the 1950s the development industry has increasingly focused on ensuring that aid benefits poor people. The MDGs agreed upon in 2000 are a clear example of an instrument that aims to ensure targeting. Since the 1980s many development organizations, not least the World Bank, have been engaged in large-scale exercises to make sure that it is possible to know how many people are poor, uneducated, and so forth. But the ways in which aid does benefit poor people can be manifold (as discussed later), and this underlies many of the debates about aid. Moreover, assessing whether aid succeeds in benefiting the poor (the subject of Chapter 8) remains a very difficult question, even within agreed frameworks like the MDGs.

Third, even when it is agreed that the world's poorest people should be the prime beneficiaries of aid, controversy arises about whether it is desirable to provide these countries with large or increasing amounts of aid. The argument, put simply, is that many of the poorest countries are not able to use aid effectively. This can be for a number of reasons, but much of the focus has been around the "governance" in these countries (discussed extensively in Chapter 5 on aid approaches that emphasize administrative and public sector reforms). The agenda of good governance is broad and calls for improvements in political and economic institutions, administrative systems and government bureaucracies, and public service delivery.

An oft-quoted and influential—but also much criticized (as discussed in Chapter 8)—World Bank working paper first published in 1997 by Craig Burnside and David Dollar showed that aid is effective *if* its recipient government has the right policies, particularly good fiscal, monetary, and trade policies (Burnside and Dollar 2000). Paul Collier and David Dollar (1999) combined an argument about the need to move aid to those countries with the largest numbers of poor people and those countries that are able to use aid effectively. In their view, based on statistical analysis comparing large numbers of countries (cross-country regressions), such reallocation could increase the numbers of people lifted out of poverty from 30 million to 80 million a year. Collier's popular book *The Bottom Billion* (2007) again stressed the need to focus on countries where most poor people are (approximately forty countries) and the need to address the development "trap" of good governance— to which he adds the need to address other traps, those of conflict, of the natural resource curse, and of landlocked countries with bad neighbors.

Fourth, a relatively recent concern about how aid is given revolves around the political nature of the aid process. Such a critique is by no means new. Chapter 3 describes the perceived failure of the Washington Consensus that dominated in the 1980s (and the aid fatigue that blamed corrupt governments for the failure of aid) and how it led to increased attention to the importance of governance for development and poverty reduction. Further, poverty reduction strategy papers (PRSPs) called for country-wide consultations to determine strategies for providing aid (discussed in Chapter 6). The attention to the institutional determinants of development led an increasing number of authors to argue that aid needs to be much more sensitive to political conditions and to calls for political analysis—such as DFID's "drivers of change"—to inform aid allocation and strategies.

A fifth question about how aid is given stresses donors' habits, that is, the patterns of behavior and incentives that limit aid effectiveness. This involves a complicated set of issues, many of which we stumble upon in the rest of the book. For example, current aid is commonly compared with the Marshall Plan, implemented after the Second World War, which disbursed large sums of money in a short period of time, as opposed to the long term and relatively small sums of money of development aid— even though, and this is only an apparent contradiction, donors suffer from what is known as disbursement pressure, that is, both in World Bank and bilateral donors, staff experience incentives for high and fast disbursement.[13] Donor procedures tend to be cumbersome and time consuming. Aid flows are often unpredictable, often following financial cycles on the side of the donors rather than demand by recipients—and donors' priorities change frequently. Many people feel that there are too many donor agencies, working in uncoordinated ways. Some argue that donors' attitudes have the potential to undermine progress, and aid has the potential to contribute to rather than to reduce conflict. With respect to fragile states, Stephen Browne of the United Nations International Trade Centre concludes:

> The donor record is patchy to say the least. And the closer you come, the worse it looks. Donors bear some responsibility for not being there, but that is not the worst accusation.

> Donors also appeared at the wrong times with the wrong attitudes. Working within their own scripted agendas, they succeeded in sometimes unpicking and undermining development progress. (Browne 2007, 32)

Finally, tied aid has restricted aid's efficiency. While the UK "untied" its aid under the Labour Government, and other OECD countries have tried to do this for some time, and although an increasing number of recipient countries qualify for untied aid,[14] many donor countries continue to make collaboration with or purchase from their national companies a condition for the provision of aid.[15]

Argument 4: Foreign Policy, Trade, and Migration Policies Matter More Than Aid

A fourth set of arguments emphasizes that aid is not as important as many of its supporters argue. There are at least three important considerations, related to the position of aid in relation to donors' foreign policies; the importance of aid compared to private financial flows; and aid's importance in relation to remittances, which (unlike aid) have rapidly grown over the last decades. I argue that it is important to contextualize aid in this way, but that none of these makes careful study of aid any less necessary.

First, as reflected strongly in writings originating in the United States aid is an instrument of foreign policy or diplomatic purposes. The United States and others provided aid as a tool in the Cold War competition, and French aid has been instrumental in maintaining a sphere of influence. The recent rise of Chinese aid similarly can be interpreted as one of its diplomatic tools. The resurgence of interest in aid in the United States was closely related to the post-9/11 agenda and the new "transformational diplomacy" (Natsios 2006). In fact, foreign-policy considerations are important for all donor countries, even for those that have made development, poverty reduction, and humanitarian relief central to their policies. Alesina and Dollar (2000) confirm, based on quantitative analysis of bilateral aid, that foreign policy and strategic considerations (along with economic needs and historical links) have a big influence on which countries receive aid.

A second important question is how important aid is in a world in which private financial flows are so large. It is often argued that broader international economic policies are more important than aid programs alone. Civil society organizations have long emphasized that for global inequalities to be reduced, trade policies need to change. This is recognized, for example, in the Treaty of Maastricht and is central to many aid ministries' efforts to influence other government departments. Donor countries are criticized for hypocrisy when they provide aid while benefiting from, for example, import restrictions and subsidies to producers in the North, foreign investment that exploits countries in the South (with advice from donors helping to open up countries to global markets), the payments of interest on loans disbursed years if not decades ago, or the fueling of conflict through the sale of arms by companies in the same donor countries. Under the leadership of Clare Short, DFID made globalization the core theme of its Second White Paper, responding to a perceived need to "make globalization work for the poor," and arguing for the need for consistency in the policies of all government departments. The Commitment to Development Index, published on the Center for Global Development (CGD) website, is an initiative that rates rich countries' policies in seven component areas (aid, trade, investment, migration, environment, security, and technology) on the extent to which they help poor countries' development. Currently, the Netherlands, Denmark, Portugal, and New Zealand ranked best; Norway and Britain fall in the middle; and Canada, Australia, the United States, and Japan score lowest.

Similarly, it has been stressed recently that the financial contributions of migrants from the South outstrip development aid. Recent estimates put remittances at about US$200 billion or more, about double official aid flows. While earlier writings emphasized the danger of "brain drain," that is, the loss of human capacity following moves by educated people to richer countries, more recent analyses have emphasized the positive contributions of migrants. Some authors stress that remittances do not suffer from the problems of aid flows (like difficulties in getting the money to the right people) and corruption.

These arguments are important, and a development agenda is about much more than aid. But aid itself does have its place. Wherever foreign-policy considerations are dominant, constituencies for the use of aid for development purposes continue to exist. And private flows, through trade or migrants, cannot substitute for the essential role aid has played, and can play, in providing countries with the preconditions for their development, including being able to benefit from private flows, from which many of the poorest countries are still excluded. There may be too few successes, but there are enough to illustrate the point that aid does matter for the places and countries that are marginalized from globalization.

So Why Are Views on the Aid Industry So Different?

The views on aid diverge for many reasons. In the first place, aid has been used for different purposes: to support allies during the Cold War, to support countries and governments considered helpful in a global security agenda, to help countries develop, to address global poverty, and so forth. Because there are many objectives for aid, views on what it can achieve differ.

Second, and closely related, there are no agreed-upon standards to measure whether aid works (see Chapter 8). Even if we discount the foreign-policy and commercial purposes of aid and instead focus on the developmental aspects, there is still an enormous variety of purposes that can be categorized as development oriented; providing humanitarian relief, promoting economic transitions and reform, promoting democracy, addressing conflict and post-conflict situations can all legitimately be classified as aid. Poverty reduction can be achieved through a range of instruments, including those that help create an environment for economic growth, policies that help provide services for the entire population (like health and education), or programs that are targeted to the poor (like microfinance or cash transfers). While the MDGs now provide a generally agreed-upon framework for measuring progress, there are still many questions about whether one can attribute any of the progress, or lack thereof, to the aid industry.

But third, the differences also can have deeper underlying reasons. As described by Jean-Philippe Thérien (2002), the ideological differences between Right and Left have exercised a great influence on framing the aid debate, and the changes in political power over the last decades have influenced the changes in the shape of aid institutions. Partly mirroring these differences are differences in perceptions about responsibilities of states, in terms of their duty to provide for their citizens, as well as their ability to promote economic growth.[16] US national public social policies, for example, are relatively ungenerous compared to their European counterparts. But private charities are larger in the United States than elsewhere. These differences are clearly reflected in patterns of aid, as we will see in Chapter 2. Similarly, there are differences in expectations about the extent to which governments can promote economic growth and how much of this should be left to the private sector; again, ideas about the ability of the state are reflected in ideas about what aid can contribute and how much should be given.

A Brief Introduction to This Book

This book is neither a critique nor a praise of aid. It will not try to answer the question "does aid work?" (see Robert Cassen et al. 1986; Roger Riddell 2007) or why it has done "so much ill" (see Easterly 2006). It will show, however, that there are no easy solutions for making aid work. As we will see, what is seen as the success of aid differs among its many different protagonists and the people who criticize the industry. Understanding the different ways in which aid is provided, the varying objectives, and different ways in which it is assessed is the key objective to which this book aims to contribute.

The next chapter provides insight into the institutions that form the aid industry: the United Nations, including the Bretton Woods institutions, IMF, and World Bank; the main bilateral organizations, and the various ways in which countries have shaped their aid programs; the role and importance of NGOs, which have grown significantly over the last two decades; and the more recent but very rapid emergence of private charities, of which the Gates Foundation is probably the most widely known. While the club of donors is very diverse, and increasingly so, the group of recipients is even more varied (this is reflected in the ways in which donors have categorized countries), with countries that are more and less aid dependent, countries that have had high or reasonable economic growth and those that have stagnated for decades, and countries that have been in conflict or are "fragile."

Approaches to development, and development studies, have seen rapid evolution since the Second World War, and Chapter 3 briefly describes this history. First, I discuss the nature of development studies, which since the early 1970s has established itself as a separate academic discipline—more so in some countries than others—with a strong interdisciplinary and a problem-oriented or applied focus. The description of the trends in approaches covers how aid approaches emerged out of late-colonial concerns, followed by a focus on reconstruction after the Second World War and support to newly independent nations. The optimism of the 1960s was followed by the period of adjustment. The turning point can be put at 1973 with the oil crisis and political change in Chile, even though in the 1970s the aid agenda continued to expand and basic needs (and later human development) became more central. The period of dominance of the Washington Consensus during the 1990s was followed by a new or renewed focus on poverty as the central objective of development aid and increasing attention to the role of governance and institutions in promoting development. Finally, while the end of the Cold War reduced the influence of foreign policy over aid, the global security agenda after 9/11 provided new directions.

Chapters 4–6 then describe the practices and different approaches of the aid industry. A key and much debated distinction has been between *projects* and *programs*, signaling the way thinking about aid and development has evolved, but also some of the dilemmas in terms of donors' preferences and the needs of recipients. A project involves financial and technical support to a distinct activity with directly tangible objectives, such as building roads or giving immunizations. A program supports recipient governments' policies more generally, for example, through general "budget support" to finance ministries. Main organizations have used a combination of the two, and choices between the two are sometimes made for different reasons. Some agencies tend to focus entirely on projects, often using implementing agencies outside the regular bureaucracies of recipient governments. The World Bank has a strong focus on programmatic loans for adjustment and reforms. With the emergence of poverty reduction strategies and emphasis on donor "harmonization" and "alignment" an increasing number of organizations have adopted a similar form of programmatic support. Chapters 4–6 describe the characteristics and rationale of the different approaches, their origins, and the successes and continuing challenges. The themes in these chapters can be identified on a continuum between program and project approaches, with practical examples drawn from recent experience.

Projects, despite criticism, are still a very important part of donor approaches, and Chapter 4 highlights the rationale for these in terms of needs for donors to show results, the possibility to be flexible and demand driven, and potential for innovation. But projects also are perceived to have many disadvantages: an overload on recipient governments, particularly but not only in aid-dependent countries; "fungibility" of funding, referring to the possibility that donor funding leads to a reduction in recipient government funding in that specific area; and the likelihood of sustainability, that is, whether projects initiated or funded by donors will be maintained. Cases of project approaches highlighted include microfinance, sustainable livelihoods projects, social funds, and practices of technical cooperation, and Chapter 4 describes LogFrames as the most important planning tool for projects.

Whereas projects focus on one-time support for countries' development, reforms and programs (the subject of Chapter 5) focus on the broader administrative and policy systems in partner countries. *Reforms* have been a key element in the development debate since the 1980s. Reforms are complex processes, often involving dozens of policy prescriptions imposed by donors on recipient governments. From the 1980s onward, sector reform and sector-wide approaches have been developed as new instruments of the aid industry, as part of a move away from project approaches to a focus on the policy environment. These approaches have had notable successes, but practices have been more varied than optimists may suggest or hope. Progress has often been extremely slow, and donors have continued to operate projects with program approaches. Other issues relate to the relationship between program approaches and cross-sectoral policy choices, the importance of capacity for policymaking, the intensely political nature of aid and reforms, and how the impact can be measured.

While always part of common knowledge, during the late 1980s donors started to emphasize the need for country ownership for successful development. Chapter 6 describes *country-led approaches* and questions of the capacity of aid recipients and the perceived need for donors to harmonize their approaches. The approach to PRSPs has been much debated in the development community, and this chapter reflects on its place in the evolving aid industry, how it emerged, what it set out to achieve, how it has worked, its successes and failures in strengthening "ownership," and whether donors can live up to the commitments this approach entails.

Chapter 7 describes cross-cutting issues. Development debates in the last decades have been heavily influenced by urges to mainstream a number of concerns: environment, gender, participation, rights-based approaches. Each of these themes has a substantial literature, and this chapter places these in the context of wider development debates, how these approaches have or have not influenced mainstream debates, and whether they have managed to obtain a central place in aid practices. It is suggested that participation has obtained a central place partly because of evidence that participation leads to better project outcomes. Environment has become a key focus because of recent concerns over climate change. Gender and rights appear much more contested with the latter receiving very little attention, and the way in which the former has been mainstreamed challenged by many activists.

How does the industry know what it has achieved? As discussed above, debates over whether aid works continue to rage. During the last decades—under the influence of changing public service management practices and pressure by treasuries on government departments to show results, presumed or real aid fatigue, and influential critiques on structural adjustment—increasing attention has been devoted to measuring what aid has achieved. Chapter 8 describes the technical approaches to such measurement, the information on which assessments are based, the advantages and disadvantages of different approaches, and whether (and the ways in which) these assessments are taken seriously by organizations, and some of the perhaps unintended impact of the need to show results.

The final chapter reflects on *major challenges* to the practices of international development. For example, has aid become irrelevant, as trade and migration agendas seem much more important for development than the relatively low aid budgets, and as global security concerns have increasingly influenced aid approaches? What does the rapid entry of new aid donors like China, India, and the Gates Foundation mean, and do they upset attempts toward harmonization of donors? There is a tension between the needs of many of the poor countries and their capacity to use aid effectively, and there may be a dilemma between a strong focus on ensuring that aid reaches the poor directly and supporting broader development processes and structures. Finally, aid is and will remain an instrument of international politics; the challenge is how to ensure that this complements development and poverty reduction.

2

The Aid Industry Defined

Every year, more than $100 billion is spent on international develop-
ment through government and international official agencies, and another $60 billion though private organizations and NGOs. This money
is spent by a wide range and ever growing number of agencies in a large
number of increasingly diverse groups of countries, partly in grants and
partly through concessional loans. It addresses a wide range of goals,
programs, and projects both for short-term emergency or relief and for
longer-term development purposes.

International assistance was provided well before the post–World
War II period. In the nineteenth century various countries provided aid
for disaster relief abroad, and US and European governments provided
support to the Soviet Union in 1921. The International Labour Organization (ILO) showed concern with and provided support to the less
advantaged in distant lands. During the 1920s France and the UK provided assistance to their colonies; this aid was small in scale but did build
roots for policies after independence. During World War II the United
States provided a small amount of funding for technical assistance to
Latin American governments in order to ease the constraints of shrink-
ing markets and to strengthen its influence in the region.

Presently, we can distinguish four main groups of institutions among
the aid industry's donors. The largest sum of money flows through bilateral channels, programs between countries, administered by aid or
foreign affairs ministries, with large differences in orientation among
them. Multilateral aid is provided by UN agencies, such as the World
Health Organization, and the World Bank and the IMF. NGOs form
the third component of the aid industry, one that has grown rapidly
during the last few decades. The fourth and newest group of agencies is
the private philanthropic organizations, notably the Bill and Melinda
Gates Foundation.

According to the DAC, ODA is

> defined as those flows to countries . . . of the DAC List of
> Aid Recipients (developing countries) and to multilateral in-
> stitutions for flows to . . . aid recipients which are: i. pro-
> vided by official agencies, including state and local govern-
> ments, or by their executing agencies; and ii. each transaction
> of which: a) is administered with the promotion of the eco-
> nomic development and welfare of developing countries as
> its main objective; and b) is concessional in character and
> conveys a grant element of at least 25%.[1]

This book refers to ODA according to this specific definition. Aid from
private organizations and NGOs is not included in these figures. Also,
as Lancaster (2007, 10) emphasizes, this definition excludes the
concessional transfers to countries that are not low-income countries,
such as Russia and Israel, which are often very important in countries'
aid programs. Further, ODA is intended to promote economic development and welfare and is provided on concessional financial terms, either
as grant or concessional loan (or a combination of the two). Technical
cooperation (also called technical assistance) is included within ODA,
and often forms a substantial part of it. The data also include funding
for both short-term emergency and longer-term development purposes.
Development, aid, and public policy are three different concepts, with
overlapping domains, as illustrated in Figure 2–1.

Figure 2–1. Development, Public Policy, Aid

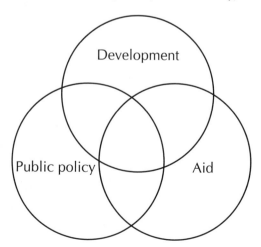

Using the official DAC definition of ODA, it is clear that the commitments made by the international community have not materialized. As a percentage of GNI, aid decreased over the 1980s and 1990s, showing an ever-widening gap between aid and the resources available in OECD countries. In 2005 over $106 billion was provided in aid, showing a sharp increase over the previous five years, but it was followed by a decline of about 5 percent in 2006 and a further decline of 8 percent in 2007. Table 2–1 shows the trend in DAC donor countries' aid volumes since 1950.

Table 2–1. Net ODA (US$ million)

	US$ million, annual average over period						% of GNI
	1950–59	1960–69	1970–79	1980–99	1990–99	2000–2007	2006
Australia	–	116	399	798	1,034	1 475	0.30
Austria	–	9	66	220	379	956	0.47
Belgium	19	88	323	557	848	1 496	0.50
Canada	34	120	730	1, 639	2, 156	2 659	0.29
Denmark	2	18	205	600	1, 502	1,954	0.80
Finland	–	4	40	299	505	646	0.40
France	568	845	1,343	3,853	7,278	7,510	0.47
Germany	63	436	1,542	3,670	6,664	7,806	0.36
Greece	–	–	–	–	73	337	0.17
Ireland	–	–	9	43	135	620	0.54
Italy	47	90	210	1,705	2,600	2,861	0.20
Japan	67	226	1,229	5,250	11,176	10,308	0.25
Luxembourg	–	–	–	10	69	219	0.89
Netherlands	25	79	627	1,637	2,844	4,325	0.81
New Zealand	–	8	41	73	116	196	0.27
Norway	3	13	184	680	1,236	2,252	0.89
Portugal	–	–	–	30	244	424	0.21
Spain	–	–	–	223	1,293	2,702	0.32
Sweden	5	44	487	1,100	1,881	2,781	1.02
Switzerland	6	12	98	379	943	1,335	0.39
United Kingdom	204	453	974	1,926	3,232	7,664	0.51
United States	1,437	3,464	4,010	8,381	9,597	17,990	0.18
TOTAL DAC	2,480	6,026	12,517	33,073	55,276	78,517	0.31

Source: www.oecd.org/dac/stats

This aid is provided for a wide range of purposes and through various means. In 2005, as Table 2–2 shows, 70 percent of the aid was provided as grants by bilateral organizations and about 30 percent by multilateral institutions (including the European Commission [EC]). Debt forgiveness (relief) was the largest component; in fact, the 2005 aid level was

Table 2–2. Aid Flows from DAC Countries by Type (US$ million and % of total)

	1989-90		2001		2005	
Official Development Assistance[a]	49,232		52,435		106,777	
1. Bilateral grants and grant-like flows:	29,066	59%	33,522	64%	83,109	78%
Technical co-operation	10,642	22%	13,602	26%	20,926	20%
Developmental food aid[b]	1,641	3%	1,007	2%	887	1%
Humanitarian aid[b]	934	2%	3,276	6%	8,720	8%
Debt forgiveness	2,466	5%	2,514	5%	24,963	23%
Administrative costs	1,900	4%	2,964	6%	4,065	4%
2. Bilateral loans	6,634	13%	1,602	3%	-976	-1%
3. Contributions to multilateral institutions:	14,300	29%	17,311	33%	24,644	23%
UN[c]	3,842	8%	5,325	10%	5,451	5%
EC[c]	3,005	6%	4,946	9%	9,258	9%
IDA[c]	3,773	8%	3,599	7%	4,827	5%
Regional development banks[c]	2,159	4%	1,491	3%	2,096	2%

Notes: US$ amounts are at current prices and exchange rates. (a) Excluding debt forgiveness of non-ODA claims in 1990. (b) Emergency food aid included with developmental food aid up to 1995. (c) Grants and capital subscriptions do not include concessional lending to multilateral agencies.

Source: OECD, DAC *Development Cooperation Report 2006*

unusually high because of large amounts of debt relief provided ($22 billion of $106 billion), especially to Nigeria and Iraq. Technical cooperation has consistently formed one-fifth to one-quarter of total aid, and it has often been questioned whether this form of aid provides as much benefit to recipient countries as other aid flows. Humanitarian aid now forms about 8 percent of total aid, showing a significant increase since 1990.

Thus, ODA is a combination of grants and loans. Grants come mostly from bilateral channels, the UN, NGOs, and private charities. The proportion of grants has been increasing and is currently almost 90 percent of ODA. The World Bank, the IMF, and some of the UN programs provide loans; although the loans are concessional (and thus have a grant element), this form of aid has rather different implications in terms of how donors organize themselves and how recipients perceive the aid provided. Finally, some of the aid is provided in a combination of grants and for example, some bilateral organizations provide so-called trust funds to the World Bank with which they can provide support that may not be feasible on a loan basis, and bilateral organizations have provided grants in combination with World Bank loans for economic adjustment loans as well as projects (Chapter 5 describes an example of this).

Aid includes a wide variety of activities, as Table 2–3 shows. The largest category, about 30 percent, is in the social sectors, but this includes funding for government reforms and civil society support. It is noteworthy that *basic* health and education, despite major campaigns over the last decades, continue to receive fairly small shares. The World Bank provides relatively large parts of total funding in these categories, particularly education, as do government and civil society. Since the early 1990s an increasing part of total ODA to these sectors has gone to the poorest countries (IDA 2007). Debt relief for the DAC members was the second largest category, but as mentioned, the year 2005 was exceptional in this respect. By comparison, economic infrastructure and productive purposes (notably, agriculture) received relatively small shares of funding, particularly from DAC members. This relative neglect has come under criticism (see Chapter 3). It is important to note that none of these purposes is necessarily better for poverty reduction than the others; building roads can be as important as building hospitals, and addressing financial management may be key for governments to provide services relatively efficiently.

Humanitarian aid forms about 10 percent of overall aid but has been among the most visible aspects of the aid industry. Many of the well-known NGOs like OXFAM arose out of a history of humanitarian assistance. The category itself includes a wide range of aid agencies and a very diverse set of activities responding to both natural and manmade disasters. Whether humanitarian aid should be classified as development aid is disputed. In this book we follow the common practice of presenting it as an integral part. Because there is a continuum from emergencies to development, aid plays an important and sometimes unexpected role in conflicts,[2] and agencies usually combine both sets of aid activities.[3]

Table 2–3. ODA by Major Purpose, 2006

	DAC	EC	World Bank
Social and administrative infrastructure	34.9	42.8	30.6
Education[a]	8.7	5.4	5.0
of which: Basic education	2.9	1.8	2.2
Health	4.7	4.3	6.8
of which: Basic health	2.9	3.1	5.1
Population & reproductive health	4.1	1.0	1.9
Water supply and sanitation	4.0	6.7	6.2
Government and civil society	8.9	22.0	7.9
Other social infrastructure/service	4.5	3.3	2.8
Economic infrastructure	11.4	15.3	28.4
Transport and communications	4.7	10.3	17.0
Energy	3.9	4.9	9.6
Other	2.8	0.1	1.8
Production	4.8	14.4	6.6
Agriculture	2.9	3.5	6.0
Industry, mining, and construction	0.8	6.8	0.6
Trade and tourism	1.1	4.1	–
Multi-sector	5.8	12.3	5.5
Program assistance	3.1	7.9	28.8
Action relating to debt[b]	22.6	–	0.1
Humanitarian aid	6.9	13.0	0.1
Administrative expenses	4.1	7.3	–

Notes: (a) Includes students and trainees. (b) Includes forgiveness of non-ODA debt. Source: http://www.oecd.org/dataoecd/52/11/1893159.xls

Rosalind Eyben in an introductory lecture at the Institute for Development (IDS) in Sussex defines aid as a transfer of knowledge and ideologies as well as financial resources. This transfer cannot easily be quantified. It comes partly through development agencies' development research programs, which we briefly discuss in the next chapter, and, of course, technical assistance. But equally important are the ideas and practices that are introduced through the conditionalities (the actions countries have to take before receiving aid), often hotly contested (see Chapter 5).

Official aid is provided by perhaps forty bilateral agencies (of which twenty-three are DAC members), twenty IFIs, and fifteen UN agencies. The following describes the main principles of organization of this enormous and ever-growing complex.

Bilateral Aid Agencies

The bilateral donors are defined by the funding that goes from national governments, mostly but not only OECD countries, to partners in poorer countries, both to government organizations and NGOs (as well as to multilateral organizations). But that is where the commonalities end. The way aid provision is organized, countries' histories and perceptions of international roles, the focus of aid and the sectors to which it is provided, and partner countries all vary a great deal. The following is only a selective description of this diversity, organized in groupings of countries that have relatively dispersed provisions within their own government systems (as in the United States), and countries where the provision of aid is much more strongly managed within and coordinated by one government agency (as in the UK and Canada), or as part of other government ministries (Sweden, Netherlands).[4] The categories used for the description derive from donor countries' predominant ideas, institutions, and interests (3 I's), which are crucially important for how aid is organized (Lancaster 2007, 18–22).

Multiple Aid Entities

Aid programs are carried out by multiple government entities in Germany, Japan, France, the United States, and "newcomer" China. In the case of Germany and Japan compensation for and reestablishing international reputation after the war played important roles in the formation of

Table 2–4. Driving Forces of National ("Bilateral") Aid Programs

	Fragmented aid programs: the US	Aid program within other ministries: the Netherlands	Aid managed by own ministry: the UK
Ideas	Tension liberalism—state as vehicle redistribution Role of US as global leader Western alliance	Social-democratic + consensus approach	Since 1997 dominance New Labour and "Third Way"
Institutions	Presidential system Influence Congress Political autonomy elements of government	Coalition governments with sustained support for aid Central role "co-financing organizations" (major Dutch NGOs)	Parliamentary system, since 1997 strong cross-party support for aid PM and Chancellor influence benefits aid
Interests	Weak constituency within government Aid lobby of NGOs Ethnic/religious groups Commercial: manufacture, agriculture, labor	Strong cross-government support NGO co-financing structure Business community	Cross-party support Strong advocacy oriented NGOs Business/consultancy community

the aid program, along with economic motives such as the need to find access to natural resources. In France the colonial past and the desire for a continued global role have played central roles. The new aid program in China—which used to be an important donor in the 1970s—is designed alongside its expanding international political role and commercial interests.[5] In all cases agencies are accompanied by varied and relatively diffuse international development objectives; in some cases this makes it difficult to describe the nature or even the size of the aid programs.

While the United States provides a relatively low share of its GNI to international aid (0.18 percent in 2006), it is the world's largest donor. It was also the first donor in the modern era of international development when it provided aid to Europe devastated by the war and to Asia in the wake of the Chinese revolution and outbreak of the Korean War (both the USSR and China soon started to provide aid to their allies). It also pressed other countries to establish their aid programs (Lancaster 2007, 28–29). Moreover, the United States also is home to an increasing number of very large private donors. The US aid program is among the most fragmented ones, with at least twenty institutions involved in aid delivery in addition to USAID; recently there has been a push for a clearer unified framework (Brainard 2007a).[6]

As described in detail by Carol Lancaster (2007), US aid is shaped by conflicting trends in thinking in the United States, dating back to the late eighteenth century: classical liberalism, which argues for a limitation of the role of the state (which contributed to the Washington Consensus), and ideas about the state needing to play a key role in redistribution. For example, reflecting a preference, relative to European traditions, for private over government-run support, private charities provided more than three times the amount of aid provided by the US government in response to the tsunami (Brainard 2007a, 20). Moreover, the US aid program has been shaped by the way the United States has perceived itself as a world power and leader of the non-communist world. Thus, national security considerations have been a strong driver of the aid program, increasingly so since 9/11. Involvement of the Pentagon also has increased significantly. However, critiques have kept aid from being used entirely for diplomatic purposes, and development has remained a core component of the aid program—and contributed to important developments like the Green revolution—though never as dominant as in some countries in Europe.

US political and administrative institutions have been influential in shaping its aid program. Political power is relatively fragmented, and the system adversarial. There are huge cultural differences between government officials and Capitol Hill staff. In its political system major elements of government are politically autonomous. The influence of private groups is large, and aid is often severely criticized. The bipolar and winner-take-all political system does not allow for smaller parties to put aid issues on the agenda—though this does not explain why development did not become a major issue during the Clinton administration. The executive and legislative branches of government both play a role in shaping policies and deciding expenditure. Congress plays a very important direct role in funding and implementation decisions, and it imposes, in Andrew Natsios's words, "hundreds of congressional directives and special budget measures," called earmarks (quoted in Flickner 2007, 225).[7] Because of the way US foreign aid has been managed, concluded Alice Amsden, it "was like the hallucinogen called angel dust—it felt good, but it had a lot of bad side effects" (2007, 71).[8]

As in other countries, there is an aid lobby in the United States. NGOs promote the use of aid for relief, development, environment, family planning, and gender equality, and have varied backgrounds, like religious organizations, universities, think tanks, and so forth. Commercial interests that influence aid include manufacturers, agricultural producers, and labor. The use of food aid has been an important—and much criticized—example of the commercial influences on aid. This has helped to reduce the US food surplus, with active support from Congress and from the NGOs that have been instrumental in delivering this aid (Wahlberg 2008).[9] Many have argued that while food aid may be important in some emergency situations, it is not an effective use of aid in normal situations.

While support for aid with developmental objectives is not absent in the United States, other interests tend to have the upper hand; in countries with a single agency responsible for aid, development and poverty reduction have more priority among objectives. The White House frequently becomes directly engaged in aid initiatives. The State Department has been the main driver of the diplomatic motives behind the aid program both during the Cold War and now in the post 9/11 period. Under President Bush and Secretary of State Condoleezza Rice "transformational diplomacy" became a prime principle of US foreign policy, influencing other countries' approaches as well. Rice summed up the increased interest as follows: "One of our best tools for supporting states in building democratic institutions and strengthening civil society is our foreign assistance. . . . One of the great advances of the past eight years has been the creation of a bipartisan consensus for the more strategic use of foreign assistance" (Rice 2008, 11). The Treasury provides money to, and directly influences, the international institutions, with a strong emphasis on fiscal responsibility. USAID is the "real" development agency, but it does not have cabinet-level status. As a result, as Carol Lancaster notes: "I found while serving as deputy administrator of USAID . . . that it was often difficult for USAID to get an invitation to high-level interagency policy discussions—even at times when development related issues were on the agenda" (2007, 101). Departments of commerce and of agriculture have been promoting the use of aid for commercial purposes but have had little influence.

In addition to initiatives on AIDS, like PEPFAR (President's Emergency Plan for AIDS Relief), which has a budget of $30 billion over five years (Lancaster 2008, 22–29), the Millennium Challenge Account is an example of an initiative with direct presidential support. A week before the Monterrey conference, President Bush announced setting up this account as a way to provide an additional $5 billion for international development:

> Countries that live by . . . three broad standards—ruling justly, investing in their people, and encouraging economic freedom—will receive more aid from America. And, more importantly, over time, they will really no longer need it, because nations with sound laws and policies will attract more foreign investment. They will earn more trade revenues. And they will find that all these sources of capital will be invested more effectively and productively to create more jobs for their people.[10]

The United States established the Millennium Challenge Corporation (MCC) in early 2004, but disbursements have remained low; as of the end of 2007 only $125 million was spent out of $4.8 billion committed (Lancaster 2008, 21). According to Radelet (2007, 104), while the MCC's basic principles of providing aid to countries with the right policies and under national ownership and participation are sound, it is too early to tell how different and innovative this initiative is.

Aid Programs as Part of Foreign Affairs

Within the aid industry Nordic countries and the Netherlands are generally viewed as having progressive and relatively focused aid programs. In these countries the departments for aid are implementing agencies or merged into the ministries of foreign affairs. The aid agencies were mostly set up in the 1950s and 1960s, starting in Norway, where an aid program was established in 1952 as a means to pacify the Labour Party's opposition to Norway joining NATO (Lancaster 2007, 30). Despite their early political origins during the Cold War, strong support for aid programs exists in these countries, and they have consistently reached the target of committing 0.7 percent of GNI to aid. Sweden even committed itself to a higher percentage.[11]

In these countries social democratic orientations exercise strong and stable influences over the aid program. In the case of the Netherlands, where the aid program also grew out of the colonial period, the tradition of coalition governments and a consensus style of policy formulation, sustained involvement of Dutch NGOs and the business community, and arguably a history of international political neutrality have contributed to a relatively stable aid policy environment, avoiding the swings experienced in the UK, for example. Dutch aid has strong ministerial and parliamentarian support, and policymakers believe in the added value of a Dutch aid program, despite its relative small size. Individual ministers have exercised great influence over the direction of the Dutch aid program, notably Jan Pronk and Eveline Herfkens, both responding to international thinking and national constituencies, and, to a lesser extent, Van Ardenne, who emphasized the role of the private sector.

The Dutch aid program is merged within the Ministry of Foreign Affairs, with an integrated administrative structure and personnel policy. Although integrated, it maintains a clear development and poverty focus, through a two-headed structure with cabinet ministers for foreign affairs and development cooperation. It is "viewed within the international donor community as a front runner with regard to its ability to adapt to new challenges and to test innovative operational approaches. . . . The Netherlands has been a leading player in consistently promoting poverty reduction" (DAC Peer Review 2006). It has remained among the most generous donors. Its aid has been relatively well targeted to low-income countries—even though attempts to focus aid on a smaller number of countries do not appear to have been very successful. Like Denmark and Sweden it has consistently interacted closely with multilateral institutions, highlighted in moves toward sector approaches, debt relief, and poverty reduction strategies.

The organization of Dutch aid reflects a national politics known as *verzuiling* (pillarization), the traditional organization of public and political life along religious and nonreligious backgrounds or pillars (Catholic, Protestant, humanist, Social Democrat). The so-called co-financing

organizations have had a central place in Dutch development cooperation since 1964, receiving core funding, but during the 1990s they also
received increased criticism and attention to quality. Since 2003 six main
NGOs receive core funding based on proposals submitted, through
which 10 to 14 percent of Dutch aid is channeled; a separate window
exists for other, usually smaller Dutch NGOs. Although the percentage
of aid to NGOs is not larger than the average for OECD countries,
Dutch aid is perceived to have a strong emphasis on NGOs, and on
working with NGOs in recipient countries.

There has been continued strong public support for aid in the Netherlands, though it has decreased slightly over the last ten years. However, as elsewhere, demands for results have increased. This contributed
to a pronounced emphasis, during the 1990s in particular, on the need
to improve the quality of aid (Schulpen 2005). First, in 1990 a white
paper set out a structured vision on poverty reduction, though it has
been argued that the operationalization of ideas was not strong. Second,
from 1993 onward Dutch policy started to emphasize "policy coherence": the importance of policies traditionally not part of aid programs
(such as the negative impact of the European Community Agricultural
Policy) but exercising great influence on poverty reduction, and hence
calling for collaboration among different government departments.[12] A
third change was increased focus on sectoral budget support to overcome the problem of project aid which had contributed to "islands of
development"—a theme that is central to subsequent chapters. Fourth,
in the mid-1990s responsibilities for implementation of the aid program was devolved to embassies. Finally, and arguably reflecting Dutch
emphasis on consensus politics, the aid program appears to have a relatively strong tradition of independent evaluation and review.[13]

This group of donors, the Nordic countries and the Netherlands,
often referred to as like-minded, shows relative stability, both in terms
of internal organization and in terms of public support—though neither is set in stone. Its embeddedness in foreign affairs has not stopped
it from being among the more progressive forces in the aid industry; in
fact, the provision of aid for "pure" development purposes in these small
countries is seen as an essential part of its foreign diplomacy.

Aid Programs as a Ministry

The UK and Canada—which now have aid ministries—demonstrate the
potential importance of political changes for donor programs. Different

Canadian prime ministers had significant impact on aid. Jean Chrétien reversed the decline in aid and prioritized Africa. Under Paul Martin, the Canadian International Development Agency (CIDA) developed a "whole-of-government" approach, integrating aid more closely with foreign-policy objectives. Directions for Canadian aid have been relatively unclear under Stephen Harper, though he has continued a focus on Afghanistan.[14]

During the last decade the UK has been one of the leading agencies in terms of both poverty orientation and as a driver of improving the efficiency of aid, under the stewardship of Clare Short, with a seat in the Cabinet, and with strong support from both the prime minister and the chancellor. In ten years DFID saw three ministers (plus a fourth, briefly, after the departure of Clare Short following a rift over the war in Iraq), and a number of junior ministers. Its main focus, however, remained the same, and DFID has gained a reputation as a trailblazer in international development, having focused its development programs firmly on the needs of the poorest countries.

As in France, the UK aid program grew out of its colonial history. The provision of financial assistance became part of the late colonial administrations. France provided aid to its colonies in the 1940s, and Britain formulated the Colonial Development and Welfare Acts 1940 (replaced in 1945). Based on Fabian views of the state and optimism about possible projects, Britain, for example, started a groundnut scheme in Tanganyika and the Gambia egg scheme. Historical links and approaches continued to play an important role. For example, the forced ujamaa villageization in Tanzania showed continuity with the British colonial policy of pressing villageization on the rural Tanzanian poor.[15]

While currently a strong separate ministry, the organization of British aid has continuously changed. Britain established development corporations for its colonies and elsewhere in 1947. In 1958 it decided to extend aid to former colonies within the Commonwealth and to some countries outside of it. In 1964 the incoming Labour government established the Ministry of Overseas Development, but in 1967 it was demoted out of the cabinet, and, in 1970, when the Conservative Party was elected, it was incorporated into the Foreign Office. It became a ministry again under the Labour government from 1974 to 1979, and the percentage of aid increased to 0.51 percent of GNI, but commercial and other motives exerted their influence. Under the Conservative government from 1979 to 1997 aid again became part of the Foreign Office, and political, industrial, and commercial objectives obtained greater and explicit weight.

When the Labour Party came into power in 1997, it established DFID, and the aid budget started to increase immediately. The orientation of aid also changed drastically, from a focus on promoting commercial and political interest to reducing poverty in the poorest parts of the world. A crucial part of the new orientation was the decision to "untie" aid; whereas previously benefits to UK commercial interests were an integral part of the aid provided, according to the white paper of 2000 and enshrined in law in the International Development Act 2002, the purpose of aid was prescribed as to further sustainable development, promote people's welfare, and contribute to the reduction of poverty. The department also has adopted targets for the proportion of aid going to the poorest countries.

The change in orientation was accompanied by rapid—and continued—organizational change. DFID rapidly increased the number of professional staff, an upward trend that only came to a halt after reductions in civil servants across the government were announced in 2002. The number of overseas offices expanded significantly, from a handful in the mid-1990s to over forty ten years later, accompanying a strong emphasis on building partnership with developing countries. Not only did the organization shift its concern to poverty reduction, but at the same time it started to focus on measuring the results of its aid efforts. Just as in all UK government departments, targets, ways of measuring achievements, and reports proliferated. A strong policy drive was highlighted by the publication of three white papers within ten years—unusual for any government department. The first set out New Labour's aspirations for international development (including untying aid); the second focused on the global economic environment, arguing for the need for trade and other government policies to ensure development; and the third highlighted the importance of governance in partner countries, reinforcing the attention paid to building partnerships.

The focus on showing the achievements of its aid program has been accompanied by an explicit acknowledgment that DFID by itself cannot achieve stated development goals. As with European donors like the Netherlands and Sweden, DFID strongly emphasized the importance of partnerships with recipient countries and the need for harmonization among donors to reduce burdens on recipients (discussed in Chapter 6). Moreover, DFID, through strong advocacy at international meetings, and though a series of "institutional strategy papers" setting out publicly the aims of the UK government to initiate reforms and achieve specific targets, has been very vocal about its belief that the international system needs reform. Finally, it has been very active in promoting collaboration with other government departments, trying to ensure that foreign and commercial policy objectives contribute to global poverty reduction. It now formally shares objectives with other departments, such as foreign affairs and environment.

There are few—if any—who have not accepted the achievements of DFID, in terms of its focus as well as its way of working. DFID greatly benefited from a level of support since 1997 that was all but absent, for example, under the Clinton administration in the United States—and most people expect that the broad support will continue. Moreover, New Labour's emphasis on modernization of government—under the pressure of strong anti-statist ideas in the UK—greatly benefited DFID in efforts to show how aid can work. Finally, the UK has a strong and issue-oriented civil society. Not only has public support for aid remained strong, but it also has a number of well-equipped NGOs that have continued to engage critically with the official aid program. In addition, it has probably the world's strongest policy-research community, which has supplied DFID with technical expertise and formed a critical voice, promoting broad public debate.

The Limits of Bilateral Aid

The brief description above of some of the bilateral aid programs shows that despite agreements over the objectives of aid, there have been significant dissimilarities in how aid programs have been structured. The way aid is provided shows clear traces of a country's public policies and respective history. Aid agencies are situated within governments in a wide variety of ways, significantly affecting the focus, implementation, and monitoring of aid programs. National pressures have influenced and continue to influence aid greatly. For example, while aid has become more important on the US political agenda over the last few years before President Obama was elected, and many of the new policies are in line with the international development consensus, this recent push was also strongly and explicitly in line with perceived US foreign-policy interests. Such influence continues to exist in other countries too. Sometimes aid agencies can shelter themselves from such pressures more effectively than in other cases, but the pressures never disappear and can become stronger, for example, as a result of national elections.

Because of the complexity of bilateral aid agencies, some observers have argued that there is a need for more multilateral (and harmonized) approaches. The channeling of aid through agencies that are independent of national interests, pressures, and the reporting requirements of national aid agencies would allow tighter focus on development purposes. It is important to emphasize how strongly the provision of aid is tied into national ideological, social, and political-administrative traditions. This chapter continues with a description of the existing multilateral system as it evolved during the twentieth century.

International Financial Institutions

Like much of the aid industry, the origins of the international financial institutions (IFIs)—a term that refers to the World Bank and the IMF, also called the Bretton Woods institutions after the place in New Hampshire where they were created—lay in World War II. At the Bretton Woods conference, the forty-five governments soon to win the war discussed rebuilding Europe and the global economic system after the devastating war and how to avoid a repetition of the disastrous economic policies that had contributed to the Great Depression of the 1930s. The British delegation led by Maynard Keynes proposed the IMF as a cooperative fund that member states could draw upon to maintain economic activity and employment. But the US plan prevailed—an IMF like a bank that would ensure borrowing states could repay their debts on time and less concerned with avoiding recession and unemployment. The IMF came to focus on fiscal stability, while the World Bank became responsible for investment in development. Over the following six decades there has been some overlap and shifting in this division (for example, when the IMF asks the Bank to contribute to stabilization after financial crises, such as in East Asia in 1997–98), but the basic difference has remained.[16]

At present, the IMF is governed by and accountable to the governments of the 185 member countries and has about twenty-seven hundred staff members from 165 countries. At the apex of its organizational structure is its board of governors, which consists of one governor from each member country. Governors meet once each year at the IMF–World Bank Annual Meetings, and twenty-four of them sit on the International Monetary and Finance Committee (IMFC), which meets twice each year. The day-to-day work of the IMF is conducted by a twenty-four-member executive board guided by the IMFC and supported by the IMF's professional staff. The IMF's resources are provided by its member countries, primarily through payment of quotas that broadly reflect each country's economic size. In 2006 total quotas amounted to $317 billion.

The IMF's main responsibilities are to promote international monetary cooperation, facilitate expansion of international trade, promote exchange stability, assist in the establishment of a multilateral system of payments, and provide resources available to members experiencing balance of payments difficulties—all arguably essential conditions for economic growth and poverty alleviation. It employs three instruments. First, the IMF conducts appraisals of member countries' economic situation, which most countries publish. Second, the IMF provides technical assistance and training to strengthen capacity in fiscal and monetary policy, banking, financial, and statistical systems. Third, the IMF provides financial assistance during balance-of-payments problems. Such support is conditional on a policy program designed and agreed upon between the IMF and the national authorities.[17] The loans have come to be known as structural adjustment loans, because they aim to help borrowing governments adjust their economies; as such, they have been widely criticized (see Chapter 5). In the 1990s the IMF, working closely with the World Bank, began to change its policymaking strategies to incorporate poverty reduction policies in addition to creating economic stability. Ten years later voices were raised to bring the IMF back to its original mandate. Recently, an increasing number of countries, like Thailand, Brazil, and Argentina, have been paying off their debt much more quickly than expected. The 2008–9 economic crisis strengthened calls to reform and again enhance the role of the IMF.

The World Bank's initial focus was rebuilding postwar Europe, and its first loan, $250 million, was to France in 1947 for postwar reconstruction. This function was soon overtaken by the much larger Marshall Plan, and the World Bank started to focus on developing countries. The function of reconstruction was picked up as a main theme again only in the 1990s, with the World Bank taking an active role in the postwar Balkans. From the start its organizational structure has been unlike that of other UN institutions. Founding governments have representatives on the World Bank's board, but voting power reflects countries' financial contribution and thus the United States has dominated many of its important decisions.[18] Currently, the Bank has about ten thousand professional staff, with capacity for development research that far outstrips any university department or think tank.

The World Bank is in fact a group of five associated institutions, of which two are the most important for the discussion here. First, the International Bank for Reconstruction and Development (IBRD) is the oldest; it focuses on reduction of poverty in middle-income and "credit-worthy" poor countries. It provides loans, guarantees, risk-management products, and analysis and advice. IBRD borrows in capital markets at low cost. It has a twenty-four-member board, with five appointed and nineteen elected executive directors, jointly representing IBRD's 184 member countries. During fiscal year 2006 it lent $14 billion for 112 new operations in thirty-three countries. IBRD has lent $420 billion since its inception in 1944.

Second, the International Development Association (IDA) provides financing to the world's eighty-one poorest countries, which are unable to borrow on market terms. The funding is highly concessional, through interest-free credits and grants financed from donor countries' contributions—which are "replenished" every three years—and IBRD's net income transfers. The resources support, for example, country-led poverty reduction strategies in key policy areas, including raising productivity, promoting accountable governance, increasing healthy investment climates, and improving access to basic services. In 2006 the IDA provided $9.5 billion for 167 new operations in fifty-nine countries. According to the World Bank website, at the end of 2007 over $40 billion became available for the period from 2008 to 2011.

The other three institutions are less directly relevant here, though they are equally large. The third, the International Finance Corporation (IFC), established in 1956, is the private-sector investment entity of the group, providing support to businesses deemed too risky by commercial investors. It has 178 members, and according to its website, it had fiscal commitments in 2006 of $6.7 billion for 284 projects in sixty-six countries. The fourth, the Multilateral Investment Guarantee Agency (MIGA), provides insurance for foreign direct investment in developing countries, providing both guarantees against noncommercial risks and advisory and mediating services. Established in 1988, MIGA currently has 167 members, and, according to its website, in 2006 it issued guarantees worth $1.3 billion. Finally, the International Centre for Settlement of Investment Disputes (ICSID) focuses on settlement of investment disputes between foreign investors and host states. According to the World Bank website, ICSID has registered 210 cases since its foundation in 1966, and it focuses on arbitration of investment disputes and foreign investment law.

The diversity of the World Bank's roles is the result of a gradual broadening of its mandate. After shifting attention from postwar reconstruction to development, it focused on infrastructure, particularly "sound" projects that could be expected to generate financial returns; it operated under the influence of economic models that emphasized accumulation of physical capital. The additional focus on poor countries was formalized with the creation of IDA in 1960—in the middle of the Cold War, and a year after the Cuban revolution.

The public focus on poverty intensified under Robert McNamara, who became the World Bank's president in 1968, after leaving the US Department of Defense during the Vietnam War. During his tenure the World Bank started to pay more attention to the question of whether economic growth did "trickle down" to poor people. McNamara created a range of new specialized departments within the bank—for rural and urban development, health and nutrition, education, and others—in effect creating a group that overlapped the functions of the UN specialized agencies. According to many, the bank overextended itself and its mandate (Mallaby 2005, 35–36), but over time the bank did build up strong capacity in those diverse areas.

While the World Bank continued to see poverty reduction as its prime mandate, the second oil crisis in 1979, following the Iranian revolution, initiated a focus on "structural adjustment lending." The rise in energy prices hit many poor countries heavily, and McNamara announced that countries would need to devalue their currencies to be able to reduce trade imbalances and to cut public spending to be able to pay back the loans, including those that countries had obtained easily in the preceding period when petro-dollars were easily available. Structural adjustment lending was conceived as a form of support to reformers, to give them some breathing space during a period of adjustment, and led a shift in development approaches from project approaches to program approaches.

By most accounts, the 1980s—during the Reagan/Thatcher years—was a relatively disastrous period for the World Bank, at least as far as its reputation was concerned. In collaboration with the IMF, its policy prescriptions for structural adjustment were broadened beyond the spheres of exchange rates and government budgets, adding conditions based on reducing trade barriers, free prices, and privatization. After McNamara, the World Bank was headed by three presidents who did the image of the Bank little good. During the 1980s increased criticisms were voiced about the presumed deteriorating quality of World Bank projects. Until the mid-1990s, the World Bank did not respond to calls to address the issues of debt relief. But it would be wrong to think poverty did not feature at the World Bank, even during the years of adjustment; for example, the bank developed high quality—though disputed—monitoring and poverty-analysis tools during the 1980s.

Following political changes in the United States and the UK, James Wolfensohn arrived at the World Bank. He changed the institution greatly, arguably rescuing it from the critiques to which it had been subjected. Wolfensohn brought in a much more informal, personal, and aggressive style of leadership intended to change the image of the bank as an arrogant institution. Against resistance from many senior staff, he accepted that the bank needed to address debt relief. This culminated in the poverty reduction strategy approach. He improved relationships with major international NGOs. He broke the internal taboo by talking about corruption, particularly after his dissatisfaction with the World Bank's approach in Indonesia, strengthening a focus on governance (see Chapter 5). He strengthened an emphasis on participation—on countries' ownership of development and participation by beneficiaries of development projects and policies (which came to be seen as crucial to success of development projects). From the early 2000s pressure increased to focus more on infrastructure and to listen more to the large borrowers. Other changes brought about under Wolfensohn included greater decentralization of country offices and much quicker quality assurance. He tried hard to change the personnel system, introduced a matrix system in which specialists simultaneously reported to technical bosses and country directors, and brought in private-sector practices such as change management.

No part of the aid industry has been under more criticism than the World Bank and IMF. The protests developed momentum under the weak World Bank leadership of the 1990s, but even under more popular and stronger presidents the critiques continued. In his in-depth description of the World Bank under Wolfensohn, Sebastian Mallaby highlights the "alternating bouts of millenarianism and contempt" as well as the "cacophony of our advanced countries" (2005, 7). The World Bank often is criticized for failure to address global poverty (portrayed as simply needing $2.50 for bed-nets to save poor Africans) and at times (for example, under the Ronald Reagan and George W. Bush administrations) undermined by contempt for and ignorance of its larger shareholder, the United States. It has been heavily criticized by international NGOs for the poverty impact of structural adjustment and the environmental consequences of World Bank projects. In fact, international NGOs have had a major impact on the World Bank, though it remains disputed whether this changed the institution's staff incentives and systems of accountability. Recent World Bank approaches undertaken at least in part in response to the external critique—such as the Comprehensive Development Framework (CDF) and the PRSPs—also came under criticism, and indeed the World Bank's and IMF's own evaluations were openly critical as well.

The World Bank's and IMF's lending have continued to be questioned. Some (for example, the Meltzer Commission established by the U.S. Congress in 1998) argue that the institutions should focus on providing support to the poorest countries and cease lending to middle-income countries, and it is often argued that the World Bank should shrink its range of activities. At the same time, an increasing number of countries—usually not the poorest—have refused to borrow from the World Bank: South Africa's post-apartheid government refused to borrow money but became a donor itself; in 2007 a number of Latin American countries set up the Banco del Sur to access funding independently from the World Bank and the IMF; and in Asian countries the need for a regional monetary fund in response to the failure of the IMF to respond adequately to the 1997 crisis has been discussed.

Multilaterals: The UN Specialized Agencies

The multilateral system of the United Nations is complex, so much so that the coordination among UN agencies ("One UN") has become a key issue. Unlike the World Bank and IMF, UN decision making operates on a one-member one-vote principle. Its aid is usually provided as grants, like most of the bilateral agencies. The UN is not an aid agency—it is primarily a political organization, with the Security Council as one of its main bodies—but it has a central role in the aid industry because of its convening power and leaders who have frequently committed themselves to international development, such as the 1995 Copenhagen and Millennium summits. The UN provides about 15 percent of total global ODA. Its total budget is about $11 billion a year (excluding the World Bank and the IMF), with the regular budget just over $1 billion in 2002, and the budget for peacekeeping about $3 billion in the same year (Fasulo 2003, 115). The UN agencies usually do not come under the same kind of public criticism as the IFIs, though there are exceptions, but there have been major concerns about their operational inefficiencies.[19]

The United Nations had its forerunner in the League of Nations, established after World War I, which aimed "to promote international cooperation and to achieve peace and security," and in organizations that are now UN specialized agencies, such as the ILO, which was created under the Treaty of Versailles, and specialized unions. The name United Nations was coined by US President Roosevelt, and the organization officially came into existence in 1945, after representatives of fifty countries met in San Francisco to draw up the United Nations Charter on the basis of proposals worked out by the representatives of China, the Soviet Union, the United Kingdom, and the United States. The image of the UN is very strongly determined by its secretary-general,[20] and the organization was much strengthened under the leadership of Kofi Annan, who served two terms between 1997 and 2006. Annan was respected by most people who worked with him, with the notable exception of John Bolton, the (temporary) ambassador to the UN from the United States during 2005 and 2006.[21]

A great deal of the work of the UN is carried out by and through its numerous agencies and funds, each devoted to a particular aspect of development. (This decentralization has led to relatively limited management power for the secretary-general.) There are about thirty UN specialized agencies—plus a number of research institutes. As traditional sources of funding have begun to dry up, UN agencies have started to look for alternatives, including corporate sponsorship. Organizations like the United Nations Children's Fund (UNICEF) have a very good record of raising private contributions.

The United Nations Development Programme (UNDP) was founded in 1965 to coordinate UN work in more than 160 developing countries, but in fact it often operates as a technical agency itself. According to a historical study commissioned by UNDP (Murphy 2006) it has been one of the main forces for democratic change across the globe.[22] Its annual budget is about $2 billion, of which $750 million is core contributions (Fasulo 2003, 115). One of its most widely known contributions has been its annual *Human Development Report* (HDR), starting in 1990, created under the leadership of Pakistani economist Mahbub ul Haq. This has provided major input to the international development debate (described in the next chapter) helping to broaden the understanding of development from a narrow perspective on economic growth. The

Human Development Index, by which countries compare their achievements as they compare their gross domestic products, has become a part of a global policy debate.

UN agencies may be best known for emergency operations,[23] which had increased in importance during the 1990s as the number of conflicts rose after the end of the Cold War; the establishment of the International Criminal Court; and the adoption of the "responsibility to protect" norm. The Security Council organizes peacekeeping operations, with a budget in 2006 of US$2.6 billion (Fasulo 2003, 53). The Office of the United Nations High Commissioner for Refugees (UNHCR), established in 1950, leads international action to resolve refugee problems, starting with support to refugees after World War II. It aims to safeguard the rights and well-being of refugees and to help exercise the right to seek asylum and find safe refuge. The UNHCR estimates that since 1950 it has helped fifty million people restart their lives. Its budget peaked in 1994 (US$1.4 billion) with refugee emergencies in former Yugoslavia and the Great Lakes region of Africa and elsewhere—and is currently just over US$1 billion. Its activities are almost entirely funded by direct, voluntary contributions from governments, NGOs, and individuals. Today, over six thousand staff members in 111 countries assist an estimated thirty million people.

Since the 1990s, and particularly after failures during the conflicts and genocides in Bosnia and Rwanda, the UN has tried to step up its efforts in peacekeeping. Under the inspiring leadership of Kofi Annan, who accepted responsibility for the failures during the 1990s, a much intensified and aggressive approach to conflicts emerged, for example, in East Timor, involving all major stakeholders. In 2005 the UN Central Emergency Response Fund (CERF) was established by the General Assembly to "speed up relief operations for emergencies, make money available quickly after a disaster and help in financing underfunded emergencies." The fund provided over $200 million in the first half of 2007, through donors contributions, with allocations to eight UN agencies and the International Organization for Migration (IOM), and humanitarian projects in thirty-five countries.

UNICEF is definitely also among the most visible UN agencies, working in some 150 countries and perceived as an important partner by many governments, with appeals for support during emergencies and a large number of celebrities as goodwill ambassadors. While perhaps 40 percent of UNICEF's work is in emergencies and humanitarian settings, in general it focuses on development and social protection of children, basic education, and HIV/AIDS and children. It annually publishes its *State of the World's Children Report,* which describes progress on and challenges related to these issues. It has a strong advocacy focus, and bases its advocacy for children primarily on the 1989 Convention on the Rights of the Child.

The ILO is a central but unique part of the aid system. It predates the UN and is a tripartite organization, bringing together representatives of governments, employers, and workers in its executive bodies. It was created in 1919, at the end of World War I, at the time of the Peace Conference, and under the influence of industrialists Robert Owen and Daniel Legrand. The United States became an ILO member in 1934, and ILO's current charter was adopted in the midst of the Second World War.[24]

The initial motivation of the ILO was humanitarian, focusing on conditions and exploitation of workers. Political and economic motivations played a role too; it was feared that social unrest or even revolution might occur (the Preamble notes that injustice produces "unrest so great that the peace and harmony of the world are imperiled"). International coordination was seen as essential to ensure countries that implemented social reforms were not disadvantaged in regard to their competitors. The ILO's executive council is elected by the conference, one-half of whose members are government representatives, one-fourth workers' representatives, and one-fourth employers' representatives. During the 1950s and 1960s the number of member states doubled, and industrialized countries became a minority. At the same time the budget grew fivefold. The ILO received the Nobel Peace Prize in 1969, but during the early 1970s the organization was faced with politicization of the East-West conflict, and the United States withdrew from the organization in 1977. The ILO supported the legitimacy of the Solidarnosc Union in Poland. During the 1990s the ILO increased its role in international councils on economic and social development while decentralizing activities and resources.

The ILO supports technical cooperation projects in the fields of employment and personnel planning, and labor-market information, through long-term projects and short-term consultancies. Regional employment teams provide technical advisory services and training courses in response to requests from countries. Technical missions for public-works programs help governments define the scope of special public-works programs, assessing technical feasibility as well as organizational and staffing needs.

One of the most widely known ILO technical programs has been the World Employment Programme (WEP). Following a convention adopted in 1964, and inaugurated in 1969, WEP was seen as the ILO's main contribution to the United Nations Second Development Decade. The concept of freely chosen employment is an integral part of a basic needs strategy (discussed further in Chapter 3). It encourages ways of meeting the basic needs of the poor through advisory services, technical cooperation, and research. ILO initiatives have focused on the so-called informal sector through the Regional Employment Program for Latin America and the Caribbean and the Jobs and Skills Program for Africa. This included gathering data; training and technical cooperation; promotion of income-generating projects for specific vulnerable groups; apprenticeships and training for production; and case studies of regulatory barriers. In 1991 the ILO emphasized the working poor—the people who work in jobs in the informal sector, on the fringes of the recognized labor market. It proposed that governments set and meet targets of creating sufficient jobs, and since 2007 employment and decent work have been included among the targets under MDG1.

The ILO's International Programme on the Elimination of Child Labour (IPEC) was created in 1992 with the goal of progressive elimination of child labor. The ILO tries to achieve this by strengthening countries' capacity to deal with the problem and by promoting a worldwide movement to combat child labor. It operates in eighty-eight countries; in 2006 its expenditures on technical cooperation projects were more than US$74 million. IPEC's partners include employers' organizations, workers' organizations, other international and government agencies, private businesses, and a wide range of civil society organizations. (An example of the program in China is provided in Box 2–1).

WHO, the World Health Organization, is the UN specialized agency for health. It was established on April 7, 1948, following advocacy by three physicians (Szeming Sze of China, Karl Evang of Norway, and Geraldo de Paula Souza of Brazil). It is governed by 193 member states through the World Health Assembly. WHO provides programs in health education, food, food safety, nutrition, safe water and basic sanitation, and immunization. Previous action plans promoted breastfeeding, production of foods to improve local diets, distribution of supplementary foods, and health education. WHO's global disease monitoring has been credited with helping to contain the spread of diseases. When Severe Acute Respiratory Syndrome (SARS) broke out in China in 2002, some of the earliest alerts were provided by an automated system that uses

---

**Box 2–1. ILO Project to Prevent Trafficking in Girls
and Young Women for Labour Exploitation
within China (CP-TING project)**

As part of the IPEC program, and with DFID funding, CP-TING is an ILO program in China (2004–9) that focuses on elimination of labor exploitation of children and women and the trafficking in girls and young women. It builds on China's ratification of ILO Convention 182 on the worst forms of child labor, including trafficking, and the *UN Convention on the Rights of the Child*. The project starts from the observation that while migration has helped many people to escape poverty, it also poses risks to which some people—particularly women and girls—are extremely vulnerable. The ILO has worked with the All China Women's Federation on a range of practical activities to address these risks and to help prepare vulnerable groups for the process of migration (rather than to try to stop people from migrating). It operates in three sending provinces (Anhui, Henan, Hunan) and two receiving provinces (Guangdong, Jiangsu). The project developed information campaigns, which have reached over one million women and girls. It helped to establish a network of female employers that has made a commitment to follow good labor practices. Women's Homes provide training and referral services. Further, the project aimed at and has been successful in informing national policymaking, for example, contributing to the drafting process of the National Plan for Action on Anti-trafficking.

---

electronic media including discussion groups, to identify signs of disease outbreaks that could lead to epidemics. A global network links 112 existing networks to monitor and respond to outbreaks of infectious diseases, and WHO has a network of leading laboratories to identify the cause of the disease and develop diagnostic tests.

The International Fund for Agricultural Development was established in 1978 to "increase food production in the poorest food deficit countries." IFAD finances agricultural development projects for food production through a combination of loans and grants. IFAD has increasingly prioritized poverty interventions, by targeting of funding to remote and unirrigated areas and by concentration on microfinance for the landless and near landless. Its program in Orissa in eastern India is an example of this approach, which evolved over the 1980s and 1990s. The approach encountered substantial and perhaps surprising criticism (see Box 2–2).

Box 2–2. IFAD Focus on the Poorest and Criticism

Southwestern Orissa is one of the most deprived regions of India, with about two-thirds of the population living below the poverty line. Fifty percent of the population belongs to so-called tribal groups or *adivasis*. The area has been in the public debate in India for decades, with prime ministers regularly visiting and announcing large programs with vast sums of money, which often remain unspent. The extreme poverty and remoteness of the area have been exploited by an insurgency group, the Naxalites, though its presence is not as large as in neighboring states.

IFAD started working in this area in the mid 1980s, after Prime Minster Rajiv Gandhi made a widely publicized visit to Kashipur, an area that more than any other symbolizes deep poverty. The Orissa Tribal Development Project (OTDP), the first of its kind financed by IFAD in India, with a value of over US$20 million, aimed to improve the livelihoods of tribal people. It was followed by the Orissa Tribal Empowerment and Livelihoods Programme (total value of US$90 million, including co-financing of DFID and WFP). While the first program had a strong emphasis on physical infrastructure and technologies—as IFAD's own evaluation stressed—the second program focused much more on building the capacity of poor people and their institutions and on enabling vulnerable groups, particularly women, to manage their own development. Key objectives of the program were to provide access to and management of natural resources, to improve access to financial services and markets, and to develop non-farm enterprises. The program was multifaceted, including employment, microfinance services, investments in agriculture, and funds for creating community infrastructure.

Criticisms of the programs have been wide ranging. It is often asserted—for example, through active electronic networks—that

---

Continued on page 49

decades of development projects and millions of dollars in government and aid money have made no difference to the area, which continues to suffer from deep poverty, health epidemics, and perennial starvation deaths (caused by poor people eating rotten food during the hungry season, for example). The development programs also have been criticized for introducing commercial activities like coffee plantations and sericulture (silk farming), thus threatening traditional livelihoods of the *adivasis* and benefiting traders, consolidating the power of moneylenders, and introducing dependency through the practice and expectations of government handouts. It is often claimed that much money has been misappropriated by project staff and partners, including NGOs, and several cases of misappropriation have been proven. Finally, it has been asserted that planting eucalyptus benefited paper mills more than the local population, and the creation of infrastructure in the area benefited large companies such as aluminum plants and other forms of mining. Indeed, exploitation of natural resource in the area has and continues to be resisted by local people.

Sources: www.ifad.org website (for OTDP and OTELP). For examples of criticism, see Tordella 2003; Das 2003; www.ainfos.ca; www.sabrang.com.

NGOs

The world of NGOs and civil society organizations is vast. In 1989 four thousand organizations existed in OECD countries alone devoted to international development (Desai 2002, 495). In Kenya, over five hundred development NGOs were operating in the late 1990s, of which 40 percent were foreign (Manji and O'Coill 2002).

The term *NGO* is applied to a range of institutions, including the charities in OECD countries (see Box 2–3), similar organizations in the South (like OXFAM India or OXFAM Hong Kong), small self-help and other organizations that often operate in one locality in very poor areas, and large organizations like the Grameen Bank in Bangladesh, which provides credit to large numbers of poor households. Development-focused NGOs are a significant part of the aid industry; on average, about 15 percent of aid flows are spent through nongovernmental channels, with, for example, the United States having a high proportion of total aid flowing through its NGOs.

Box 2–3. OXFAM UK and Elsewhere—From Relief to Development to Advocacy

Oxfam is one of the most widely known NGOs. Oxfam UK's network of shops selling donated items and handcrafts from overseas, run by twenty thousand volunteers, has given it its brand name and provided a main source of income since the late 1960s. Like many UN agencies, its origin lies in the Second World War. In 1942 the Famine Relief Committee tried to persuade the British government to allow supplies through the blockade, and it raised funds for war refugees and displaced people. The Oxford Committee for Famine Relief, consisting of businessmen, church, and university representatives, met for the first time in October 1942. After the war the Oxford Committee continued and broadened its focus: first, to relief of suffering in wars by providing food, clothing, and grants, and to "other causes in any part of the world." It changed it name to Oxfam in 1965. In India, Oxfam GB set up a registered society in 1978, which in the mid 1990s changed its status to the independent agency SVARAJ.

Oxfam Director Howard Leslie Kirkley was chairman of the UK Publicity Committee for the UN World Refugee Year in 1959–60, which gave Oxfam high visibility. During the 1960s Oxfam's income expanded, reflecting increased attention to poverty worldwide. Oxfam profiled itself as presenting a different picture of poverty—poor people not as passive victims but human beings with dignity—and education and informational materials focused on causes of poverty and suffering. Oxfam's overseas operations, increasingly managed by field directors and focused on employing local people, supported self-help schemes in water supplies, farming practices, and health. Relief work in the Sahel in the late 1970s stressed traditional ways in which communities survived and tried to ensure that local people kept control of the schemes in which they were involved. During the 1970s Oxfam started to focus on advocacy and to lobby at the global level, providing research on and analysis of the causes of poverty in relation to pesticides, food aid and aid more generally, and third-world debt.

Sources: www.oxfam.org.uk; www.svaraj.in; www.oxfamblogs.org.

Charitable activities were significant during colonial rule. NGOs, often working in close collaboration with bilateral or multilateral organizations, came to play an increasingly important role in formulation and development policy in the 1950s. There is a strong view among the current official aid agencies that nongovernmental partners have a key role to play in implementation of aid programs, because they have local knowledge and capacity. They are critical during emergencies, when official aid channels often cannot reach the populations affected.

NGOs became more popular as the critique of governments in developing countries increased and a neo-liberal paradigm was becoming stronger. Over time, the advocacy role of NGOs has become stronger, supported by electronic media, expanding into a new transnational civil society (Batliwala and Brown 2006). In the South this has entailed advocacy for rights as well as piloting new approaches. NGOs have increasingly moved into the monitoring of government policy. African NGOs, for example, developed a toolkit for monitoring policies (CAFOD, Christian Aid, Trócaire undated) in the area of gender. Box 2–4 illustrates an example from Cambodia in the area of the environment.

Box 2–4. Civil Society Monitoring of Environment in Cambodia

A proposed $470 million aid package in Cambodia in 1999 included a condition that there should be independent monitoring of log processing and export. The need for independent monitoring was identified at a donor meeting in order to ensure Cambodia government compliance with promised forestry reforms. IMF and World Bank support became conditional on the signing of the deal. With donor funding, the British environmental and human rights group Global Witness became the official independent monitor of Cambodia's forestry sector. The independent monitoring role complemented the new Forest Crime Monitoring Unit and inspection teams from the Forestry Department and the Ministry of Environment, both of whom receive donor funds to support monitoring. The government terminated Global Witness's activities in 2003 and banned members of the organization from entering the country in 2005.

Source: www.globalwitness.org.

In the North, NGOs play a key role in the development debate. They are influential in large organizations like the World Bank, particularly during the tenure of Wolfensohn, who cultivated relationships with a vocal NGO community. Influential issue-focused advocacy efforts by many NGOS include the Make Poverty History campaign, the Jubilee Debt Campaign, and Jubilee South (see Box 2–5). Since 1999 Jubilee South has built up a network of social and political organizations to strengthen continued advocacy for debt relief, illustrating a new dimension of globalization and the aid industry. It claims about eighty-five members in forty countries. According to its website "Jubilee South asserts that we—the peoples of the South—are the real creditors of a massive ecological, moral, social, financial, and historical debt." In its view this debt has been "imposed on us by the IMF, the World Bank, other international financial institutions (IFIs) and Northern governments to further their own profit and interests."

Box 2–5. The Jubilee Debt Campaign and Its Impact on IFIs

Since the mid 1990s the Debt Crisis Network has organized meetings on debt with African leaders, aid agencies, unions, and churches, raising the profile of the indebtedness of poor countries and the impact this has had on poor people. The pressure contributed to the heavily indebted poor countries' scheme launched by the World Bank and the IMF in 1996. This initiative was widely criticized for providing too little relief too late, and an international debt campaign continued to grow.

In Britain in October 1997 the Debt Crisis Network transformed itself into the Jubilee 2000 Coalition. A broad-based campaign crystalized and began to mobilize under this banner, including black refugee groups, trade unions, and organizations like the Mothers Union and the British Medical Association. Well-established NGOs like Christian Aid, CAFOD, WDM, and TearFund campaigned strongly in support of the Jubilee 2000 campaign. Churches organized Jubilee 2000 meetings, petitions were distributed, and people chained themselves to railings, resulting in one of the largest demonstrations ever organized in the UK.

Source: www.jubileedebtcampaign.org.uk.

Another example of the importance of NGOs is their influence on large development projects. The World Bank, responding to NGO criticism, has carefully assessed dam projects, withdrawn some large and controversial projects, and developed detailed environmental and social guidelines (safeguards) in project preparation. In India influential groups have vigorously opposed large projects like the Narmada dam and the influence of the World Bank in the country's policymaking. In September 2007, at JNU in Delhi, a group of organizations organized a People's Tribunal on the Impact of the World Bank Group in India, which highlighted that "local groups have been opposed to the often-disastrous intervention of multilateral agencies in India's economy and development. Specifically, the retrogressive impact . . . is being felt throughout the country by almost all marginal and impoverished sections of society" (worldbanktribunal.org website). International NGOs also have played an important role in the discussion on economic adjustment, and particularly the importance of social spending for poverty reduction.

While NGOs, which tend to be close to beneficiaries and able to reach poor people effectively, have been commended for the role they play within the aid industry, they also come under regular criticism. As Box 2–6 shows, relationships between governments and NGOs are not always collaborative.[25] Their impact tends to remain limited, and smaller organizations tend to lack professional capacity. NGOs are not representative of beneficiary groups. They are outsider organization working for deprived groups, but they are not membership-based organizations of the poor, as is the Self-Employed Women's Association (SEWA) in India (Chen et al. 2007). As with government organizations involved in the aid industry, NGOs too are scrutinized for their use of money, and coordinating bodies such as GiveIndia have emerged that help the public evaluate the credibility of NGOs.

It is sometimes argued that NGOs working in the South are an invention of the aid industry. The number, for example, of NGOs has increased very rapidly in Vietnam since the late 1980s; in 2003 international NGOs disbursed $90 million per year. But partly because of its communist history, the country does not have a concept that resembles NGOs or civil society, and the introduction of these terms resulted in misunderstandings and disputes (Salemink 2006).

Some argue even more critically that the work of NGOs, particularly as it is associated with the neo-liberal development model, "contributes marginally to the relief of poverty, but significantly to undermining the

---

Box 2–6. NGOs and Governments as Adversaries

The example from the development project in Orissa highlighted that the different players in the aid industry are often competitors rather than collaborators, and that their views on development can be radically different. Agragamee, an organization set up in the early 1980s, is devoted to supporting tribal communities in poorest parts of India. It has been heavily involved in and often praised for programs that reach the poorest (such as watershed projects) and supporting grassroots organizations. The organization resisted the exploitation of minerals by large companies, arguing that this would loot the tribal areas of Orissa. It withdrew from the collaboration in the IFAD project described in Box 2–2 because it believed that the voices of project beneficiaries were not given sufficient attention. The government revoked Agragamee's license in 1998 after a violent incident between villagers and companies (the nature of which remains disputed). While the organization's license was restored the next year, for government officials the organization and the incident continue to illustrate that NGOs can be "anti-developmental."

Source: www.agragamee.org.

---

struggle of African people to emancipate themselves from economic, social and political oppression" (Manji and O'Coill 2002, 2).

With their great diversity and differing views, NGOs are an important part of the aid industry. They often form the face of the industry, have increasingly been part of dialogues about the shape of the industry, and are more visible than their share in total aid flows—15 percent— would suggest.

Private Foundations

More recently, the aid industry has expanded enormously through the entrance of private foundations, which have typically focused on specific international health and other social-sector issues. At one end of the spectrum is the incidental support, which is now large scale; examples include responses to large disasters like the tsunami or the Gujarat and Sichuan earthquakes, which generated huge support among diaspora communities, private companies (particularly in China), and individual support worldwide. For instance, according to reports on the Internet, Dr. Kumar Bahuleyan, a dalit or untouchable from Kerala who made millions as a neurosurgeon in Buffalo, New York, in 2007 donated $20 million to his native village to establish a neurosurgery hospital, health clinic, and spa. Hindu Aid coordinates efforts of Hindu organizations in the UK engaged in development work, with a task force to respond to natural disasters like the tsunami, during which it helped to bring together offers of support from the South Asian community in the UK. And the initiative set up by Mo Ibrahim, a Sudan-born businessman, aims to contribute to better governance, for example, by awarding a prize to good leaders when they step down.

The biggest change to the aid industry has come from the large foundations, often US-based. The United States, which provides a relatively low percentage of its national income to aid, provides by far the largest sums of private money. In 2006 total US donations reached $295 billion—about the gross domestic product of Poland, or an average $2,000 per US household—though only a relatively small proportion of this is for poverty or development purposes, either at home or abroad.[26] For a long time the Rockefeller and Ford foundations have made significant contributions to international development. During the 1980s pharmaceutical companies started to donate drugs to eliminate particular diseases; this developed into successful collaboration among a range of agencies, as Box 2–7 describes.

More recently, the Bill and Melinda Gates Foundation has become particularly important, with resources far outstripping the annual budget of many of the traditional agencies. In 2004 the Gates Foundation provided 134 grants for international causes, worth US$1.2 billion. The Ford Foundation was the second-largest foundation in terms of grants—on average much smaller—worth US$258 million (Kharas 2007). In an even more recent development, the Bill and Melinda Gates Foundation moved into the agricultural sector in 2007, launching (with the Rockefeller Foundation) the $150 million Alliance for a Green Revolution in Africa.

While Bill Clinton did not make international development a key element of his US presidency, he started the Clinton Foundation and the high-profile Clinton Global Initiative (CGI), following the example of previous US presidents since Jimmy Carter. Like a private not-for-profit UN, CGI brings together global leaders, former heads of state, business executives, scholars, and representatives of NGOs to work together for a

---

Box 2–7. Medical Companies Contribute to Health

In October 1987 Merck announced it would donate the human formulation of its big-selling veterinary antiworm medicine, ivermectin (brand name Mectizan), intended to combat river blindness (onchocerciasis). Over 100 million treatments were made possible in the next decade or so. In 1998, nearly 25 million people were treated in thirty-one countries in Africa, Latin America, and the Middle East. This successful program has been emulated by a number of other drug companies. In 1996 the British drug company Glaxo Wellcome started donating its antimalaria drug. SmithKline Beecham (with WHO) launched its albendazole program in 1998, with the ambitious twenty-year goal of elimination of a parasitic disease (lymphatic filariasis) that can lead to disfiguring elephantiasis and serious male genital damage. In the same year Pfizer announced it would donate its best-selling antibiotic, Zithromax, as part of a large, integrated, five-country effort to control trachoma, a disease that can lead to blindness and that typically affects the poor.

These initiatives have also been criticized. Companies have been accused of using these programs as public-relations exercises, possibly even undermining the case for free trade in drugs. Some argue that the programs are not easy to administer, particularly in poor countries, and that these initiatives may be advanced at the cost of other important programs (for example, meningitis and yellow fever control). But it is generally accepted that the initiatives have saved millions of people from crippling diseases.

Source: Peter Wehrwein, "Pharmacophilanthropy," *Harvard Public Health Review*. Available online.

---

common cause.[27] The Clinton initiatives focus on education, energy and climate change, global health (for example, contributing to cutting the price of anti-retroviral drugs for poor AIDS victims), and poverty alleviation. Members have made over six hundred commitments since CGI's launch in 2005, with $9.15 billion committed in 2006. Like the Gates' efforts, Clinton's organization shows a strong business approach to philanthropy.

The Recipients—How Is Aid Allocated?

If aid donors are diverse, recipients are even more so. Europe was the main recipient of the first large aid program after World War II. Before that war, and continuing through independence, relatively small sums were provided to the colonies of European powers.

Currently, depending in part on how aid is defined, large numbers of countries receive aid. An overview of the amounts each country receives shows enormous diversity. Even the Netherlands' aid program, despite attempts to concentrate efforts, in 2004–2005 provided aid to thirty-six focal partner countries, but Dutch funding can be found in no fewer than 125 countries. All poor countries receive some form of aid or another, including the countries that themselves provide aid, like China and India. Recipients of large amounts of aid include Iraq, Afghanistan, and the DRC—all countries in or emerging from conflict. With broader definitions of aid, many middle income countries are included. A fairly large number of countries have graduated from low-income status (or, like China, will do so soon) and will no longer be eligible for aid. In some recipient countries aid forms a tiny fraction of public financial resources; in many countries in Africa aid can make up more than 20 percent of public finance.

Data from the OECD DAC show that aid is relatively well targeted: one-third of total bilateral donor resources go to countries classified as least developed, and another one-third to other low-income countries. There has been an increase in the proportion of aid that goes to Sub-Saharan Africa, from about 20 percent in the 1960s to over one-third of total ODA today (IDA 2007). The OECD DAC figures presented in Table 2–5 show that the largest recipients in Africa in 2007 were Sudan, Cameroon, the DRC, Zambia, Ethiopia, and Nigeria (which received a large amount of debt relief). Countries in conflict, notably Iraq, Afghanistan, and the Palestinian areas, receive large amounts of aid. Central and South Asia receive about 15 percent of total aid. India receives very little aid per capita, even less than China.

Donors' choices of aid recipients and the flow of money are the result of several factors. First, colonial history has played an important role, explaining, for example, the importance of British aid in India, French aid in Francophone Africa, and Dutch aid in Indonesia (the Indonesian government suspended Dutch aid in 1992).

Second, political and strategic considerations that were central to aid relations during the Cold War continue to influence the directions of aid: the increase of aid to middle-income countries during the 1990s; the scale of aid provided to Turkey, Israel, Pakistan, and more recently Afghanistan and Iraq; and the fact that donor countries tend to provide more aid to recipients that support them in votes in the UN.

Third, recipient countries' needs are important, both in terms of economics and levels of poverty. Aid to many countries is not as high as popular opinion might think, often $50–$100 per capita (though these are significant amounts in countries where the average per capita income is $500–$1000). Aid is fairly well targeted to the poorest countries, though much improvement still can be made.[28]

Fourth, aid flows partly follow policy performance, that is, the extent to which recipients' policies are in line with certain political and institutional conditions. Countries with democratic structures, for example, receive more aid from DAC donors, and economic policy improvements are important in decisions particularly to provide program aid.

Fifth, donors over time have developed categorizations of aid recipients, emphasizing that many poor countries do not have the institutional capacity for development and receiving large sums of money. Countries categorized as, for example, fragile states, are assumed to need aid instruments and decisions on sums of money that are radically different from those relating to more stable poor countries.

Sixth, large low-income countries such as China and India form a special category. They receive relatively little aid, at least measured on a per capita basis, but they have had great economic and poverty-reduction success despite this. Very little aid goes to the large number of poor people in both countries—estimated even now to be around 130 million in China and 250 million in India—but both countries have relatively good fiscal positions (particularly China) to address their problems with poverty.

The aid industry's recipients are inevitably diverse, probably increasingly so; motives for supporting countries vary; and donor responses have become increasingly differentiated. Recipients represent a range between aid-dependent countries and those that receive very little aid and indeed are rapidly becoming donors themselves (Maxwell 2006). It is thus important to understand the working of the aid industry in the specific context of countries.

Conclusion

The world of aid is tremendously diverse in terms of backgrounds, motivations, ways of operating, and how these have evolved over time. As

Table 2-5. ODA by Recipient Country, US$ million

	2000	2001	2002	2003	2004	2005	2006
Nigeria	84.33	107.5	215.	199.84	314.63	5944.74	10819.59
Iraq	84.08	100.8	85.05	2094.98	4393.82	21824.7	8487.83
Afghanistan	87.51	322.86	985.92	1199.67	1701.06	2168.21	2404.57
Sudan	90.26	107.64	232.26	332.02	847.92	1459.56	1518.14
Cameroon	213.48	351.18	435.99	751.56	572.07	336.16	1505.25
Congo Dem. Rep. (Zaire)	102.71	143.36	351.01	5009.49	1164.99	1036.58	1500.36
Viet Nam	1246.2	819.52	746.04	967.7	1184.8	1253.17	1306.5
China	1256.18	1079.76	1211.51	1139.47	1584.87	1692.92	1173.68
Serbia	592.91	631.11	1921.28	852.99	583.73	812.44	1169.24
Pakistan	475.06	1110.09	702.45	536.26	382.22	792.84	1144.89
Zambia	486.24	274.11	359.52	591.88	745.81	822.5	1115.19
Ethiopia	379.49	367.08	489.22	1033.33	1024.74	1185.09	1024.09
Tanzania	778.7	939.09	908.87	965.64	1028.7	860.31	991.71
Mozambique	623.53	720.21	1660.99	697.06	731.25	760.21	938.31
Uganda	578.16	386.3	466.07	587.28	683.85	690.74	938.19
Colombia	178.47	372.32	426.11	767.06	481.66	572.63	917.05
Kenya	292.99	270.45	288.07	320.28	470.79	510.06	761.17
Palestinian adm. areas	306.44	280.19	410.18	490.81	605.33	569.74	754.42
Indonesia	1543.98	1345.16	1162.	1580.45	-117.38	2242.06	688.44
India	650.34	904.51	785.31	384.33	14.55	850.13	653.08
Ghana	376.	386.71	404.98	471.43	913.29	602.8	594.65

Source: OECD DAC, www.oecd.org

Jan Cedergren, the chair of the DAC Working Party on Aid Effectiveness, puts it:

> A layperson observing today's aid industry might be understandably baffled by the sheer number of aid actors, funds and programmes. The last time the OECD counted, there were more than 200 bilateral and multilateral organisations channelling official development assistance. Many developing countries may have more than 40 donors financing more than 600 active projects, and may still not be on track to achieve the Millennium Development Goals. (Cedergren 2007)

Historical differences provide a partial explanation for different opinions about whether aid works. But the aid industry is even more complex than that, because of the diverging and rapidly changing paradigms that underpin these differences, at least partly (see Chapter 3). Donor approaches change rapidly, and many agencies appear to be in a constant state of internal reform and restructuring. Many agencies continue to have a wide and often expanding range of involvement. The World Bank, for example, has increasingly included work on health and education and has become one of the largest funders of research on poverty, while it continues to be heavily involved in large infrastructure projects, in supporting adjusting economies, and in undertaking a large number of projects with other funders often combining loans and grants. And the number of agencies continues to increase, each bringing in its own background, objectives, and approaches.

Further Readings

Most major international organizations and NGOs provide information on their websites. For bilateral donors, many country histories exist.

Degnbol-Martinussen and Engberg-Pedersen (2005), *Aid: Understanding International Development Cooperation*, provides a textbook introduction.

Lancaster (2007), *Foreign Aid: Diplomacy, Development, Domestic Politics*, provides a very useful comparison of aid programs in the United States, Japan, France, Germany, and Denmark.

The edited book by Paul Hoebink and Olav Stokke, *Perspectives on Euro-pean Development Co-operation* (2005), includes chapters on the main characteristics of sixteen European donors.

Among the many books and critiques of the World Bank, I recommend Sebastian Mallaby's *The World's Banker*, which focuses particularly on the years of Jim Wolfensohn's presidency; and Steve Berkman, *The World Bank and the Gods of Lending*, which argues that the World Bank's inward-focused bureaucracy is unable to address mismanagement. A good paper on NGO engagement with the World Bank is Ebrahim and Herz (2007), "Accountability in Complex Organizations."

Helleiner and Momani (2007), "Slipping into Obscurity?" gives a good overview of challenges for, pressures on, and reform proposals for the IMF.

Linda Fasulo (2003), *An Insider's Guide to the UN*, provides an overview from a US perspective of the wide range of responsibilities of the United Nations and its internal workings.

A good introduction to the civil society organizations in a sense broader than development-focused NGOs is Batliwala and Brown (2006), *Transnational Civil Society: An Introduction* (2006).

Official definitions of aid can be found in the "Glossary" section of the www.oecd.org website.

3

The Evolution in Thinking about Aid and International Development

The field of international development is marked by very rapid changes and trends—indeed, it is often argued that it suffers from fads and is rife with "buzzwords" (Cornwall 2007). Some of these changes have been driven by political considerations of donors, sometimes short term, sometimes long term. In the context of the Cold War, practical alliance to one of the two camps was often much more important than theoretical differences over development models. Sometimes changes have been the result of more technical considerations; for example, during the 1990s many started to argue that international development had neglected the "productive" sectors of agriculture and infrastructure. And over the decades since the 1960s the areas of engagement of international development have expanded, engaging at political levels as well as central administrations, and with organized civil society and NGOs as well as directly with households and individuals (Degnbol-Martinussen and Engberg-Pedersen 2005, 39–44).

Different approaches to aid also have been the outcome of radically different views, theories, and thinking. This chapter discusses the main approaches in international development, organized chronologically mainly since the end of World War II. While these provide a good overview of the main issues as they evolved over the last six decades, it is important to keep in mind that such periodization—like any categorization—implies significant simplifications. While certain approaches can be characterized as dominant throughout these periods, different views continued to exist, apparently diverging movements appeared on the scene, and—as highlighted in the previous chapter—different donors often held radically different ideas.

The Study of Aid and International Development

International development and aid have been studied from different institutional positions. A number of think tanks—mostly in the North—have contributed directly to the management of the aid industry (such as the Overseas Development Institute [ODI] in the UK) or to monitor aid practices (such as the CGD in Washington DC). Others position themselves more remotely from the aid business, studying development processes more broadly, and are often very critical of aid practices (such as the IDS in the UK and the North-South Institute in Canada). Research on development and aid also takes place at institutes that focus on training professionals, such as the Institute of Social Studies in the Netherlands and a range of institutions focusing on development practices. While aid is examined closely in development studies, development studies looks at issues that are much broader than the aid industry itself.

Aid itself has been studied from varying theoretical angles (Lancaster 2007, 3–4). Realist perspectives highlight the role of foreign aid as an instrument of political power. Marxist or "dependency" scholars see aid as an instrument to maintain positions of control in world capitalism. Scholars in a liberal tradition emphasize aid as a reflection of collaboration between states. A "constructivist" lens and social-democratic theories emphasize that foreign aid is an expression of norms and ideas intended to assist in the improvement of quality of life, while "deconstructivist" approaches focus on aid practices as discourse and ways of exerting power. Much of the literature cited in this book has a strong emphasis on the management of aid; this literature has been criticized by authors that emphasize the importance of personal relationships in aid (Eyben 2008).

As Lancaster notes, none of these theories adequately explains the complexities of aid. Its principles almost always reflect a combination of motives. Aid practices tend to take their own dynamics, as all policies tend to do, through the institutions responsible for their implementation. Further, the interaction of development analysts or students with practitioners is not straightforward. In fact, the industry continues to struggle with the question of how research influences policymaking, while it is equally possible that policy influences research, particularly when much of the development research is directly funded by the aid industry itself.

For many European countries the aid industry had its origins in the colonial period, and early development projects were set up by colonial administrations. Academic research informed the colonial administration: schools of Oriental or African studies trained colonial officers, and anthropologist helped to educate administrations about local populations. There has been much continuity between the colonial and postcolonial periods. For example, economic theories that emphasized dualism between modern and tradition sectors were first articulated during the colonial period—by the Dutch economist Boeke, for instance, with reference to Indonesia. Moreover, as Kothari (2006) has pointed out, there was a fair amount of continuity in terms of personnel through former colonial officers who stayed on after independence to work in universities, government departments, and the new aid industry.

Academic approaches to aid in the two decades after World War II were dominated by economic theories, of *modernization* in particular as described below. From the late 1960s, particularly in the UK, the area of development studies started to grow. The IDS was the first center in the North that focused explicitly on development as a subject, and it has remained one of the largest institutes in the field. The number of institutes and research centers on development has continued to increase, while in many places development is studied as part of other fields, notably international relations, public administration, and (mainstream) economics. In many cases the study happens at postgraduate levels, though Canada, for example, has seen recent growth in the number of development studies programs at undergraduate levels.

A problem-oriented nature has been the first defining feature of development studies. From its origin development studies has been seen as the science or discipline that will help address the most urgent problems of poverty in the South. At present, students of development are motivated by concerns about deprivation and look for ways to assist in solving problems, usually in other countries that are shown in the press and through public campaigns.

Second, from its origin in economics, development studies moved on to become defined as strongly interdisciplinary. The motivation for this has typically been the problem-oriented nature of development studies; development problems were increasingly recognized to be multifaceted and multisectoral, and therefore multi-disciplinary or interdisciplinary approaches became a defining feature of the field.

The interdisciplinary approach has been contested, however. The World Bank and its exceptionally large group of top-class researchers—

who produced nearly four thousand publications between 1998 and 2005 alone (Banerjee et al. 2006)—played an important role. By far the largest number of its researchers are economists. Organizations like the International Food Policy Research Institute (IFPRI) also tend to be dominated by economists, though they too have increasingly adopted a multi-disciplinary approach. While understandable in many core areas of work for organizations like the World Bank, poverty studies and even some of the policy analyses that developed during the 1980s and 1990s were also dominated by economists. The debate on poverty analysis, which is described in Box 3–1, reflects this influence.

Political science also has had much less influence in the development debate than economics. As described later in this chapter, development theories started to pay more attention to institutions during the 1990s, but even then methods of economics continued to shape the approach to studying institutions, and even politics. Moreover, anthropologists have engaged relatively little in development studies, even in poverty analysis. "The relationship between anthropology and development has always been difficult," writes Ralph Grillo (2002, 54). Influential anthropologists like Evans-Pritchard distanced themselves from applied areas of study after World War II. No anthropologist was involved in setting up the UK's ODA in the mid 1960s, for example, and it was not until 1978 that an anthropologist joined the World Bank[1] and anthropologists began to focus on critical analysis of aid discourse and power relations.

Who Studies Development?

The World Bank houses the single largest group of development economists. Development think tanks include the ODI in London; the ISS in The Hague, which was set up by the minister of Development Cooperation; and the OECD Development Centre. The CGD, based in Washington DC, makes direct contributions to the aid industry by organizing debates and publishing the Commitment to Development Index. The role of NGOs and transnational civil society in development research has been increasing as well, often offering insights critical of or alternative to those put forward by organizations like the World Bank.

While large development-studies think tanks play an important role in the donor countries, fewer have sprung up in the South. Nonetheless, strong development-studies institutes exist in Thailand, the Philippines,

Box 3-1. The Debate on Poverty Analysis and Development Studies Disciplines

Poverty analysis rapidly gained importance during the 1980s, when the World Bank in particular came under criticism for distributing aid that failed to help the poor, and the World Bank responded with new or renewed efforts to assess the scale of poverty, particularly in Africa. The main form of poverty analysis was through large-scale representative household surveys, and donor agencies invested in implementing surveys and building capacity. The main indicator of poverty became the poverty headcount, a measure of the number of people living below a poverty line (national or international, such as dollar-a-day). A second measure is the so-called poverty gap, which describes not only how many people live below the poverty line, but also how far below that line, the extent of their poverty (a measure that became important in measuring the impact of microfinance projects, for example).

Poverty analysis was criticized heavily because of two main issues (central to many development-studies debates in the 1990s): its single focus on the income dimensions of poverty, and the focus on quantitative analysis of poverty based on household surveys. The critique highlighted the need for the study of health and education and access to assets as central components of poor people's well-being, and also as preconditions for economic growth. Increasingly, studies claimed that measuring people's income neglects the dimension of vulnerability, that is, the risk that households may fall back into poverty. The critique of quantitative poverty analysis was associated with the growth of participatory poverty analysis and participatory approaches more generally, and finally a strand—promoted, for example, by Ravi Kanbur, the lead author of the 2000/2001 *World Development Report*—that advocated for integration of qualitative and quantitative analyses. Poverty analysis within development studies has remained dominated by economists, much more so than poverty analysis in the UK, where sociologists play a much more important role. Poverty analysis also suffered by neglecting the societal and political influences on poverty, focusing heavily on measurements and indicators rather than explanations.

The best sources for studying a combined qualitative and quantitative approach to poverty analysis are http://www.q-squared.ca/ and Kanbur 2005.

Zimbabwe, India, and Bangladesh, with IDS Nairobi possibly the world's oldest development institute (established in 1965). In China no tradition of development studies has developed. Of course, much of what is taught and researched as development in Northern development institutes is taught in higher education and research institutes in the South.

Research organizations also exist within the UN system, though they usually operate on an autonomous basis. They often have limited amounts of core funding and rely on donors for research grants. For example, UNRISD, the United Nations Research Institute for Social Development, was set up in 1963 with a grant from the Netherlands. It currently has an annual budget of about $4 million, and it depends on both core funding (mainly from bilateral donors) and grants for specific projects. Similar institutions are WIDER (World Institute for Development Economics Research) based in Stockholm, which recently carried out major research projects on economic inequality, and the IILS (International Institute for Labour Studies). The IILS is closely linked to the ILO and was, for example, among the first organizations to focus on social exclusion in the development-studies debate of the mid 1990s.

One of the most important scientific organizations supported by the aid industry is CGIAR (Consultative Group on International Agricultural Research). Created in 1971, it currently employs more than eight thousand people in over one hundred countries, including thirteen countries in the developing world. It promotes sustainable production, supports national agricultural research systems, encourages research on policy that affects agriculture, and works directly on germplasm (collection of genetic resources for an organism) improvements and collection.

There have been significant efforts to strengthen research capacity in the South. Canada's International Development Research Centre (IDRC)—a Crown corporation that reports to the Canadian Parliament rather than CIDA—supports applied research, expert advice, and building local capacity in developing countries in order to undertake research and innovate. Its 2006–7 annual budget was Can$135 million (less than, for example, DFID's research program, which does not have a strong and explicit capacity focus). The department for research cooperation of the Swedish International Development Agency (Sida) supports partner-country development research as well as Swedish research activities relevant to developing countries.

The African Economic Research Consortium was established in 1988 to strengthen research capacity related to the management of economies in sub-Saharan Africa; it is supported by bilateral and multilateral donors, private foundations, and African organizations. The consortium was created with an assumption that good economic policy needs (1) a strong group of locally based professional economists to conduct policy-relevant research, and (2) research agendas that are determined locally rather than by donors. Collaborative research projects on poverty, for example, contributed to the preparation of PRSPs, and an electronic network among participating universities facilitates information sharing and access to global resource centers.

Despite these efforts to support capacity building in the South, it is probably fair to say that development-studies knowledge has continued to be concentrated in the North. While aid agencies strengthen their own think tanks—not necessarily by design but through the work they commission—capacities in many countries in the South have not developed at the same pace, with a few notable exceptions. Over the years there has been criticism that when aid agencies started to focus their efforts on primary education, they failed to support higher education and research. Indeed, aid agencies have often been ambivalent about the need to support research capacity, finding it hard to identify the impact of such support.

Development Studies in the 1950s and 1960s: Optimism, "Kick Starting" Economies

With independence, development became the core objective of all newly established governments. The study of poor countries became a separate subject, highlighted by Sir William Arthur Lewis, among others. Lewis argued that standard economic models are less relevant to poor countries (Lewis 1954).

The early period of independence was one of great optimism. Even though many economists did not believe economic growth rates could achieve levels much above 1 to 2 percent, new governments expected to be able to modernize the economy while simultaneously addressing the historical injustice of the colonial era. The optimism was fueled throughout the 1950s and 1960s by a growing world economy, booming markets for exports of primary commodities, and low energy prices. While aid was heavily determined by donors' security concerns in the context of spreading communism, donors looked favorably on newly established countries in which elites took active roles in modernizing economies.[2]

While socialism experienced great popularity across the former colonial world and the international community was heavily influenced by the Great Depression and the devastating Second World War, economic policies emphasized planning. Five-year plans became common across the South, with industrialization through import-substitution central to many countries' objectives. Simple economic models provided the necessary theoretical support, while food aid contributed to keeping agricultural prices low and thus shaping favorable conditions for economic development. Until the late 1970s international-development thinking assigned a primary and entrepreneurial role to government, and models that are now recognized as failures—such as the socialist model promoted by Nyerere in Tanzania—found widespread acceptance.

The development model that dominated this period emphasized economic growth. Social objectives were seen as complementary to or resulting from increasing national products. Poverty reduction seldom emerged as a specific priority; it was expected to emerge from better infrastructures and employment-intensive growth. The path of development was seen as linear; Walter Rostow's 1960 book, *The Stages of Economic Growth*, for example, used the image of an airplane taking off. Modernization was thought to start in the industrial sector, which would pull the agricultural sector along; as a result, thinking was focused on urban areas. There was little interest in the rural sector where most of the poor lived and worked, although the US Alliance for Progress in support of Latin American land reform in the 1960s was a short-lived exception.

The main economic framework emphasized the role of investment, as highlighted in the one-sector economic Harrod-Domar model. In the absence of sufficiently high savings rates, foreign aid was seen as providing countries with the necessary capital to "kick start" their economies. Economic frameworks were believed to be able to predict the amount of aid and investment needed. During the 1950s, funding of infrastructure projects was popular (see Chapter 4). While there was no increase in total amounts of aid, the 1960s saw the establishment of bilateral aid programs, with financial as well as technical assistance, and a strong focus on productive sectors.

But, as in other periods, development thinking in the 1950s and 1960s was not undisputed. In the 1960s, notably through the work of Theodore Schultz, human capital (along with physical capital) was seen as important, and issues of education and fertility were put on the agenda. From the early postwar period onward, despite aid's emphasis on large infrastructure projects, community-development models had some popularity among the international community, as they did in India, where the modernization view promoted by Nehru was balanced by Gandhian traditional and village-oriented views.

A more radical critique, particularly of the modernization theories, was formulated by a group of Marist-oriented authors, mostly Latin American social scientists. This came to be known as dependency theory, rooted in the United Nations Commission for Latin America. For dependency theorists, underdevelopment was not only the result of failure to modernize, or identical with a traditional or native state, but the result of the expansion of global capitalism and colonialism, through which the South became underdeveloped. Dependency theory made little impact on mainstream thinking within the aid industry, but its ideas are reflected in the movements and writings that see the World Bank and IMF as instruments used to maintain global capitalism and injustice.

Economic thinking during the colonial period emphasized a dualism between modern and traditional sectors. This became deeply ingrained in the developing thinking of the 1950s and 1960s and remains influential even today. Statistical systems started to record economic activity and employment in the modern and large-scale sector, where in general better working conditions and pay prevailed and some social security benefits were provided. Thinking about employment and migration was dominated by dual models (like Lewis's), and the idea that modernization involved transfer of labor from a traditional agricultural sector, with an unlimited supply of labor, to a modern sector.

Thus, development thinking in the early postwar period was already a mix of ideas. Emphasis on growth and modernization was combined with thinking about the need for human capital, education in particular. And while there was much acceptance and promotion of models of planning and socialism, in line with the Keynesian economics of the time, the thinking about the push toward modernization was also informed by the perceived need to contain communism. It is worth noting that Rostow's book about modernization had the subtitle *An Anti-Communist Manifesto*, and Rostow was not only an economist but also an adviser on US national security affairs.

The 1970s: The Short Era of Redistribution

Levels of aid, which had remained constant since the mid 1950s, increased during the second half of the 1970s. But in terms of development thinking, the 1970s—once again—was a period of opposing directions. Whereas the 1960s still was a period of great optimism, cracks appeared in the early 1970s. It was a period of adjustment, and a process of global liberalization began with the collapse of the economic regulation that had dominated since the end of World War II. The year 1973 saw both the first oil crisis, though the impact was not as severe as the crisis in 1979, and the fall of Allende in Chile and resultant advent of what many Latin Americans have regarded as the classic form of neo-liberal structural adjustment under an authoritarian regime.

In the same year Robert McNamara explicitly committed the World Bank to a focus on poverty reduction. In a famous speech in Nairobi addressing the World Bank–IMF meeting of 1973, he emphasized the extent and persistence of rural poverty and pledged to increase and transform aid. Thinking at the World Bank in the 1970s was influenced by Chenery, who, as chief economist under Robert McNamara, put inequality and redistribution on the agenda, questioning the idea of "trickle down"—the assumption that economic growth would automatically benefit the poor—which had dominated earlier thinking. The early 1970s was also a period of radical debate about the new international economic order and the "right to development."[3]

Other players in the aid industry also started to emphasize poverty from the late 1960s onward, and they too shared the doubts about modernization and trickle-down paradigms. The late 1960s and 1970s saw a mass of experiments with targeted interventions, reflecting the growing focus on poverty among donors. Reconstruction in Bangladesh in the early 1970s challenged the predominant aid strategies for doing far too little for the poor. Canada's Pearson Commission and Dutch and Scandinavian donors expressed worries that growth from aid was inadequately translated into poverty reduction, and they began to attempt a more rural, decentralized, small-scale project bundle. Britain's first white paper on aid in 1964 had started to prioritize poverty; its chief economist, Dudley Seers, in an IDS article (1967/69) argued that development was about much more than national income and should include normative concerns based on basic needs and distribution.

While food aid became less important as a donor instrument, the aid industry started to pay more attention to agriculture, increase lending, and help remove technical constraints, redressing the relative neglect during the 1950s and 1960s. Debates started to see agriculture as productive—as part of economic growth strategies—rather than a traditional sector that would shrink with modernization. Reflecting on failures of large projects of the earlier period, participatory approaches to agricultural development became more popular. Compared to the earlier period, development economics became more sophisticated in its understanding of the interaction between traditional and modern, rural and urban sectors, and ideas of balanced growth and inter-sectoral linkages came to the forefront of debates. IFAD was established in 1978 with the mandate to increase food production in the poorest food deficit countries and for the poorest people. Michael Lipton's much-cited 1977 publication, *Why Poor People Stay Poor: Urban Bias in World Development*, contributed to a shift of focus toward agriculture. He argued that development was designed by and for people in urban areas. He estimated that while most poor people (between 60 and 80 percent) lived in rural areas and depended on agriculture, they received no more than 20 percent of development spending.

The 1970s was also the period when employment took center stage in the international development debate. The ILO's World Employment Programme, founded by Ajit Bhalla, signaled a shift away from growth-oriented models, recognition of the scale of world poverty, and focus on the creation of productive employment and provision of public services. The program was seen as an answer to the authoritarian turn that the process of modernization had taken in many post-colonial (and post–Cold War) contexts. The 1976 ILO conference, for example, emphasized that strategies and national development plans and policies should promote employment as a priority.

An important contribution during this period was the introduction of the term *informal sector.* The term was coined by anthropologist Keith Hart in 1971, and the ILO adopted it in a report on employment in Kenya in 1972. The term highlighted the problem in less-developed countries as that of the "working poor"—people in occupations in which they earn a low income in precarious labor relations—rather than unemployment. During the 1980s and later, much research focused on the growth of the informal sector, particularly as it related to the process of globalization and liberalization, which was thought to increase the size of the informal sector and undermine the rights and entitlements of people in the formal sector (though in many poor countries the formal sector had never been larger than between 10 and 15 percent of the labor force).

In the 1980s Peruvian researcher and lawyer Hernando de Soto made an important contribution to the debate from a liberal economic perspective. His 1986 book *El Otro Sendero* ("the other path," referring to the extremist group Sendero Luminoso, or Shining Path) described people in the informal sector as entrepreneurs who were hindered from making economic contributions by government rules and regulations.

Questions of migration occupied a central part in debates on employment. While earlier migration was seen simply as a part of the transition from traditional to modern sectors, and by and large as a positive phenomenon, over time views and approaches became more diverse. There has been a longstanding concern among policymakers and academics alike that migrants from rural areas congested cities and drained their resources. Many rural development programs have attempted to reduce "out migration"—usually with little success. The most important model of rural-urban migration, the Harris-Todaro model, describes migrants as economic agents who weigh the difference between the expected earnings from formal-sector urban employment against the expected earnings in the village.

A "basic needs" approach was central at the ILO and elsewhere during the 1970s, that is, an emphasis on satisfaction of basic needs and inclusion of people in decision-making processes. Nobel Prize winner Amartya Sen's book *Poverty and Famines*, written for the World Employment Programme, stressed that starvation does not happen because no food is available, but rather because people do not have access to food. The book presents four case studies of famines—Bengal 1943, Ethiopia 1972–75, the Sahel during the early 1970s, and Bangladesh in 1974. Sen also emphasized the role of democracy and the free press in averting large-scale starvation, and his 1999 *Development as Freedom* has been interpreted as one of the theoretical foundations of "rights-based" approaches.

Thus, during the 1970s, the international development debate moved from one centered on growth to one more explicitly focused on poverty, redistribution, basic needs, direct anti-poverty interventions, and participatory approaches to rural development. Yet there were trends that conflicted with this increased concentration on poverty. First, donors and recipients faced financial constraints due to the sharp rise in oil prices and increasing balance-of-payment pressures. They cut back on long-term or "soft" projects, including anti-poverty programs, and financial support to maintain essential imports started to become more important. Second, a growing part of aid came from new donors (Japan, OPEC countries) who, like the United States, World Bank, and Western Europe earlier, concentrated on infrastructure projects. Third, while the 1970s debate and donor policy continued to see the state as a key actor in development, a reaction against state intervention was beginning. For example, reviews showed that massive, state-subsidized credit, labeled "for the poor," was failing to reach the poor, stimulate agricultural growth, or even to sustain financially viable lending. The backlash against support for state intervention reached its full force in the 1980s.

1980s: Adjustment

The 1980s were dominated by structural adjustment programs, and donor approaches shifted attention to program lending and targeted interventions to ameliorate the effects of crises. The 1980s has often been regarded as a lost decade for development, though whether adjustment caused the failure or was a response to development problems is debated. In any case, Mexico defaulted on its external debt in 1982. This started the "debt crisis," which came to be a major rallying point of advocacy-oriented NGOs and resulted, for example, in the Jubilee 2000 coalition. As financial crises increased, the Bretton Woods institutions designed packages intended to enable countries to stabilize and address balance of payments problems in the short run, and to liberalize and restore economic growth in the longer term.

While the 1970s was characterized by a basic needs focus, the most significant theoretical development of the 1980s was the emergence of the Washington Consensus—even though it would be a mistake to assume that this ever was a true consensus, as opinions always remained diverse. The so-called consensus highlighted the need for policies of fiscal discipline, market-determined exchange and interest rates, protection of property rights, liberalization, privatization, and openness to trade. During this period an increasing proportion of aid was provided with a large number of "conditionalities" regarding adjustment of the economy and state intervention.

Contrasting earlier optimism about the state as a key agent for development, during the 1980s the state came to be associated with development problems, ranging from low economic growth to continued and sometimes even increasing poverty. It was strongly argued that the state should focus on its minimum functions, including "getting prices right." As Albert Hirschman noted in 1981, the "state . . . was charged with intellectual responsibility for whatever had gone wrong" (quoted in Fritz and Rocha Menocal 2007, 540). This was the case in particular for Africa, but was also true in Latin America. Studies of the East Asian economic successes showed how important state intervention was for development, but these studies did not receive as much attention as the studies of failures in Africa and, to a lesser extent, in Latin America.

Many observers have proclaimed the Washington Consensus a fiasco. But it is probably fair to say that the evidence is mixed. On the one hand, for example, in a large number of countries fiscal and monetary stability was achieved during the 1990s. On the other hand, growth performance was not uniformly favorable, and it has been acknowledged that the "supply response" to adjustment measures has been weak and that the developments in the fast-growing economies of East Asia did not follow the path of the Washington Consensus.[4] While the evidence on the impact of adjustment on development and poverty was mixed, the critique of adjustment did lead to a renewed focus on poverty, including a drive to measure the extent of poverty, particularly in Africa.

The development debate became increasingly influenced by policy research at the IFIs, and the influence of UN agencies like ILO and WHO declined as the World Bank expanded its areas of investment and expertise. Controversies over structural adjustment dominated the debate, for example, on user fees. Under the influence of the fiscal crisis in Africa and elsewhere, affordability of services became an increasingly important concern.[5] A World Bank paper by M. Thobani (1983) argued that charges in education were necessary because governments could not afford the total subsidy required. But concerns for poverty were also present in the paper; Thobani argued that with fiscal constraints governments would ration services, which would hurt the poor, and that introduction of user fees would help expand access for the poor. The conclusion about the positive impact of user fees was strongly challenged in a major critique of the social and economic policies under structural adjustment commissioned by UNICEF on "adjustment with a human face" (Cornia, Jolly, and Stewart 1987). The study describes how adverse economic developments and consequent stabilization and adjustment policies affected vulnerable groups, especially children, and included a critique of the adoption of user fees in primary health and education.

The question of social spending remains hotly debated in the development-studies debate. On one side, particularly influenced by NGOs like Action Aid, is the view that the World Bank and IMF have forced governments in poor countries to keep spending on social sectors low. On the other side, the IMF and the World Bank argue that under fiscal crises governments need to address their spending, but that they have not forced governments to reduce spending on education and health more than other sectors. Moreover, the World Bank has produced research showing that a large percentage of the additional donor funding available for debt relief has been spent on social sectors. Also, its recent research has shown that since the 1980s investments in agriculture suffered more than that in social sectors.

Ensuring that the poor benefit from health and education services has become an increasingly important concern within the social sectors also. In the context of crisis and adjustment the World Bank and regional development banks turned their attention to "add-ons" designed to reduce the pain of adjustment for the poor. The Bolivia Emergency Social Fund was followed by the Program of Action to Mitigate the Social Cost of Adjustment (PAMSCAD) in Ghana, both schemes set up in decentralized and participatory ways and primarily designed for the people who had lost jobs and livelihoods as a result of retrenchment. Also, donor attention shifted toward innovative targeted projects, such as the World Bank's support for the Tamil Nadu Integrated Nutrition Programme and IFAD's support for Grameen in Bangladesh.

Although the 1980s was perceived as a lost development decade, there was much progress in theories of development, including a proliferation of statistical information, allowing economists in particular to develop increasingly sophisticated models of national economies (including general equilibrium modeling) and models for comparing achievements across an ever-larger number of countries (using cross-country regressions). Development economics achieved a better understanding of the role of human capital for economic growth and of the links between trade and growth. Moreover, new institutional economics started to emerge and played a central role in the 1990s.

The 1980s was clearly a period of economic crises and structural adjustment. The World Bank and the IMF in particular received increasingly bad press at the same time that their areas of work rapidly expanded. Development, nonetheless, became an increasingly important element among the various motives given for aid; and relatively more aid, and on softer terms, became available for the poorest countries (Lancaster 2007, 39). The development debate became increasingly heated, the number of NGOs continued to grow, and the field of development studies was enriched with the work on the "human face of adjustment" and following that the HDR, which is described next.

The 1990s: Poverty Back on the Agenda, and the Rise of Governance in Development Studies

Although the end of the Cold War led to a decline in interest in development at higher political levels, the 1990s ended not only with greatly increased attention to aid, but also to poverty. The Washington Consensus continued to be criticized, even though many of its basic principles have never been abandoned.[6] IFIs were increasingly pressed to respond to the critique, as James D. Wolfensohn clearly did after he became president of the World Bank. The financial crisis in Asia in 1997, followed by radical political changes in Indonesia, provided impetus to the development debate on poverty and to aid more generally. During the period the study of development broadened to include an emphasis on institutions and governance.

Among the World Bank's annual *World Development Reports*, the 1990 edition on poverty is often seen as most important. It brought poverty "back on the agenda," and it did so through a model of economic development that became very influential. It proposed a two-part strategy for tackling poverty: promoting labor-intensive economic growth, and investing in health and education. The report noted that people who are vulnerable to shocks and unable to benefit from growth require protection in the form of "safety nets."

The first HDR was published that same year, under the leadership of Pakistani economist and finance minister Mahbub ul Haq and Indian Nobel Laureate for Economics Amartya Sen. The principal motivation behind the HDR, according to Sen, was the overarching preoccupation with the growth of real income per capita as a measure of the well-being of a nation. Physical expansion of an economy, as measured by per capita GDP, does not necessarily mean that people are better off in terms of health, freedom, education, meaningful work, or leisure time. According to the 1990 HDR: "People are the real wealth of a nation. The basic objective of development is to create an enabling environment for people to enjoy long, healthy and creative lives. This may appear to be a simple truth. But it is often forgotten in the immediate concern with the accumulation of commodities and financial wealth." The Human Development Index (HDI) was introduced as a measure of human development, to provide an alternative to the common practice of evaluating a country's progress in development based on per capita GDP. HDI tables comparing countries' performances have drawn the attention of governments and international organizations to improving services in health and education.

Box 3–2. The Human Development Index

In order to broaden the development debate beyond income poverty, the HDR introduced the HDI. This index measures countries' achievements in terms of

- a long and healthy life, measured by life expectancy at birth;
- knowledge, measured by the adult literacy rate and the combined primary, secondary and tertiary gross enrollment ratio; and
- a decent standard of living, measured by GDP per capita in purchasing power parity (PPP) (in US dollars).

The HDI is a composite index; it is based on separate indices for each of these dimensions. These are calculated on the basis of minimum and maximum values, and performance is expressed as a value between 0 and 1. The HDI is calculated as the simple average of those three factors.

Since the first HDR, new composite indices for human development have been developed: the Gender-related Development Index, the Gender Empowerment Measure, and the Human Poverty Index.

Economic development studies have become increasingly complex. During the 1980s studies on growth included increasingly sophisticated understanding of links with, for example, trade, and in the middle of the 1990s it became possible to relate data on growth to data on income, poverty, health, and education. This was the result of two developments. First, an increasing number of surveys, often supported by donors, on income, education, and health became available, particularly in Africa. Even the importance of social relations and connections was considered a source of economic growth, and the concept of social capital, which allowed the measurement of these social relations, was introduced. The concept was also heavily criticized.[7] Second, it became possible to compare data on poverty when an internationally comparable set of prices became available. The dollar-a-day measure of poverty was the result of this. The dollar does not represent an actual dollar, to be converted with normal exchange rates; rather, it represents a consumption bundle containing the minimum necessities in different parts of the world.[8]

During the 1990s thinking about agriculture and how it relates to development more broadly also continued to change. The "sustainable livelihoods" approach (Chamber and Conway 1992; Scoones 1998) was rapidly adopted by a number of agencies; bringing together different strands of analysis, it was based on participatory approaches to project formulation and implementation and on analysis that highlighted the ways in which poor communities manage their relationship with environmental change. While having a clear impact on aid practices in the late 1990s, its popularity also declined quickly; it is not mentioned in the 2008 *World Development Report* on agriculture, for example.

Perhaps the major change in development thinking during the 1990s was the increasing attention to the role of institutions, or governance, in development thinking (and in the policies of new leaders like James Wolfensohn), which contributed to new approaches of sector support and PRSPs. Writings on the post–Washington Consensus show approaches to economic policies that define a wider role for public policies. According to Nick Stern, who thought there was nothing wrong with the principles of the Washington Consensus, it

> said nothing about governance and institutions, the role of empowerment and democratic representation, the importance of country ownership, or the social costs and the pace of transformation. The development community has learned the hard way, through the setbacks of the structural adjustment programs in developing countries of the 1980s, and the transition of the 1990s in eastern Europe and the former Soviet Union, that these elements are at the heart of the development challenge. (Stern 2002)

The new approaches take into account many of the earlier critiques, concluding that the policy prescriptions were not wrong—certainly not regarding the need for macro-economic stability—but that they were insufficient. The new approaches stress the complementary role of the state with regard to the market and hope that processes of democratization will support a vibrant market economy.[9] The importance of governance for the provision of services was highlighted in the 2004 *World*

Development Report. The governance approach includes emphasis on economic growth for poverty reduction, and the role of the private sector and trade. But it also recognizes the importance of national ownership of the development agenda, empowerment of people, and basic health and education as essential ingredients in development and poverty reduction.

The newly built consensus based on human development and participation and empowerment was illustrated in the 2000/1 *World Development Report* entitled *Attacking Poverty.* This report highlighted the central role of economic development in reducing poverty, but also that poverty is an outcome of economic, social, and political processes that interact and can reinforce one another. The report used a new three-part framework for analyzing and addressing poverty: expanding poor people's opportunities, empowerment, and security.

Thus, while emphasis on adjustment did not disappear, during the 1990s the development agenda and development thinking changed radically. This was highlighted in the response to the 1997 Asian financial crisis. The IMF response was heavily criticized by authors like Joseph Stiglitz. But 1997 also was a turning point from the "aid fatigue" and declining levels of aid. Moreover, rather than merely emphasizing short-term stabilization after the crisis, the response implied a strengthened emphasis on poverty reduction and protecting the poor from the effects of crises, an emphasis that was equally strong after the 2008 financial crisis. With this renewed emphasis, development thinking increasingly focused on the political and institutional conditions that contribute to growth and development. Under the influence of the 1990s critique of development aid, an increasing number of studies also looked at the conditions under which aid works.

Since 2000: Broadening Development Agenda Continues, Emphasis on Results, Growth Returns

As of 2008, there have been no signs that the attention to poverty is decreasing or that the broad and multi-disciplinary perspective on development is narrowing. The emerging security agenda after 9/11, like growing concerns over international migration, influenced aid practices, but the development community responded quickly by emphasizing the need to look at the links between poverty and causes of extremism and insecurity. Similarly, the growing concerns over climate change, following the efforts of Al Gore, the Stern report in the UK, and reports of the Intergovernmental Panel on Climate Change (IPCC) were quickly followed by development reports, such as the 2007 *Human Development Report*, that looked at links between poverty and climatic conditions and changes. Analysts quickly developed methods to measure the impacts of the 2008 financial crisis. Development studies thus continues to be dynamic, growing, and increasingly diverse. But the last decade has also seen a rethinking—or continuous debate—on at least three fronts: the link between economic growth and poverty reduction, approaches to governance and institutions, and more critical consideration of the results of development aid.

The publication of the 2000/2001 *World Development Report* was marked by controversy. The main author and coordinator of the report—Ravi Kanbur, former World Bank economist and now professor at Cornell University—resigned because the report's authors were pressured to emphsize economic growth and change the order of the chapters on the three main themes of opportunities, empowerment, and security. World Bank and US treasury officials believed that analysis of growth had to be the most important business of the World Bank, and—even though *World Development Report* does not represent World Bank policy—there was a perceived need to ensure that a chapter focusing on growth would come first.

During the preparation of the report there was another significant but less discussed controversy. A paper by Lundberg and Squire (1999), using internationally comparable data,[10] found evidence that during processes of economic growth, the poorest were not always benefiting. The World Bank then put a lot of effort into arguing that growth did benefit the poor; one of its most widely cited publications on the growth-poverty links was Dollar and Kraay's "Growth *Is* Good for the Poor" (2002). The question of rising inequality did not receive much attention from the World Bank at the time, thought it did become the central subject of the 2006 *World Development Report*.

The focus on institutions and governance has continued into the twenty-first century and has been enriched in two aspects. It has become increasingly clear that the donor literature on good governance produced too many requirements to be practical. The list of necessary reforms has grown exponentially, including participation, accountability, predictability of government action, transparency, free information flow, rule of law, legitimacy, constitutionality, sociopolitical pluralism, decentralization, market-oriented policies, and concerns for socioeconomic equity and poverty. The optimism of the early 1990s about implementing good governance has given way to an understanding of the influences of local context in the implementation of reforms and more focused and realistic ideas about "good enough governance" (Grindle 2002). Such governance tries to target fewer but more important and feasible interventions.

The emphasis on good governance led to calls for better understanding of local politics. Forms of political analysis were introduced in agencies, for example, Sida's "power analysis," World Bank's Institutional and Governance Reviews; and DFID's Drivers of Change. The term *political economy* became common, emphasizing that politics and power cannot be separated from economics. Politics also entered the development debate through the Monterrey Consensus (discussed in Chapter 1), which stresses that governments in developed and developing countries need to build public support to translate development aspirations into action and emphasizes the need for political leadership in the South for undertaking institutional and policy reform, and in the North to strengthen solidarity with poverty reduction efforts in the South.

Development studies have become increasingly concerned with the results of development efforts. This is a major theme in Chapter 8 herein, but it is worth highlighting here the surge in analysis of aid effectiveness, which highlighted that aid should be given to countries with large numbers of poor people *and* those that have governments that are *able* to use aid in an appropriate way and committed to using it. Also, the adoption of the MDGs by 189 nations at the United Nations in September 2000 boosted the political advocacy of aid as well as being a new input into the field of development studies. In some aid organizations the MDGs came to form the basis for reporting on the agency's work, as clearly illustrated in DFID's 2007 *Annual Report.* Major analytical work was undertaken to assess the progress at the mid point of the MDG period, July 7, 2007; the general conclusion was "substantial but uneven progress." The MDG targets for the year 2015 and progress to the midpoint are summarized in Table 3–1.

The field of development studies, which has provided most of the theoretical underpinnings for the aid industry, as well as fierce critiques, is very diverse and dynamic. Many of the classics in development studies, in fact, have been strongly polemic. The list in Box 3–3—a very limited and personal choice of publications—suggests that significant paradigm changes occur approximately every ten years.[11] Moreover, even within those periods, views on development have differed.

Table 3–1. Millennium Development Goals and Progress

Millennium Development Goals	Targets for 2015	Progress at Midpoint, July 7, 2007
1. Eradicate extreme poverty and hunger.	Reduce by half the proportion of people living on less than a dollar a day.	Global progress is good, but MDG will not be achieved in Africa. (on target)
	Reduce by half the proportion of people who suffer from hunger.	Global target unlikely to be met. (lagging)
2. Achieve universal primary education.	Ensure all boys and girls complete primary schools.	Good progress since late 1990s, but Africa has a long way to go. (lagging)
3. Promote gender equality and empower women.	Eliminate gender disparity in primary and secondary education, preferably by 2005, and at all levels by 2015.	Gender gap is closing, but slowly. (lagging) Progress in labor market access.
4. Reduce child mortality.	Reduce by two-thirds the mortality rate among children under five.	Child survival rates, worst in sub-Saharan Africa, show improvement. (on track)
5. Improve maternal health.	Reduce by three-quarters the maternal mortality ratio.	Half a million women continue to die during pregnancy or childbirth. (lagging)
6. Combat HIV/AIDS, malaria, and other diseases.	Halt and begin to reverse the spread of HIV/AIDS.	HIV prevalence has leveled off, but deaths from AIDS continue to rise in Africa. (lagging)
	Halt and begin to reverse the incidence of malaria and other major diseases.	Faster progress is needed to achieve malaria target. (lagging)

Continued on page 85

Millennium Development Goals	Targets for 2015	Progress at Midpoint, July 7, 2007
7. Ensure environmental sustainability.	Integrate the principles of sustainable development into country policies and programs; reverse loss of environmental resources.	Deforestation continues; biodiversity continues to decline; greenhouse gas emissions outpace sustainable energy technology. (lagging)
	Reduce by half the proportion of people without sustainable access to safe drinking water and basic sanitation.	Meeting water target requires extraordinary efforts. (water on track; sanitation lagging)
	Achieve significant improvement in lives of at least 100 million slum dwellers, by 2020.	Expansion of cities making slum improvements more daunting. (lagging)
8. Develop a global partnership for development.	Develop open, rule-based, predictable, nondiscriminatory trading and financial system.	No agreements in trade negotiations.
	Address special needs of the least developed countries, landlocked countries and small island developing states.	Development aid falls despite commitments; little progress in doubling aid to Africa.
	Deal comprehensively with developing countries' debt.	Debt burden continues to lighten.
	Develop and implement strategies for decent and productive work for youth.	
	In cooperation with companies, provide access to affordable essential drugs in developing countries.	
	In cooperation with private sector, make available new technologies, especially information and communications technologies.	

Sources: The data for the first two columns is from the www.un.org website. The description of progress is from the MDG 2007 report, and text in parentheses is from the DFID *Annual Report* for 2008, annex 3. The official UN site of MDG indicators is http://mdgs.un.org/unsd/mdg/Default.aspx.

Box 3–3. Five Decades of Development Debate

1954: W. A. Lewis defines a new role for development economics, distinct from standard economics.

1967: Dudley Seers defines the role of development studies as distinct from colonial economics and emphasizes that development is about much more than national income.

1977: Michael Lipton notes that development planning has ignored rural areas, where most poor people live.

1987: Giovanni Andrea Cornia, Richard Jolly, and Frances Stewart's *Adjustment with a Human Face* presents a major critique of the structural adjustment programs imposed by World Bank and IMF.

1997: Deepa Narayan's *Voices of the Poor: Poverty and Social Capital in Tanzania* establishes within the World Bank the utility of participatory methods in development.

2007: The 2008 *World Development Report* highlights the need to refocus on investment in agriculture.

   For a much broader list of choices, see Simon 2006.

There are no rights or wrongs among the different approaches described in this chapter. Any policy will be the outcome of diverging and sometimes clashing views. Development studies as a field of academic inquiry has been very closely linked to development practice, though many of its researchers have also remained critical and at a distance. When aid organizations increasingly focused on poverty, particularly during the 1990s, studies of international development evolved in parallel. Particularly since the period of adjustment, knowledge about the numbers and characteristics of the poor has greatly increased. Since the 1980s development studies has highlighted the multi-dimensionality of poverty, and paid increasing attention to issues of empowerment, governance, and security. Its multi-disciplinary approach has contributed much to improved understanding of processes of economic development, how these can be promoted, and the role of governance and institutions in these processes.

   In my view development studies faces two main challenges. First, because it remains strongly focused on informing the practice of donor organizations, it has continued to be dominated by academic institutions and think tanks in the global North. A count of quotations by ODI researchers in the 2006 *World Development Report* showed that the vast majority of studies were produced in the North.[12] According to an independent evaluation of World Bank research in the last decade the institution's enormous capacity for research is not always used in an independent way: "The panel had substantial criticisms of the way that this research was used to proselytize on behalf of Bank policy, often without taking a balanced view of the evidence, and without expressing appropriate skepticism. Internal research that was favorable to Bank positions was given great prominence, and unfavorable research ignored." (Banerjee et al. 2006, 6).

Many of the countries that lack capacity for public policymaking also lack the capacity to produce research and evidence to inform those policies. The aid industry has made important attempts to support research capacity in the South, but these have been outweighed by the investments in development research among and within Northern institutions, sometimes through tying research funding, sometimes because global research competitions are much more likely to be won by Northern institutions with long-established links with the donors. Over the coming years we will witness how the expansion of donors like China, India, Brazil, and South Africa will change this international arena, but capacity in the poorest countries continues to be a major challenge.

Second, there has been a tendency in international development efforts to equate poverty reduction with development itself. Much poverty analysis in particular has focused on identification of characteristics of the poor rather than the causes of and particularly the policies that lead to or sustain poverty. Writings on governance and institutions have improved much on the earlier Washington Consensus and on the understanding of links between markets and state intervention, but conceptualizing the politics of public policymaking and how the international community relates to these politics remains challenging. Debates on scaling up aid indicate that even if the analysis is restricted to fairly narrow measures of economic growth, many questions remain, and these questions are likely to be even more difficult if the analysis includes the role of public policy in shaping political contestation and social contracts.

Development studies continues to comprise different understandings of the relationship between growth and economic policies, on the one hand, and poverty and inequality, on the other. Researchers at the World Bank continue to differ: while David Dollar in 2000 strongly emphasized that "growth *is* good for the poor," authors of the 2006 *World Development Report* took pains to emphasize that inequality matters too, and Martin Ravallion at an IFPRI conference in Beijing in 2007 pointed out that "growth is not an anti-poverty policy." For others, growth is not enough, or never enough, as Armando Barrientos stressed in a DFID conference in December 2007.

In addition, camps remain divided about the importance and role of the state in relation to the private sector. Till the 1970s the state was seen as a key agent of development. During the 1980s "rolling back" the state became a predominant theme. PRSP approaches (described later) implied some return to state-led development. And lessons from East Asia also provide challenges to conventional wisdom. The debate on investment in social sectors continues to be divided between views that stress the need for increasing investment in health, education, and social security, and those that emphasize, for example, the limited resources available nationally and the need to invest in infrastructure and agriculture. In the end, these differences are only partly technical; they are strongly informed by different values, different national histories and traditions of public interventions, and different ideas about what the core of development is and ought to be. Debates like these will continue.

Further Readings

Isbister (2003), *Promises Not Kept*, gives a concise introduction of the main theories of development and underdevelopment.

Stern (2002), *Dynamic Development*, provides a good description of the evolution of the Washington Consensus.

Tarp (2000), *Foreign Aid and Development*, offers a more detailed overview of development thinking, for example, in the chapters by Erik Thorbecke (tracing five decades of development thinking), Irma Adelman (discussing the role of government in economic development), and Hjertholm and White (placing foreign aid in historical perspective).

The UNDP's annual *Human Development Report* was launched in 1990 and broadened the poverty debate by stressing its multi-dimensional nature.

Woolcock (2007), "Higher Education, Policy Schools, and Development Studies," posits an interesting view on what students in development studies should learn: skills of data collection and analysis; reframing given ideas for diverse groups; and negotiation and conflict mediation.

World Development Report (1990) is one of the most influential World Bank reports; it introduced the growth paradigm that has continued to be important.

4

Development Projects:
Rationale and Critique

In the previous chapters there have been many references to development "projects" and to a move away from projects to "program" aid and "sector" approaches. These terms are important in order to understand the ways in which aid is provided by different agencies in different periods of time. Projects, the original way of providing aid, assisted countries that were short of savings and technological capabilities but also took the form of integrated rural development. Program aid and sector approaches evolved partly out of the debt crises of the 1970s and partly out of problems created through project aid, as well as a focus on the broader set of institutions within countries that is essential for providing public services and conditions for development in general.

Late colonial authorities developed projects, often in agriculture. The World Bank started to develop infrastructure projects that could be expected to generate financial returns, and this moved on to integrated rural development projects under Robert McNamara. More recent project approaches include sustainable livelihoods approaches, microfinance projects, and social funds. As described in Chapter 3, during the 1950s and 1960s, the main economic theories emphasized the low savings rates in developing countries and saw foreign aid as the means to "kick start" economies. Funding projects was the way the aid industry tried to help developing countries to "take off," and, despite recent changes, the majority of aid is still delivered as projects (Roger Riddell 2007, 180), in a range of sectors, provided by small NGOs and large organizations like the development banks, and ranging from a few thousand to hundreds of millions of dollars.

While the design and implementation of projects is now a common and well-established practice of development agencies, the aid industry had to find ways of institutionalizing this in the newly established bureaucracies. Judith Tendler provides an interesting description of the workings in USAID and the World Bank in the early years of the industry. Infrastructure projects became popular for two reasons: first, the belief that accumulation of fixed assets was the key to development; and second, the pressure on officers in development agencies to spend large amounts of money within short periods of time (these development agencies were relatively small and newly created bureaucracies—the World Bank had barely made the transition from a reconstruction to a development agency at that time).

But projects were not generated automatically. "The initial position of the Bank was that preparation of a project was the responsibility of the borrower; if the Bank became involved, it could not thereafter be sufficiently objective in appraising the project. Though buttressed by logic, this position soon gave way to the pressure of events. 'Experience has demonstrated that we do not get enough good projects to appraise unless we are involved intimately in their identification and preparation.'"[1] Over time, this has become the common practice. Development practitioners do not simply respond to demands from partners for loans or grants but actively engage—supported by bureaucracies that encourage disbursement of loans or grants—in discussions about possible new projects.

As we will see throughout the next chapters, projects (and programs) exist in a wide range of areas, not all clearly related to poverty reduction. There are at least two reasons why the range is so wide. First, not all aid agencies have a narrow focus on poverty reduction; much assistance is provided to development more generally, and as described earlier, the focus on poverty is a relatively recent phenomenon. Second, even if agencies have a strong focus on poverty, they emphasize that there are different ways in which poverty reduction can be achieved and that the preconditions for sustainable poverty reduction are broad. So, for example, DFID distinguished three types of activities: *enabling* actions that support economic growth or more effective governments; *inclusive* or broadbased actions that benefit the entire population; and *targeted* interventions of which the benefits go directly to poor people.

The objective of this chapter is to provide an understanding—and a number of examples—of project approaches, their characteristics, whether and how they "target" the poor or development in a broader sense, and advantages, disadvantages, and critiques of these approaches. While the distinction between projects and programs is crucial for understanding approaches to international development, it is also important to emphasize that donor agencies normally use a combination of different approaches.

Project Management

A project approach involves a focus on a specific area of intervention for donor involvement. It targets the use of funds for specific activities for which objectives and outputs, and the inputs required to achieve them, have been defined. Aid projects are defined as specific and distinct activities with concrete outputs. Goals, results, and measurements of success are specific to the project. Activities include tangible objectives, like building schools, water tanks, or roads. They can also consist of "gap filling," that is, delivering technical expertise, skills, or "capacity development" more generally.

Projects have a clear, distinct, and time-bound rationale, which is often described in a project cycle that moves from identification through implementation to evaluation (see Figure 4–1).

Figure 4–1. The Project Cycle

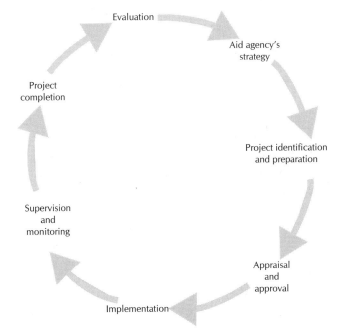

In the 1970s and 1980s, with aid agencies becoming increasingly professional, it became common to describe and report project objectives in the forms of Logical Frameworks, or LogFrames. The LogFrame, now a common management tool, is used to improve the design of interventions. It usually consists of a matrix, typically four-by-four. In the rows it describes (from bottom to top): inputs, outputs, outcomes, and impacts (the development goal). The four columns describe objectives, measurement indicators, ways of measuring these, and the assumptions or conditions that may influence success and failure. The systematic approach in the LogFrame is meant to facilitate planning, execution, and evaluation of a project, with periodic reviews measuring performance against a specific level of the LogFrame. The LogFrame, however, has been criticized for its mechanistic character, for not allowing adequate description of complex policy processes and indirect consequences, and for neglecting personal relationships, cultural sensitivity, and potential conflicts.[2]

Though international agencies have emphasized the need for projects to be "owned" and implemented by local agencies—government or otherwise—in practice the form of management has varied a great deal. At one end of the spectrum are special implementing agencies, often with international personnel; they have been responsible for the direct management of projects. At the other end are projects undertaken by government or other local agencies; the role of international staff is restricted to supervision and evaluation.

Technical Cooperation and Capacity Development

Technical assistance or technical cooperation, which forms approximately one-quarter of total ODA, has come under heavy criticism. It is a project approach but also usually part of program approaches (discussed in the next chapter). While most agencies see technical cooperation as an integral part of their work, Germany has set up a separate but government-owned agency for technical cooperation, GTZ. Consultants and NGOs often play a key role in the delivery of this form of support.

Technical cooperation focuses on strengthening capacity to promote development rather than simply providing money or other benefits to poor people. DAC defines capacity development as follows: "Capacity development can be understood as a process whereby people, organizations and society as a whole strengthen, create, adapt and maintain capacity over time. Promoting capacity development refers to what outside agencies do to facilitate or catalyze capacity development. Not all TC or TA . . . in donor statistics is capacity development, and there are other parts of aid that do qualify as capacity development" (OECD DAC 2006, 9).

Technical cooperation focuses on the transfer of knowledge and skills, which can be technical, economic, organizational, or other. It aims to strengthen capacities of organizations, and individuals, for development and poverty reduction. Such cooperation can be directly with civil society or grassroots organizations, promoting livelihoods or enhancing the status of women, for example, or organizing and training communities of poor people. But a great deal of technical cooperation is less directly related to working with poor communities. For example, donors have supported reform of and strengthening of capacity of finance ministries (through secondment and technical training), of offices of personnel or human resources, and of public utilities responsible for infrastructure (see Box 4–1).

Infrastructure Projects

Infrastructure projects, the model of the early aid industry, are still key to early phases of reconstruction efforts after disasters. Infrastructure was, and still is, a key constraint to "kick starting" economies. Infrastructure projects are ideally suited for large-scale investments, with distinct outcomes and relatively easily calculated rates of return; despite risks and long pay-off periods, they have attracted increasing amounts of foreign capital. In the initial period programs focused on large investments for state-owned enterprises. Currently, most of the aid for physical infrastructure (transport, communication, energy) has been provided by Japan, the United States, the EC, the World Bank, and more recently, China.

Infrastructure projects may be large or small. Large infrastructure projects include the World Bank's highway projects in Morocco, where donor support gradually moved toward programs constructing and improving thousands of miles of roads.[3] While overall donor funding for infrastructure has decreased, infrastructure and transport have remained among the largest sectors within the World Bank (perhaps 15 percent of all lending, with 20 percent of that in Africa). The work on highways has been celebrated as a development success.[4] For international donors

---

Box 4–1. Technical Assistance for Electricity Industry, Orissa, India

In the first half of the 1990s the government of Orissa, with support from the World Bank and techical assistance grants from DFID, took the initiative to reform its electricity industry. Objectives of the reform included reducing the industry's enormous losses; rationalizing the generation and supply of electricity; enhancing the industry's competitiveness and the participation of private entrepreneurs and investment; and improving the quality of services. When DFID's overarching focus became poverty, this technical assistance specified a development and poverty-reduction objective: with the pre-reform losses it would be difficult for the government to have any policies benefiting the poor, and better electricity provisions would benefit the entire population, including the poor.

Substantial amounts of money were spent on consultancy, both local and "highly rated consulting firms of international repute." This form of technical assistance was thought essential to prepare the blue-print reform (Orissa was among the first states to undertake this) and to develop systems of operation management, financial control, and contract management. Official government reports and various external critiques have emphasized that the utilities were unable to absorb the advice fully, and remained dependent on the international consultants, thus possibly weakening rather than strengthening the organizations themselves.

Source: Orissa Electricity Regulatory Commission at www.orierc.orgdfidweb
.dfid.gov.uk/prismdocs/ARCHIVE/INDIA/51806411.doc.

---

it is not merely about roads but a precondition for poverty reduction and economic growth. Much of the infrastructure supported by donors has been in smaller projects. Increasing emphasis has been put on village roads, because these are more directly relevant for the poor and because they tend to receive less emphasis in existing national government programs. In these smaller-scale infrastructure projects, community participation tends to receive greater emphasis.

Failure in infrastructure projects also became a key focus of the critiques of international development. Large failed projects—wide roads that are not used, inappropriate blue-print approaches, and lack of maintenance—have contributed to this image. Support for building dams has been heavily criticized by NGOs, leading to a withdrawal from these forms of funding. According to the critiques, infrastructure symbolizes lack of attention to the poor—and even the "anti-poor" nature of development. With the onset of the debt crisis, moreover, long-term investment suffered because of the expense of repaying countries' debt. With the 1980s focus on markets, the failure of state and public-sector units to build and run utilities was increasingly highlighted.

Over time, while donors have continued to pay attention to smaller and community-based forms of infrastructure, for larger infrastructure projects the private sector has become more important. Growing amounts of private foreign capital has come to finance infrastructure projects. And the models of delivery of infrastructure projects has changed, moving away from government-managed projects toward more private-sector participation and so-called public-private partnerships, and with the IFC playing an increasingly important role.

While infrastructure provision often has been criticized for being the preserve of engineers, with planners focusing on technical goals and operational efficiency, over time approaches have become more sensitive to questions of economic development, poverty reduction (with much analysis highlighting the importance of, for example, roads as a precondition to escape poverty), and to the need to adapt approaches to different conditions in developing countries. Increasing attention is being paid to the demand for infrastructure, willingness to contribute, and decentralization in implementation and management of infrastructure—though the critique that the infrastructure provided does not benefit the poor remains. The emphasis during the 1980s on privatization was succeeded by new thinking about and introduction of new forms of ownership and financing of infrastructure provision.

The "aid fatigue" of the 1980s and 1990s hit the infrastructure sector particularly hard. Infrastructure ODA for low-income countries has declined in relative terms—in the case of Sub-Saharan Africa from 29 percent of ODA in the first half of the 1990s to 19 percent between 2000 and 2004.[5] The urge toward privatization of government services and cost recovery was indirectly responsible. As described by Kessler (2005), while privatization in many places has been and still is disputed, a key problem has been that the expected private finance has not been forthcoming, particularly in the water sector.

More recently, the aid industry has renewed its attention to infrastructure. There have been a number of reasons for this. Recipient countries have started to focus more on the need for infrastructure, particularly in Africa where investments have suffered most as a result of the debt crisis. Organizations like the World Bank have come to realize that they continue to need the large projects, with relatively predictable disbursements. Recently, China, India, and the Gulf nations have been rapidly increasing their funding in infrastructure in Africa.

From Integrated Rural Development to Sustainable Livelihoods

Approaches to rural development have been as diverse as any of the other development fields. An IFPRI article in 1997 identified nine different agricultural paradigms since the 1960s: commercialization via cash cropping, community development, basic human needs, regional integration 1 (national food self-sufficiency), regional integration 2 (Food First), structural adjustment 1 (demand management), structural adjustment 2 (growth with equity), supply shifters, and sustainable development (Delgado 1997). Since then, DFID, for example, witnessed the rapid rise and subsequent decline in popularity of the sustainable-livelihoods approach followed by renewed attention to agriculture as part of a broader economic growth agenda. This section focuses on two of the major project approaches: integrated rural development and sustainable rural livelihoods.

Approaches to rural development were informed by the experience of the Green Revolution. Between the mid-1960s and the mid-1970s agriculture in parts of Asia and South America rapidly modernized. The period witnessed massive adoptions of improved cereals, mainly wheat and rice, and of improved crop technologies, including use of fertilizers, irrigation, and management practices. Asian countries doubled their rice production per capita per year. Yet despite successes in increasing food supply, Green Revolution progress did not necessarily translate into benefits for the poor. It was the better-off strata of rural society that gained access to better incomes generated by the introduction of technology. Women often lost job opportunities as a result of modernization. In addition, the Green Revolution has been criticized for reduced genetic diversity, increased vulnerability to pests, soil erosion, and water shortages, among other things.[6]

During the 1970s the goals of equity and poverty alleviation entered explicitly into thinking on agriculture, which previously had focused on commercialization that benefited both poor and rich. Under McNamara, the World Bank became especially concerned with poor farmers and started an approach that aimed to address their multiple problems simultaneously. That approach was called integrated rural development (IRD).

IRD highlighted rural poverty as a part of wider socioeconomic development, and as the result of limited access to resources. It defined the development problem as integrated and multisectoral, highlighting the multiple functions of agriculture in the development process and the need for simultaneous development in different sectors and areas, for example, technology, training, research, and marketing. IRD projects often addressed issues of rural food production and distribution, nutrition, health, child welfare, and off-farm employment opportunities and rural enterprise initiatives. Planning units to coordinate multisectoral projects were set up in core ministries, often linked to a national board. NGOs started to play an increasingly important role, but planning tended to have a strong top-down character.

Within a decade the approach was considered a failure, partly because emerging financial crises challenged its potential. The institutions created under the projects were often very complex, and coordination was both difficult and time consuming. Expectations regarding planning capacity were overly optimistic, and the need and potential for local planning underestimated—issues that also became core to participatory approaches developed later.

The sustainable-livelihoods approach that emerged in DFID, UNDP, IFAD, and OXFAM was portrayed by some as a radical departure of past practices, while others have described it as a revitalized version of the IRD approaches of the 1970s. The term *livelihood* was made popular by the Advisory Panel of the World Commission on Environment and Development, and subsequently by Chambers and Conway in a 1992 paper. *Livelihood* was defined as people's capabilities, social and material assets, and activities needed to make a living. *Sustainability*, a key addition, was defined as the capacity to cope with and recover from shocks while maintaining capabilities and assets as well as the natural resource base. This was presented as a new approach to analyzing rural life and poverty, which put people at the center of development.

The sustainable-livelihoods approach, like IRD, focuses on multisectoral and integrated development. It emphasizes that the poor derive their livelihoods from many sectors, jobs, and other sources of income. Therefore, standard approaches to labor markets or focusing on specific sectors were thought to be inadequate, particularly in most marginalized areas. The sustainable-livelihoods approach emphasizes the diversity of rural households' strategies, including not only agricultural production but also diversification and migration. A sustainable-livelihoods approach focuses not only on poverty and deprivation but also on poor people's resources and assets. An "asset pentagon" shows this multi-dimensionality of people's livelihoods and the relationship among their assets (see Figure 4–2).

Figure 4–2. Livelihoods Framework: Assets

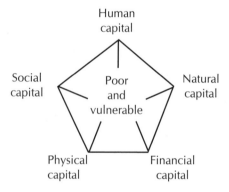

Source: Adapted from www.livelihoods.org (originally designed by Scoones 1998).

The sustainable-livelihoods framework built on lessons from poverty analysis, which over time had come to emphasize the multi-dimensionality of poverty and issues of vulnerability (people's situations are not static, people move in and out of poverty, and slightly better-off people also can be at risk of losing their income). Moreover, in a new wave of emphasis on participation, and following in particular work by Robert Chambers and Gordon Conway (1992) at IDS Sussex that reflected on past problems caused by, among other things, paternalism of development professionals, it put participation and empowerment at the center of this development approach. The sustainable-livelihoods approach thus aims to work across a range of sectors, as most governments and donor agencies tend to work along sectoral lines. In the case of the project in China described in Box 4–2, project priorities as defined through a participatory approach include a wide range of services and therefore require the cooperation of and counterpart funding by the different line agencies involved.

Following from the focus on participation, but in practice much less developed, the sustainable-livelihoods approach also highlights the importance of policy dimensions. This was also partly a response to the critique that technical project approaches paid little attention to the policy environment in which they functioned. The framework thus stressed the importance of strengthening policies and institutions—at the local level through direct participatory processes, but also at higher levels of policy formulation and implementation—for enhancing poor people's livelihood options.

The sustainable-livelihoods approach also has come under criticism. In agencies like DFID, where the approach was seen as a major priority for a few years, attention shifted to other issues, in fact away from agriculture all together. The 2008 *World Development Report, Agriculture for Development*, for example, did not mention the approach. The sustainable-livelihoods approach has been criticized for its ambition to work across a range of sectors. In the project in China ensuring cooperation from the many different line agencies involved and ensuring that the program matches the participatory plans developed have continued to be challenging. Finally, some have argued that a focus on agricultural productivity must be maintained in situations where food insecurity prevails.

Microfinance

Since the 1980s microfinance has become a widely praised instrument of the aid industry. Its development was based on the understanding that regular financial systems in many countries failed to provide financial services to the poor. In the 1960s many countries experimented with massive subsidies and credit, but in the 1980s this approach was heavily criticized. In the early 1980s the now-world-famous Grameen Bank in Bangladesh started with a group-based lending approach, subsequently

Box 4–2. Poor Rural Development Communities Project, China

Since 2005 the World Bank and DFID have jointly provided support to the Chinese government for a rural development project in eighteen counties in three of its poorest provinces (Sichuan, Guanxi, and Yunnan). This is the fourth in a series of World Bank poverty projects in China that has generally been considered very successful. The objective of the project is to improve security of livelihood for the poorest people and to encourage their participation in project design, implementation, monitoring, and evaluation. The funding is provided through a World Bank loan (US$100 million), a DFID grant (US$32 million, which reduces the interest rate of the loan), and counterpart funding from the Chinese government as well as project beneficiaries (US$42 million).

By 2005 China was no longer among the poorest countries. But, it was argued in the project document, the number of poor people in resource-poor areas was still very large, forming a large proportion of the world's poor, and to address this required innovative development approaches. The approach had the following main components:

- A participatory approach, through involvement of poor people in all stages of the project, and through increased involvement of NGOs. International assistance is critical in promoting such approaches in China.
- The project is targeted to China's poorest population, those who live in remote and mountainous areas and often belong to ethnic minorities.
- It is a multisectoral project, providing access to education and health in the poorest areas as well as improvements in infrastructure and diverse forms of agriculture. The project is based on a belief that focusing on one sector alone fails to address the needs of the poor, which are multisectoral, as highlighted in the participatory analyses.
- The project has a substantial financial allocation and technical inputs for capacity building in order to improve management

Continued on page 103

> capabilities of government staff and to promote the use of a participatory approach.
>
> - While directly benefiting large numbers of poor households in the eighteen poor counties, the project also aims to influence the government of China's broader poverty strategy. The government has had a very proactive strategy in using such projects as part of its economic development programs and reforms, including strengthening management capacities to international standards.

adopted by many microfinance institutions around the world, including some OECD countries. The number of studies on the subject and assessments of the effectiveness of such projects and institutions grew exponentially.

Microfinance programs target finance to poor people. Small and easily accessible loans are very important to fund new economic activities or to provide support during crises. Because the loans are small, it is unlikely that the rich will capture program benefits, which makes microfinance an effective anti-poverty investment (it avoids the so-called leakage problem). Grameen provides credit to groups of women with little or no land. Staff members who have gone through extensive training assess households' wealth through visual indicators like housing quality and other assets. This is a quick and fairly reliable mechanism, allowing a rapid increase in program coverage in contexts where little information about income exists. In many programs loans are provided to groups instead of individuals. In the absence of collateral, the groups are jointly liable for the loan; this is key to keeping up repayment rates.[7]

The assessment of how well these services have been targeted has been a major policy and analytical question. In the case of Bangladesh lack of land is regarded as a "proxy" for poverty; the quick assessment done by Grameen bank staff is generally a good indicator of the overall wealth of the household. In other cases, like the small-farm-loan project in Thailand in the mid-1980s, finance was targeted to villages that had been identified as poor. In Indian states village councils identified poor household eligible for loans. However, even in the celebrated Grameen case, targeting errors occur. The literature distinguishes two kinds of such errors: "inclusion error," which implies that people who are not poor get benefits (in the case of Grameen, for example, people without land who are not poor), and "exclusion error," which means that people who are poor do not get benefits (for example, people with a little land who are still poor).

These schemes have had enormous success and are regarded as both an effective and sustainable way to provide poorer households with loans. The approach is sustainable because the repaid loans can be used to expand services and increase coverage to larger populations. Indeed, successful programs like Grameen's have shown very high rates of repayment, unlike earlier state-led approaches with little emphasis on or success in repayment rates.

Such programs have also met with criticism. There are reasons why the poorest may be excluded, either by project staff or the groups themselves, particularly if there is high pressure for repayment. And some studies have pointed at possible negative social consequences. For example, Grameen borrowers have to sit on the floor, chant slogans, and so on, which can be stigmatizing. While group formation may enhance the "social capital" of its members, failing to repay loans may damage social connections. There has been a lively debate about whether providing loans to women empowers them or creates further tensions within the household. Perhaps the most important question is whether the loans have a sustainable impact on income or well-being. Can the poorest people actually use loans for economic investment? Many loans are used for consumables, and new small enterprises often fail. Concluding that microfinance lifts large numbers of people out of poverty may be too optimistic, but overall the approach has proven very successful.

Social Funds

As described in Chapter 2, throughout its history the World Bank has emphasized poverty reduction, though it was only in the 1990s that poverty became an overarching objective. During the 1980s, when economic stabilization and adjustment were the core concerns, the World Bank started to look for ways in which the impact of economic crises could be ameliorated, focusing on people directly affected by these crises. The "social funds" approach emerged and has continued to expand. It also has been adopted by regional development banks and often has been co-financed by other donors. In 2000, social funds existed in over fifty countries, with the World Bank and the IADB the largest funders. World Bank financing was estimated at about US$3.5 billion from 2001 to 2005, with government and donor co-financing total expenditure amounting to almost US$9 billion. Though social funds have remained a small part of social security activities in most countries, they are a significant part of the government budget in a number of countries.

The first funds emerged in the late 1980s as emergency measures to alleviate the direct effects of structural adjustment and economic shocks. The Emergency Social Fund in Bolivia aimed to address the social costs of adjustment, particularly the unemployment of miners laid off after the collapse of tin prices and the closing of state-run mines. The Program of Action to Mitigate the Social Cost of Adjustment in Ghana and the Program to Alleviate Poverty and Social Costs of Adjustment in Uganda were set up in a similar vein. Social funds have been less important in Asia, but social-fund support was given to the District Poverty Initiative Project in India. In Thailand a social fund was created to establish a new economy after the 1997 crisis, and Indonesian agencies share many operational characteristics with social funds.

Social funds are provided as a regular loan to countries, usually co-financed with a contribution from the recipient, and sometimes with additional grant funding. Social funds are primarily an intermediary that channels resources to small-scale projects for poor and vulnerable groups. The funds appraise, finance, and supervise implementation of small projects—but do not implement them. They operate institutionally and organizationally distinct from government sectoral policies and services. Organizational setup varies, from autonomous agencies outside regular government bureaucracies to locations within a ministry or office of the president, or within the finance ministry, but with a substantial degree of independence. The central administrative entity disburses funds to intermediary organizations including local government, private firms, and NGOs. Many funds set up procedures that aim to overcome the problems of time-consuming, bureaucratic, and poorly administered procedures associated with the public sector. They recruit staff at higher rates than civil service standards—as civil-service pay scales are too low to attract the best professionals—and sometimes on performance contracts. They aim to avoid complex disbursement and procurement procedures, and funds are given great control over their budgetary procedures.

The funds respond to demand from local groups, usually within a set menu of eligible and ineligible projects. Social funds are intended to take quick and targeted actions to reach poor and vulnerable groups. They aim to be "demand led." They stimulate participatory development initiatives by providing small-scale financing to local NGOs, community groups, small firms, and entrepreneurs and also provide pre-investments to promote broad-based participation. Beneficiary co-financing is central in order to ensure that projects respond to demand and are likely to be sustained after project funding comes to an end. Social funds have experimented with a range of community contracting models.

There is much diversity in social funds supported by donors. They have been set up in the poorest countries and in former communist countries marked by crises of social security systems. They balance multiple objectives, with much variation in the kinds of activities they can support, and a range of different institutions has evolved. Over time, the emphasis has shifted from short-term emergency relief toward more general development programs. In line with an evolving World Bank social-protection strategy, social funds have moved from a focus on coping with risk to a more aggressive strategy dealing with risk mitigation and risk reduction, and with longer-term objectives. Social funds have come to pay more attention to popular participation and have become a main instrument for facilitating Community Driven Development (CDD) (see Chapter 7).

Social funds have been praised for their rapid disbursement, flexibility, and ability to respond to demand from poor communities.[8] Of course, impact and project quality have varied: beneficiary-executed projects were found to benefit from broad participation in project definition and meet the perceived needs of the community; private organizations and NGOs scored less well, usually because of project complexity and lack of continuity and capacity; while interventions through line ministries have tended to lack participatory practices and the resources to supervise interventions and work closely with beneficiaries.

Another concern about social funds is related to the potential conflicts between efficiency goals and the need for time-consuming and costly processes of community ownership and decision making. There are potential tradeoffs among reaching the poor and demand-led approaches, the varying interests involved, and the need to enhance the capacities of communities to participate. Only a small proportion of the funds could be categorized as really demand oriented, and reviews have raised questions regarding the adequacy of the methodology to formulate community needs. Social funds—as with other forms of support provided to communities (Gaspart and Platteau 2006)—can even increase corruption.

Finally, social funds tend to create new structures rather than working to reform existing government institutions; they react, often driven by donors, to the slowness of public-sector reform. There is evidence of negative effects of social funds on other national and local policy and public-sector institutions. Setting up a parallel system, with conditions for staff much better than those in mainstream public institutions, may harm the morale and efficiency of government staff elsewhere, while—some argue—support should focus on tackling tough issues regarding transparent and accountable government structures. Phasing out or integrating of social funds into existing structures also does not seem to be a focus at planning stages. Finally, establishing funds may displace other sources of funding. As with other projects, social funds suffer from so-called fungibility, the risk that ministries reduce their allocations to areas that are targeted by social funds.

Critique of Project Approaches

Projects thus have come a long way from their origins in the late-colonial period and the early infrastructure projects of the period, in which the emphasis was on "kick starting" economies of the former colonial countries and overcoming the savings' gap through straightforward and visible projects. During the 1980s countries' financial crises made many of the projects financially unsustainable, but even before that a serious critique of project approaches had emerged (Mosley and Eeckhout 2000). The list of perceived problems with projects is long; the following presents half a dozen often interrelated issues.

First, development projects can undermine local ownership. The aid industry rapidly discovered that demands for projects were not easily or quickly forthcoming, and the entrepreneurs of the industry had incentives to go out and design projects rather than sit back, and donor countries often had economic interests in supplying certain goods. There are many stories about highly inappropriate projects, but even in the better cases, local ownership can be limited. And certainly where grants rather than loans are involved, recipients do not have strong reasons to say no to offers of aid.

Sustainability is a second concern, directly related to the question of ownership. Many infrastructure projects have had a bad record of maintenance. Technical cooperation does not have a strong record in many places (and therefore became unpopular during the 1990s, often because the broader environments needed to sustain improvements do not exist.

Third, aid projects have imposed large burdens on recipient governments, particularly aid-dependent countries, but even the Indian government—for whom aid is only a small proportion of government budgets and administrative capacity—has limited the total number of donors. Each project comes with its own reporting requirements. Aid projects, usually offering better conditions, often attract better-skilled people from government services.

Fourth, projects and technical assistance have often become isolated islands of excellence. With a strong focus on project outputs, donor projects have contributed little to broader government strategies. Project managers cannot be held accountable for changes at policy levels above the direct project, and evaluations usually do not address the wider environment (even though project documents often state aims to that effect). As we saw in the description of social funds, aid projects tend to create parallel structures and increase administrative burdens.

Fifth, projects suffer from fungibility of funding. Aid to particular projects or sectors may lead governments to reduce their own contributions to these areas. Unless aid agencies have insight into government planning and budgeting procedures, this is difficult to ascertain.[9]

Sixth, projects often are not only a heavy burden on governments, failing to contribute to wider development planning, but in some cases also may actively undermine government policy. In countries heavily dependent on foreign aid, projects can undermine resource planning. Budgets of many countries receiving aid show, for example, large year-to-year fluctuations in spending on sectors that receive substantial aid. Projects can undermine local accountability; for example, elected leaders can attract voters because of impressive new bridges or schools.

Not all projects, of course, suffer from all or even some of these problems. Many of these issues have been addressed by newer generations of projects. In the case of larger countries, with aid flows that are small relative to total country or government resources, projects can continue to prevail, often successfully and often with a focus on innovation.[10] Many of the problems also pertain to the newer instrument of the aid industry, the program approach, which is described in the next chapter. It is clear that the success of projects probably depends at least as much on the broader policy environment than on the project design itself. This leads to the paradox that aid projects are less likely to succeed in places where they are most needed and with weak governance than in places where they are many poor people with governments that have the capacity and are committed to development and poverty reduction.

Conclusion

Project approaches have been much criticized since the 1970s or 1980s, for a variety of reasons, including lack of ownership and the need for a broader environment that would enable the success of projects, which often remained islands of excellence. Yet development projects have been and continue to be the bread and butter of the aid industry, despite changes toward program approaches. The World Bank continues to fund projects, including major ones in the infrastructure sector, along with other forms of lending. This partly suits its own incentive to maintain stable and high levels of lending, informed by the idea that lending needs to provide benefits more directly than can be shown through supporting government budgets. The bilateral agencies that have forcefully argued for changes away from project approaches also continue to fund projects, and the new agents within the aid industry have continued to expand numbers of projects.

Projects suit the aid industry very well, with its disbursement pressures, need to show results, potential to be flexible and demand driven, and potential for innovation. But they also can fulfill very important needs in recipient countries. In the end, it is probably the ways in which individual projects are supported, both in terms of quality and ownership by recipients, rather than a project per se that determines whether a project is a success or not.

5

Hard-nosed Development:
Reforms, Adjustment, Governance

During the 1970s the aid industry increasingly made poverty reduction part of its core business. But a number of developments challenged this. Financial sustainability became an increasing concern, first gradually, but dramatically so after the second oil crisis. This led to an emphasis on economic reforms and structural adjustment, which gave at least a part of the aid industry a very bad reputation and the 1980s the title "lost development decade," but this in turn led to new development approaches. Theories on development moved from Washington to post–Washington Consensus, as we saw in Chapter 3. In this and the next chapter we focus on the accompanying changes in the practices of the aid industry.

The term *structural adjustment* raises more heated debate than probably any other term in international development language. The first section provides a very brief overview of what structural adjustment means, where it originated, and of the main elements of the critique directed at this approach, which came to dominate the 1980s. While there are good reasons to disagree with the fiercest criticism—related to the necessity of adjustment, and whether it has caused poverty—this section concludes that differences in views are likely to remain. Undoubtedly, the critique of adjustment exerted considerable influence on newer approaches.

The second section focuses on two sets of related problems that accompanied adjustment. First, under adjustment, aid agencies—particularly but not only the IMF and the World Bank—imposed *conditionalities*—conditions for policy or administrative changes, such as establishing financial stability—that had to be implemented before loans or grants were given. Increasingly, this was seen as undesirable and alternatives were proposed. Second, the focus on restoring economic growth had relatively little success, and for the aid agencies it became increasingly clear that economic growth required good governance and a wide array of government functions and capacities, such as tax policies, civil service, and public enterprise reform. These are complex processes, and aid agencies came up with long lists of prescriptions; implementing them is a continuing challenge. Moreover, the focus on governance made it increasingly clear that development, and hence providing aid, is a political process. Recently aid agencies have started to develop approaches that try to incorporate this understanding. The resulting dilemmas suggest that the questions that were highlighted with the use of conditionalities continue to influence the workings of the aid industry.

The problems that emerged with structural adjustment, combined with the critique of the projects approach of the aid industry, resulted in a move toward program and sector approaches, which are described in the third section of this chapter. Projects focus on "one off" and clearly traceable support to countries' development; program aid, reforms, and sector-wide approaches focus on the broader administrative and policy systems of the recipients of aid. While the principles of these newer approaches are sound, progress in implementation has remained limited, and despite commitments to increase funding using program approaches, project funding continues to prevail.

Structural Adjustment Lending

Structural adjustment was a response to debt crises that emerged after the oil crises of the 1970s. Brazil, Mexico, and Poland were among the countries that fairly suddenly were unable to service their debts. The IMF—because of its mandate to ensure global financial stability—and the World Bank became the key agents in addressing the so-called debt crisis, and the response received widespread attention because of its focus in poor countries on reducing government expenditure, reducing state intervention, and promoting liberalization.

Structural adjustment has been applied as a simple term in the critiques of the aid industry, in particular of the World Bank and the IMF. But it consists of multiple objectives and instruments. It has involved not only the IMF and the World Bank but also some of the bilateral agencies. The subjects of adjustment are usually countries' governments, though in the case of India the World Bank worked directly with state governments, which have a fairly large degree of fiscal policy autonomy.

Structural adjustment has characterized policy changes in the North as much as the South. The discussion here focuses on how the aid industry approached adjustment and the impact on the recipients of aid.

Structural adjustment programs (SAPs) consist of two main sets of measures.[1] The first is *stabilization*: immediate and short-term steps to address countries' internal fiscal and external balance-of-payments crises. Recommendations typically included:

- Devaluation of the currency, so imports are reduced and exports become cheaper and more competitive.
- A civil-service and public-sector wage freeze and reduction of the government's salary bill in order to address government expenditure and inflation.
- Reductions in the subsidies of public services and products, such as food and other basic commodities, health and education, and pensions, in order to reduce government expenditure.

The second main set of measures is called *adjustment* measures. These are meant to follow a phase of stabilization and designed to enhance government efficiency, economic growth, and competitiveness in the medium to long run. SAPs often include the following measures:

- Civil-service downsizing (reducing the number of civil servants). This is usually combined with attempts to reform the civil service and public sector in order to increase efficiency and, for example, improve recruitment and promotion procedures.
- Economic liberalization to enhance economic efficiency by reducing and streamlining regulation, liberalizing prices, reducing explicit and implicit subsidies, reducing taxes on productive activities, promoting privatization, and minimizing the importance of state monopolies.
- Export promotion is considered key to addressing debt crises as well as promoting economic competitiveness. Recommended measures include reducing constraints in obtaining foreign exchange and promotion of diversification, usually away from a focus on agricultural goods for which prices had been declining.

Over time, SAPs have been adapted a great deal. The distinction between stabilization and longer-term economic development was made clearer, resulting in a separate mechanism to fund activities for economic recovery: the Enhanced Structural Adjustment Facility (ESAF). While initially a blueprint approach, over time local circumstances came to feature more in SAPs. Aid agencies have greatly increased their country knowledge, presence, and technical capacity commensurate with the wide range of areas implied in SAPs. They have built up close relationships with country governments, and—as the case of Uganda described in Box 5–1—tried to convince external audiences that there would be good cooperation. Along with financial assistance, aid agencies provided technical support and assisted governments in building the capacity for economic and financial management (for example, through long-term assistance to financial-systems reforms or secondments to finance ministries). Box 5–2 provides an example of such a loan, the Orissa Socio-Economic Development Program, provided by the World Bank in 2004 after many years of preparation, and with initial collaboration by DFID. This is not a typical example of adjustment. India's conditions are very different from those in many African countries, and the loan was provided to a state rather than a country, relying heavily on fiscal reforms agreements between Orissa and the Centre, but it does illustrate the main aspects of this aid approach.

Box 5–1. Uganda, the Showcase of Adjustment

Uganda is often held up to show the beneficial effects of structural adjustment and positive relationships with the aid industry. James Wolfensohn and other donors worked very closely with its government, led by President Museveni. Many of the new aid modalities were piloted and successful in Uganda. Indeed, during the 1990s Uganda, after it emerged from dictatorship and civil war, achieved significant economic growth (including growth in agriculture) and poverty reduction. Aid dependency was reduced. Reforms had much local "ownership," though critics have pointed out that this facet has remained fragile.

There was a clear intention to communicate that the relationship was working, as both the World Bank and the Ugandan government gave Peter Chappell permission and unprecedented access to film *Our Friends at the Bank* (First Run/Icarus Films), which emphasizes the close relationship between the two, despite difficult discussions about military spending to fight an insurgent movement.

Box 5–2. Orissa Socio-Economic Development Loan Project

The Orissa Socio-Economic Development Loan Project was the first in a series of projects to support the medium-term program for the socioeconomic development of Orissa, not only India's poorest state but also probably the one with the most severe fiscal stress. Salaries of government employees alone outstripped its revenue. The loan was provided by the World Bank, and initially DFID contributed a separate grant (before the Indian government decided it did not want grants for adjustment purposes).

The project aimed to stabilize the fiscal situation and to introduce growth-enabling reforms, reinforcing government initiatives to accelerate economic growth and to improve public-service delivery to reduce poverty. Expected benefits included:

- more rapid economic growth;
- improved fiscal performance and reduction of public-sector borrowing; and
- enhanced quality of governance and service delivery.

Two overarching policy documents were scheduled to be produced: one on poverty reduction by the newly established Poverty Task Force, and a *Vision 2020*.

The Orissa program was thought to entail significant risks: implementation of the reform program could be slower than planned because of institutional capacity constraints; opposition by powerful interests could slow down the pace of reform; non-adherence to the targets set in the Medium-term Fiscal Reform Framework could derail Orissa's adjustment path. However, several factors contributed to a mitigation of these risks: government had already implemented up-front actions, laying the foundation for subsequent reforms; and the World Bank ensured that significant technical assistance was available, to follow through on the reform measures supported by the operation, while close attention was also paid to sequencing reforms.

The contents of the program were presented in a policy matrix, a part of the project appraisal document. This matrix shows the large number of policy actions or reforms required for disbursement of

Continued on page 116

funds, including the creation or strengthening of systems to monitor outcomes, and an emphasis on strengthening communication about the reforms to the Orissa public. This list was the outcome of long discussions; preparation of the project took several years. Some policy areas were subject also to separate collaboration with the World Bank and others. Which items to include were often subject to heated discussion, and it was commonly argued that the list of policy actions was too long and that the project should focus on core areas of fiscal adjustment and governance reforms.

The policy matrix highlights the gradual approach to reforms. Some reforms had already begun and are still continuing, such as power-sector reform, which had received donor funding for many years. Many of the actions consisted of drafting plans, policies, legislation, and research proposals (such as tracking government expenditure). Some were more concrete actions (such as increased prosecution of cases of corruption). And a few highlighted specific outcomes of these policy actions (for example, price realization).

It is important to highlight here how radical a departure SAPs were from previous project approaches. They greatly enhanced the role of the IMF—which was set up as and continues to be a global financial rather than an aid institution—in the affairs of the poorest countries. Because of this new emphasis, governments lost a great deal of autonomy in managing their public policies, particularly in financial planning.

Aid in this form, particularly from the IMF and the World Bank, comes with *conditionalities*. "[A] conditionality consist of actions, or promises of actions, made by recipient governments only at the insistence of aid providers; measures that would not otherwise be undertaken, or not within the time frame desired by the providers" (Killick 2002, 481). Donors justify the use of conditionalities because they are purported to improve economic policy, economic growth, and ability to repay debts. Conditionalities in policy-based lending do not follow a standard blueprint but differ by type of country. In "better performing" countries they focus on financial stability, financial sector depth, or a competitive environment for the private sector, for example; in "poor performing" countries they have a stronger focus on public-sector management and institution building, property rights, budgetary and financial management, efficiency of revenue mobilization, public administration, and corruption. In each country the mix is different.

Conditionalities imposed through SAPs and related approaches have and continue to be heavily criticized, for a variety of reasons. Many argue that conditionalities undermine governments' space and duty to formulate policies. Uvin, for example, argues that imposing conditionalities is unethical (2004, 59). Specific policy recommendations or conditionalities also have been criticized. Retrenchments of civil servants and public sector workers and privatization have been heavily contested by the people directly affected and their labor unions; and reduction of spending in health and education has continued to be a main theme of criticism by NGOs. Over time, it has become commonly accepted that conditionalities do not produce the intended results and can even be counter-productive.[2] The approaches described later in this book were partly a result of this critique, emphasizing the need to enhance ownership of the policies. More directly, donors have increasingly looked at past records of reforms as the basis of decisions to provide loans. In the Orissa example described in Box 5–2, the policy matrix referred to (an alternative to project LogFrames), lists past, current, and future reforms.

A second issue to highlight is that the list of measures does not feature reduction of poverty. It has been argued that the agencies involved did not care about poverty reduction, but this is a simplification; in my experience, even the hard-nosed reformers were usually committed to poverty reduction. Some argued, however, that poverty could not be addressed until some of the basic economic problems and government failures were dealt with. In the case of adjustment in Orissa, experts thought that it would be undesirable to discuss increased spending in the health sector or poverty-reduction programs while all government financial resources went to salaries of civil servants and public-sector employees; financial losses, particularly in the power sector, as well as public finances and government functions, had to be rationalized first in order to "create fiscal space."[3]

As mentioned earlier, there has been an enormous amount of debate about the impact of structural adjustment on poverty, and global debt-relief campaigns and the PRSP approach have made poverty much more central.[4] Killick's (1999) summary assessment however is more positive: "Overall, the strongest criticisms that SAPs cause poverty are not born out, and concern about poverty effects is not a sufficient reason for deferring adjustment. But SAPs have done avoidable harm and could be made more pro-poor" (1999). In the first place, it is important to consider whether there were alternatives to adjustment. It is unlikely that countries would have been better off if they did not address high inflation and financial deficits—though over time it has been recognized that there are different ways in which these problems can be addressed. Second, implementation of programs was often partial and experienced much slippage. Partly as a result of this, the impact on economic recovery and growth, and therefore also on poverty reduction, remained limited. Third, many of the elements of adjustment do not have a direct or immediate link to the main causes of poverty. Efforts to stimulate job creation existed, but with relatively little success. In the case of Orissa, issues of land and forest produce by marginalized groups are central to poverty reduction but received very little attention in the policy discussions.

Fourth, structural adjustment has had a direct impact on particular groups and hence created new forms of inequalities. Civil servants and public-sector enterprise workers lost their jobs as a result of reform. In the case of Orissa, the reforms were accompanied by training and retirement schemes. In many countries, social funds (discussed in Chapter 4) also were set out to ameliorate the direct impact. Changes in prices and subsidies as a result of reforms also have had an impact on both producers and consumers, but the direction of this has varied, and some of the changes, like devaluation, did benefit some poor groups. Fifth, the introduction of user fees and the reduction of subsidies in health and education have been much criticized. However, overall, and partly as a result of the critique, the spending in these sectors has been protected, though much social spending does not benefit the poor. In the case of the Orissa project, the policy actions that were promoted tried to shift spending toward primary education, but this is not easy to achieve.

Finally, as highlighted in Killick (1999), the impact of reforms and adjustment also depends on political and other forms of power. Many countries' leaders and their constituencies paid little attention to poverty reduction. In the case of Orissa's state leaders, political analysis clearly showed that power was held by a very small elite, hardly accountable to large groups of deprived groups and with little incentives to make existing government programs work properly (De Haan 2008). Many of the policy measures that are part of adjustment programs do not affect these power relations, which in any case are difficult to change because people in power are usually able to block reforms that would affect their position.

This section has not tried to provide a final assessment of the impact of adjustment but merely to present an overview of the different positions in the debate. Whatever the rights and wrongs, for the purpose of this book two issues are of central importance. First, the debate about adjustment and the impact it has had on the recipients of aid is likely to continue, in part because different ideological positions are involved and technical assessments are unlikely to overcome them. Second, the critique of adjustment has led to changes in approaches of the aid industry, including conditionalities.

Conditionalities, Good Governance, and Politics

Among the most important changes in development thinking in the 1990s was the increased attention to governance. The field of governance is very broad, and relevant in all programs, sectors, and projects (see Box 5–3). It has moved from a more narrow focus on the operation of government institutions, and now usually is meant to inform development approaches with an understanding of processes of power and authority and of institutions beyond governments as well. In addition, it focuses attention on issues of legitimacy and accountability.

Sub-Saharan Africa: From Crisis to Sustainable Growth, published in 1989, was the first World Bank document to mention governance.[5] It argued that "a crisis of governance" was behind the "litany of Africa's development problems" (World Bank 1989, 60) and defined *governance* as the "exercise of political power to manage a nation's affairs." "African governments . . . need to go beyond the issues of public finance, monetary policy, prices, and markets to address fundamental questions relating to human capacities, institutions, governance, the environment, population growth and distribution, and technology" (World Bank 1989, 1). Key elements of this good governance agenda included economic liberalism; civil service reform and increasing accountability, transparency, elimination of rent-seeking, and managerial efficiency; political pluralism, participation, decentralization, and democracy; social justice, respect of human rights, freedom of expression and association; and upholding the rule of law.

The emphasis on governance resulted from a number of factors. First, the increased attention to governance coincided with the end of the Cold War. Increased engagement with the former Soviet Union and other transitional countries focused attention on the role of institutions

---

Box 5–3. Governance Defined

In 1996 the Governance Working Group of the International Institute of Administrative Sciences described the following aspects of governance:

- Governance refers to the process whereby elements in society wield power and authority, and influence and enact policies and decisions concerning public life, and economic and social development.
- Governance is a broader notion than government, whose principal elements include the constitution, legislature, executive and judiciary. Governance involves interaction between these formal institutions and those of civil society.
- Governance has no automatic normative connotation. However, typical criteria for assessing governance in a particular context might include the degree of legitimacy, representativeness, popular accountability and efficiency with which public affairs are conducted.

Source: www.gdrc.org.

---

in development. Second, globalization contributed to increasing harmonization of institutions and norms of governance, reinforcing the attention paid to the role of institutions in development.

Third, interest in governance followed recognition that many of the reforms during the 1980s had failed. This was in part because they had been technocratic in nature, with quick-fix technical solutions and blueprint approaches, with little attention paid to local conditions and weak institutional capacity or to questions of legitimacy, incentives and motivation of political and administrative leaders. Further, the policy prescriptions and conditionalities under structural adjustment had not worked, as recipient governments did not have the capacity or the political will to implement them.

And fourth, the emphasis on governance was part of the new developments in economics and signaled the move from the Washington Consensus to the post–Washington Consensus (Stern 2002). The large financial crises, like that in Mexico in 1995, also had led to a reconsideration of earlier approaches. While the crises of the later 1970s led to an emphasis on reducing state intervention, the crises of the 1990s pushed experts to look more closely at the institutions that govern market and financial processes, a trend that has been reinforced after the 2008 global financial crisis.

The emphasis on governance also coincided with increased focus on aid allocations intended to ensure that grants or loans were provided to partners that were likely to use aid effectively.[6] Governance indicators became a key component of aid delivery. The World Bank now uses annual policy and institutional assessments to determine resource allocation, rating countries against a set of sixteen criteria grouped in four clusters: (1) economic management; (2) structural policies; (3) policies for social inclusion and equity; and (4) public-sector management and institutions.[7] Despite the large number of indicators, such assessments still have a narrow focus considering the wide array of existing governance or political dimensions, such as informal political voice or influence, and inequality. Questions remain about how the indicators are constructed, what they really measure, and their hidden assumptions (for example, rules associated with liberal-democratic societies).

The emphasis on governance has led to the development of instruments to analyze and support better governance, and increasingly also to address conflict. Table 5–1 illustrates this diversity, listing nine areas or instruments of governance work.

The governance paradigm has come under criticism from different sides. For critical observers, the emphasis on governance meant a less radical departure from the Washington Consensus than suggested by some. Mosse and Lewis's anthropological study of social processes and aid relationships in the "new global aid architecture" argues that emphasis on policy reform was part of a new "managerialism" in international development, and a more intrusive form of aid: "The *means* of international aid have expanded from the management of economic growth and technology transfer to the reorganisation of state and society needed to deliver on targets" (Mosse and Lewis 2005, 5).

A predominant critique that was more internal to the aid community came from Merilee Grindle. She developed the idea of "good enough governance," in a paper for the World Bank at a time when the PRSP approach had become popular (Grindle 2002). The paper highlighted that the expectations for poor countries regarding governance performance and policy reform were unrealistically high. The "must be done" lists

Table 5–1. Agencies' Instruments to Analyze Governance

Area or instrument	Description	Examples/ Studies
Civil service reform	Interventions that affect the organization, performance, and working conditions of employees paid from central, provincial, or state government budgets.	*Comparative Experience with Public Service Reform in Ghana, Tanzania and Zambia,* by M. Stevens and S. Teggemann.
Drivers of change	Approach to apply political economy analysis to the development of a donor strategy.	*Uganda's Political Economy,* by Joy Moncrieffe.
Fragile states	Countries in which the government does not deliver core functions to the majority of their people.	The OECD in 2005 produced draft principles for good international engagement in fragile states, presented for field testing.
Human rights	Donor approaches to promoting human rights use a diverse range of tools. They vary between different donors and NGOs, including the extent to which rights approaches are integrated in development work.	SIDA, 2003, *Country Strategy Development: Guide for Country Analysis from a Democratic Governance and Human Rights Perspective.*
Institutional development	Main concern is helping organizations to improve performance, focusing on both formal and informal aspects of organizations.	Institutional analyses are part of most adjustment operations, such as that described in Box 5–2.
Justice	An accessible and effective justice sector is essential for development and includes security of property and protection of assets; access to legal protection; and effective justice institutions for economic growth.	DFID program Justice and Poverty Reduction: Safety, Security, and Access to Justice for All.

Continued on page 123

Area or instrument	Description	Examples/ Studies
Measuring governance	Indicators to measure governance to assess governance capacity and performance; understand determinants and impacts of good governance; facilitate domestic debate; and identify priority areas for aid allocations.	UNDP, "Sources for Democratic Governance Indicators," 2004, UNDP, Oslo. World Bank, Country Policy and Institutional Assessment.
Public financial management and accountability	Encompasses government capacity to raise revenues, set spending priorities, allocate resources, and manage the delivery of those resources effectively .	Standard part of preparations for donor funding.
Voice and accountability	Emphasis on creating inclusive spaces for dialogue between citizens and the state (e.g., in PRSP, PSOA); support to citizen-driven initiatives, such as participatory budgeting, community scorecards, and watchdogs.	R. Eyben and S. Ladbury, 2006, "Building Effective States: Taking a Citizens' Perspective."

Sources: GSDRC website and author.

presented by donors to partners were huge and often did not highlight priority areas or advise on sequencing of actions. She argued for donors to focus on minimally acceptable government performance and civil society engagement. But this idea did not provide a clear guide to making decisions, as Grindle acknowledged in an article five years later. She highlighted, again, the need to prioritize and to choose interventions depending on local contexts, informed by an understanding of possibilities for and dilemmas in promoting change and the impact of specific interventions or reform (Grindle 2007). As highlighted also in a paper by the OECD DAC Network on Governance, capacity development had an "overemphasis on what were seen as 'right answers,' as opposed to approaches that best fit the country circumstances and the needs of the particular situation" (OECD DAC 2006, 3).

But even a narrower agenda of governance brings us back to the question of conditionality. The new agenda partly resulted from the idea of the importance of governance for development and poverty reduction, and that aid allocation should follow governance indicators. It has been emphasized that loans and grants should be disbursed against past performance; however, future actions are critical in donor decisions. Indeed, a 2007 report by the IMF's Independent Evaluation Office suggests that despite efforts to reduce and streamline conditionalities, many of the problems continued to exist. According to Tom Bernes, office director, "Progress had been made in better aligning IMF conditionality to its core areas of responsibility and expertise, but about one-third of conditions continued to reach outside these areas" (Aslam 2008).

A further complication was due to the renewed focus on politics. In the aid industry governance is not the same as politics (see de Haan and Everest-Phillips 2006). A project approach enabled ways of working that allowed aid to stay away from politics as much as possible, and even the early approaches to governance in the 1990s often had a technocratic character. But more and more, and with the increased attention to local contexts and questions of legitimacy of reforms and participation, the issue of politics moved center stage. Moreover, a donor focus on corruption and increased accountability to taxpayers brought about the realization that donors were part of recipient countries' politics.

In governance analysis it became increasingly apparent that reform feasibility required better understanding of local politics. The 1990s showed that "political will" and "political context" needed to be understood much better; for example, that legal reforms should not be seen as solutions without understanding whether new laws are really needed or will be implemented, rather than reformist governments and activist judges applying existing laws to changing contexts.

The Monterrey Consensus in 2002 confirmed that politics is at the heart of development, domestically and internationally. While acknowledging that geopolitical considerations continue to play a key role in aid allocation, according to the Monterrey final report:

> Governments must build within their countries—both developed and developing—the public support necessary to translate their collective vision into action. That would require political leadership—in the developing countries to overcome the many difficulties in undertaking institutional and policy reform, and in the developed countries to develop engagement and solidarity with the developing countries in their efforts to reduce poverty. . . . To translate the draft Consensus into action will involve a process of arriving at politically acceptable decisions at the national and international levels. There is a need for strong political will. (UN 2002)[8]

A growing number of instruments started to integrate politics into aid delivery. Forms of political analysis have been introduced in a number of agencies through DFID's Drivers of Change and the World Bank's Institutional Governance Reviews, with a strong focus on sources of corruption, as well as the use of the term political economy in various agencies.

Sida's (2006) "power analysis" focuses on helping to understand "underlying structural factors" that create incentives and disincentives for pro-poor development, a form of political analysis that tries to highlight potentials for "transformative" processes. Analysis of actors, interest groups, and structures is meant to show where "real power" in a society lies, how power is distributed, what kind of power is being exercised, and how. It highlights both formal and informal power relations and structures. For example, it focuses on why resources and authority are not transferred to lower levels of government in the context of support to decentralization, why women are not allowed to inherit land, or why human rights tend to be neglected. Finally, it also intends to show the impact that development cooperation has on power relations and aims to identify agents and incentives for change.

For the aid industry, this raises more questions than it answers. Political analysis almost inevitably is disputed, and the credibility of donor-commissioned studies remains an issue. Further, as an ODI paper on public financial management puts it, "The apparent consensus that politics matters begs the question of what reformers should do when the necessary political impetus is weak or missing" (Hedger and Kizilbash Agha 2007). As a DAC Network on Governance paper noted: "Tensions are emerging between corporate objectives and the implications of Power and DOC analysis, which emphasise the prime importance of local political process and incremental change, in the face of pressures on donors to meet short term spending targets, and to be accountable to their own taxpayers" (OECD DAC 2005).[9]

Aid modalities tend to remain technocratic: monitoring of progress is very much and increasingly outcome focused, with little analysis of the whys, the causes, and the political economy of change. Political analysis remains absent in many of the new aid modalities, including cash transfers and sector approaches, and (perhaps understandably) in attempts to raise taxation in developing countries. Finally, the question of democracy has remained a key unresolved issue in the debate. On the one hand, even the most hard-nosed development professionals share a commitment to democracy, and the end of the Cold War provided a good deal of optimism about transitions to democracy. On the other hand, some of the development success stories happened under non-democratic regimes, at least by Western standards, and it will remain to be seen how the contours of this debate will change now that China is becoming an increasingly important player in the aid industry.

The questions raised by the thinking on governance and politics are by no means easy ones. Imposing conditionalities through grants or loans is now generally thought to be undesirable. However, the debates on conditionality also point to some dilemmas in the aid industry that merely avoiding the term will not resolve: sustainable poverty reduction requires the right conditions, with a governance agenda that is and will remain (or even becoming increasingly) challenging, while aid agencies continue to have to show the result of their efforts.

Program and Sector Approaches

The aid industry has moved, or has tried to move, from a project approach to a program approach. Under the financial crisis the 1980s saw dramatic expansion of conditional aid lending (or general program aid, or budget support[10]), which we described in the section on structural adjustment—quick disbursing loans in the form of program lending to help meet balance of payments and public-sector financing requirements, linked to recommendations for economic policy and institutional reform. The idea of program aid as it received currency in the 1990s was slightly different, partly a reflection of the problems of the adjustment approaches of the 1990s and partly a response to the problems of project aid.

We first focus on donor initiatives at the levels of sectors, particularly sector-wide approaches, which were first promoted by agencies like Danida. This is followed by a discussion of implications of "vertical initiatives." Sector-wide approaches imply that "all significant funding for the sector supports a single sector policy and expenditure programme, under government leadership, adopting common approaches across the sector and progressing towards relying on Government procedures for all funds" (Foster 2000, 9; see also Brown et al. 2001; Walford 2003).

Box 5–4. Elements of Sector Approaches

- Existence or development of a comprehensive sector policy and strategy.
- An annual sector expenditure program and medium-term sectoral expenditure framework.
- Donor coordination, steered by recipient governments.
- Major donors providing support within the agreed framework.
- Donors committed to gradually increasing reliance on government financial and accountability systems.
- A common donor approach to implementation and management.

Alongside increased emphasis on allocations to social sectors, this aid modality was a response to three issues (Foster 2000, 7–8). First, as already mentioned, donors found that conditionality did not work. Sector approaches became a way of providing support to governments, based on their commitment to and track record in providing services for poverty reduction, a theme that was described as a shift from "conditionality" to "ownership." Emphasis was on working within government management structures and responsibilities. It has remained focused on donor dialogue with governments: civil society organizations often are involved in service delivery, but not central to planning, at least not to the extent that PRSP approaches involved civil society in consultation.

Second, sector approaches focused on creating and supporting a sound policy environment. Rather than donors directly funding services, as in the project mode, sector approaches provide funding to promote changes in policies and institutions, including changes with respect to budgeting, thus forming the preconditions for nationwide services. This is thought to be particularly important in sectors where public funding is a substantial part of overall spending, which partly explains the predominance of programs in education and health.

Third, questions of budgeting have been central to sector-wide approaches. The projects provided by donors, often many at the same time, led to fragmentation of the budgeting process. Much spending was outside regular government budgets, and financial oversight focused on accountability to donors rather than to finance ministries and parliament. The proposed solution was that "government and donors should work together to implement a single, coherent expenditure programme which prioritises the use of all sources of public funding" (Foster 2000, 8).

In 2000, approximately eighty sector programs were in existence. These were mostly in health and education. There has been coordinated support to poverty monitoring, for example, but much less in, for example, the agricultural sector.[11] In the area of social "safety nets," social funds and cash transfers have continued to remain the dominant approaches,[12] with Ethiopia's Productive Safety Nets Program, started in 2005, providing multi-year and predictable resources, a possible exception. One example of a sector approach is that which exists to support the justice sector in Uganda since 1999 (Sserumaga 2003). Most of the sector programs are in Africa, reflecting the greater need for donor coordination in poorer and more aid-dependent countries. Though they do exist elsewhere, including in India, where the government has worked actively to reduce the numbers of donors and to ensure their coordination, and principles of sector support have been applied in multi-donor support to the national primary education and health programs.

There is recognition that the approach has led to successes, addressing problems created through previous support and concretely improving services and health and education outcomes. Successes have been achieved in Uganda and Ghana, for example, reflecting general agreements between government and donors; sector approaches have been behind government programs for universal primary education, for example. Sector support may have helped to enhance political commitment, efficiency in resource use, and capacity for policy formulation and implementation. For donors, sector-wide approaches have contributed to aid coordination.

On the down side, it has been noted that the process of establishing joint-donor support is usually very time consuming. Monitoring frameworks tends to be complex and costly, and limited capacity in many countries continues to hinder effective implementation. Showing how such long-term processes link to impacts on poverty on the ground can be challenging. There may be conflicting policy objectives between sector approaches and strengthening decentralized governance structures, for example (Land and Hauck 2003). Some recipient governments have felt joint donor responses a potential disadvantage, as this also involved the risk of a complete halt to support. And finally, even with sector approaches, discrete projects and particular donor emphases have continued to thrive.

The emphasis on sector approaches has been promoted mostly by the older players in the aid industry, many of whom committed themselves to increasing funding in social sectors: a substantial number of bilaterals, the World Bank, and UN specialized agencies, though they all use slightly different definitions (Abby Riddell 2002). However, there is a substantial number of new and often private donor agencies, particularly in the health sector, referred to as vertical initiatives. The old players in the industry often support these, too, responding to political pressure. Pharmaceutical companies have donated particular drugs to eliminate disease, and the last decade has witnessed the rise of "new philanthropists," who donate large sums of money for specific health-related projects. Vertical initiatives often focus on individual or groups of diseases. There are now dozens of health funds and partnerships with the Global Fund for AIDS, Tuberculosis, and Malaria (which is thought to be very effective, with a minimum bureaucracy, and high impact, for example, distributing thirty million anti-malaria bed nets), the Global Alliance for Vaccines and Immunisation, and the International Finance Facility for Immunisation among the largest.

The impact of these initiatives on the issues discussed above and to which sector programs are meant to be a response is as yet unclear.

Jeffrey Sachs expresses doubt about the focus on improvement in public institutions; when the per capita spending in health is less than $10 per head—which it is in many poor countries—even the huge resources for HIV/AIDS are still only a portion of what is required. But the commitments for increasing aid are made in the face of the clearly documented doubts about government capacity, fragmentation of initiatives, and donor overload. Further, the recent vertical initiatives may imply a move away from the state as central actor in providing legislative frameworks and standards and toward "a multiplicity of new—and largely unaccountable—actors in the health arena," with public–private partnerships "as potentially radical new systems of global governance" (Poku and Whiteside 2002, 192). The particular aid modality also has implications for the balance of power within public policymaking, strengthening particular agencies in regard to others. Also, it is likely that international support will remain volatile, and there are questions about the sustainability of many well-funded initiatives.

In a useful paper for CIDA that compares program aid and project aid, Lavergne and Alba use the expression *program-based approaches* as an extension of the concept of sector-wide approaches:

> A program is an integrated set of activities designed to achieve a related set of outcomes in a relatively comprehensive way (mostly health, education) . . . a way of engaging in development cooperation based on the principle of coordinated support for a locally owned program of development. (Lavergne and Alba 2003)

Aid programs, in contrast to projects, emphasize coordinated planning in a sector or area, and intend to support locally owned programs of development. Authors are usually quick to add that this does not mean blueprints. Instead, unlike projects, programs develop in a dynamic fashion with often changing directions and a plurality of approaches while being based on agreed-upon sets of goals or outcomes, typically formulated as MDGs or national equivalents. Also, program approaches are not advocated for all circumstances; Foster and Leavy emphasize that approaches need to be appropriate to specific country circumstances, and they provide ways of choosing depending on a range of factors (Foster and Leavy 2001).

The defining elements of program approaches are the following:

- They highlight the need for and try to promote *leadership* by recipient countries. This is particularly important in aid-dependent countries, where policymakers have often been busy servicing the requirements of donors.
- While projects have clearly defined time spans and related outputs, program approaches recognize that the various elements of successful support are likely to take a *long time* to develop and will continue to evolve once they are in place.
- In assessing progress, the *direction of change* rather than particular levels of achievement for each element is important. For example, the leadership for a program or reform may not be very strong, but what is thought to matter in assessing progress is the direction in which this is moving, that is, whether indicators show that the leadership is strengthening.
- A program implies a *single budget* framework, integrated into common budgeting and execution processes, not a range of projects financed outside countries' regular budgets. Funds can be earmarked for specific activities, depending on specific situations and goals, but the approach emphasizes reducing targeting of funds and using budget support and pooled funding.
- A program implies *donor coordination*. International agencies in a country agree to jointly support a government-led program and aim to harmonize the donor procedures in their planning, implementation, and monitoring. This has led to "joint accountability."
- The approach commits donors to increase gradually the *use of local procedures* for program design and implementation, financial management, and monitoring and evaluation. The approach focuses on reducing transactions costs and encouraging greater flexibility in the use of funds, while simultaneously reinforcing local systems.

While the principles of the program approach appear sound, problems have been pointed out. First, designing programs is extremely complex. The number of qualifying criteria remains large. Even though these are no longer conditionalities, as used previously, and programs are based more on ongoing and completed actions and reforms, a large number of policy intentions and plans remain central to qualifying for support—and to successful implementation. Questions of fiduciary risks and corruption remain, and seem even more pertinent in program approaches as donors have less control over money flows when they rely more on recipient government systems, and the increased accountability that support requires remains among the most difficult challenges. In the discussion on aid modalities, the aid industry has also emphasized the need to take account of country specificity, for example, in "fragile" and "post-conflict" countries (Collier and Okonjo-Iweala 2002, Manor 2007).

The question of donor coordination remains a difficult one, and one that, with the increasing fragmentation of the aid industry and continued and sometimes strengthening political motivations for aid provision, is unlikely to go away. In practice, the use of program aid remains fairly limited, as few donors have committed themselves to the approach, and within program approaches donors continue to fund distinct projects. The incentives for donors—to spend money, to show results in their organization, and to show achievements to the taxpayers—also can be in conflict with the aim to enhance ownership, which almost inevitably makes processes longer and outcomes less clearly defined, at least from the viewpoint of the donor. Almost inevitably, measuring success or progress becomes more difficult, certainly compared to the straightforward indicators that are common in project approaches.

Conclusion

While traditional structural adjustment has disappeared—although some argue it has not, as we will see in the next chapter—many of the old questions remain. In the early 1980s the state was charged with responsibility for whatever went wrong, but ten or twenty years later it was recognized that rolling back the state's role did not provide the solution. In extreme cases of fragile states, development and sustainable poverty reduction clearly are not achievable, but in less extreme cases it has become increasingly clear that state capacity—or governance—is critical, and that strengthening that capacity ought to remain a critical element of providing aid.

This poses a dilemma for the aid industry and makes its objectives ever more ambitious. Strengthening governance capacity is essential, but it is also a very slow process, too slow in the view of people like Jeffrey Sachs, who argues that health conditions in Africa are so severe that countries simply cannot afford to wait. Building up capacity is critical, but the aid industry does not have a very good record in capacity support. Donors also need to show results, and most taxpayers expect this to be in schools, or hospitals built, number of kids brought into schools or lives saved—long-term support to financial management within ministries simply does not provide the good "photo opportunity" that ministers of donor countries require. Sector reform and sector-wide approaches are relatively new instruments, part of a move away from project approaches to a focus on the policy environment. They have had notable successes, but practice has been more varied than optimists may suggest.

Further Readings

For an excellent and concise discussion of structural adjustment and poverty impact, see Killick 1999.

A good chapter on government failure in Tanzania is Doriye 1992.

The GSDRC website provides documents discussing sector-wide approaches and instruments to assess the wide range of governance; see, for example, Institute for Health Sector Development 2003a and 2003b.

The CIDA primer on program approaches, Lavergne and Alba 2003, gives a good theoretical introduction (even though practice has remained limited).

6

Country-led Approaches
and Donor Coordination

In the late 1990s a number of pressures on the aid industry came together. Concerns about achievements of the aid industry continued to intensify, and the accumulated knowledge stressed the need for stronger recipient country "ownership" and improved partnerships with donors as well as collaboration among actors within countries. Simultaneously, global civil society increasingly pressed for debt relief, and the agreements reached on providing debt relief stressed the need to make enhanced resources more results focused—particularly poverty focused.

Within the aid industry these pressures led to the three sets of initiative described in this chapter. First, the World Bank introduced the Comprehensive Development Framework (CDF) to improve the effectiveness of aid through a long-term, holistic framework with country-led partnership. More or less simultaneously, the United Nations introduced an assistance framework that stressed similar principles as a foundation for more coordinated operations by UN agencies. Second was the initiative that brought civil society into close collaboration with the major agencies—the Poverty Reduction Strategy Papers—which became the way through which debt relief, and later aid more generally, was meant to be disbursed. Third, the aid industry made the coordination of its own activities an increasing focus, leading to clear agreements and targets, but with continuing challenges imposed by the political and administrative imperatives of each aid agency.

Comprehensive Frameworks at the World Bank
and the United Nations

Among the drastic changes that were introduced by James Wolfensohn at the World Bank was the introduction of the CDF. He announced this in early 1999 with much fanfare, though few people around him saw it as path-breaking as he thought it was, and some argued that it would mean increased conditionalities. The CDF was piloted in thirteen countries in 1999. In a joint note with Stanley Fischer, IMF director, the CDF was presented as

> a means by which countries can manage knowledge and resources to design and implement effective strategies for economic development and poverty reduction. It brings together many current trends in development thinking and is centered on a long term vision—prepared by the country through a participatory national consultation process—that balances good macroeconomic and financial management with sound social, structural and human policies."[1]

The CDF had four main elements. First, referring to the World Bank's emphasis on short-term macroeconomic stabilization and balance of payment pressures, Wolfensohn stressed the need for considering longer-term structural and social considerations: to expand education and health, maintain infrastructure, and train officials. Development strategies, Wolfensohn thought, should have a long-term vision and be comprehensive, or holistic, and embrace social and structural issues alongside concern about stabilizing the economy.

Second, Wolfensohn stressed that the aid industry had put too much emphasis on measuring project inputs and disbursement levels. He felt more emphasis needed to be put on finding out what the impacts of these efforts are on people and their needs. Thus, development performance should not be measured by inputs and outputs but assessed by outcomes and impacts, by results on the ground. This mirrored a broader move of the industry toward "results-based management" (see Box 6–1).

Third, while asserting that some of the donor-driven aid delivered under structural adjustment had been effective, Wolfensohn accepted that many of the difficult adjustment measures had not been sustained, and sometimes had even been undone. While by no means new, this acceptance brought to the fore the idea that if countries have greater say in shaping reforms, governments are more likely to be committed to seeing them through. Therefore, the third element of the CDF stressed that goals and strategies needed to be "owned" by recipient countries,

---

Box 6–1. Results-based Management

While many different interpretations and perceptions exist, results-based management (also called management for results or performance management) is generally seen as a management strategy that focuses on outcomes and impacts and on how organizations' human and financial resources can best be used to optimize outcomes. The LogFrame discussed in Chapter 4 is a common management tool used for this purpose, though its use precedes that of results-based management. The use of results-based management in the aid industry follows the popularity it gained as part of the "new public management" reforms of the early 1990s, which brought market strategies into public management. It has become a central theme of the aid effectiveness agenda and includes an emphasis on engaging all stakeholders in the process.

Source: http://www.mfdr.org; Binnendijk 2001; Hatton and Schroeder 2007.

---

and the goals and strategies needed to be shaped through a process with broad citizen participation. To ensure effective use of human and financial resources, the CDF emphasized partnerships among government, civil society, the private sector, and external assistance agencies.

Wolfensohn was concerned by how the World Bank was perceived in the countries within which it worked; he did not want it to be seen as arrogant. Further, building on the point about ownership of development efforts, he had become convinced that partnerships and mutual trust were critical and that the asymmetrical power relationships needed to be addressed. The fourth aspect of the CDF framework, therefore, emphasized that recipient countries should take the lead in aid relationships, that they should be in charge of coordination, and that they should actively manage the process rather than be led by donor preferences. It was highlighted that partnership and coordination of efforts can enhance the capacity of governments to manage foreign development assistance. The framework encouraged coordination to improve efficiency and coherence in the use of financial flows and services and to take advantage of synergies among development partners. As with the later PRSPs, papers on the CDF were quick to add that the CDF was not a blueprint. It was meant to be voluntary; countries were to decide on priorities and programs. When other initiatives emerged, particularly the PRSPs, the language changed from *framework* to *principles*.

While Wolfensohn was pushing for changes at the World Bank, from 1997 UN Secretary-General Kofi Annan was trying to make the United Nations a more effective and efficient institution. He stressed the strong links between peace, security, poverty reduction, sustainable human development, and the promotion of and respect for human rights. He called for the UN to develop a coherent vision and unified approach to the development goals. In addition to developing a Common Country Assessment, this push also resulted in the development of the United Nations Development Assistance Framework (UNDAF), for which guidelines were issued in April 1999. The UNDAF is meant to be a collective UN response to national priorities and needs. An example of the UNDAF for Uganda, a country that was among the leaders in developing the UNDAF, is given in Box 6–2.

When the PRSP became the most common instrument or plan by recipient countries, the UNDAF was presented as the UN's business plan in support of them. In a letter to Wolfensohn in May 2001, Kofi Annan stressed: "It is the responsibility of governments to be at the centre of all coordination efforts on assistance. Too often a bewildering surfeit of diagnoses and programming modalities has strait-jacketed national responses and imposed high transaction costs. . . . The task now is to ensure consistent quality country-level partnership that reduces costs and overlap and boosts our overall impact."[2]

In 2003 the World Bank published an evaluation of the CDF approach.[3] While critical, the publication of reports like these did illustrate the World Bank's commitment to engage with external commentators, and they provide more insight into the working of the World Bank than the working of the United Nations. Four main findings are worth highlighting, as they have relevance for our discussion here. First, progress in the World Bank's country-led approach—to give recipient countries the leading voice in aid management—was found to be far from even. Some donors did better than others, and the approach worked better in some countries and in some sectors than in others.

Second, the long-term and comprehensive development frameworks often ended up as long wish lists. The evaluation stressed that the objectives were often not translated into affordable priorities with proper budgets, and hence their operational use and ability to make clear policy choices remained limited. The evaluation also stressed the need for capacity building to enable formulation and implementation of development

Box 6-2. The Uganda UNDAF, 2006-10

The UN framework for cooperation in Uganda was set against the challenges of rapid population growth, low life expectancy (forty-six years), a poverty ratio of 39 percent, gender inequality, 800,000 children aged 6-12 years who had never attended school, high infant and maternal mortality, and HIV prevalence of 6 percent (with dramatic improvement from 18 percent). Corruption and human rights violations were still big issues, though improvements had been made. Civil war had uprooted more than one million people.

The UN system declared its support of the government's attempt to achieve the MDGs and the objectives of the national Poverty Eradication Action Plan. The UNDAF was intended to support decision making, enhance collaboration, and reduce transaction costs. It stated that expected outcomes were, among other things, to address the development challenges through a multi-dimensional approach; to focus on equal opportunities, empowerment, sustainability, governance, and human rights; to contribute to efforts to minimize the impact and to halt the spread of HIV/AIDS; and to reduce the regional disparities through the creation of an enabling environment for peace, resettlement, reintegration, and socioeconomic recovery.

The UNDAF committed the United Nations to multi-dimensional partnerships with the government, NGOs, the private sector, bilateral donors, and among the UN agencies themselves. The strategy revolved around dialogue and collaboration, and it aimed to link aid coordination to ongoing reforms. It also considered regional cooperation with other countries and international agencies in the context of security challenges in Uganda. The resources available to implement the UNDAF included the allocations by each participating UN organization as well as the resources that organizations expected to mobilize over the period.

Coordination among UN agencies was a key message in the UNDAF. It stated that programming of UNDP, UNICEF, UNFPA, and WFP were fully "harmonized" within the UNDAF and accorded with the Poverty Eradication Action Plan, while specialized agencies UNHCR and WHO were guided by country programs. Five UNDAF working groups were set up to meet regularly and served as the main mechanisms for implementing and monitoring the UNDAF, and joint mid-term and end-of-cycle evaluations by the government and various development partners were envisaged.

plans, including support for public-sector reforms and institutional development.

Third, among the principles of the CDF, progress on strengthening a results orientation—measures of impact on people rather than inputs and disbursement—was found to be "the most elusive." This principle was overly demanding, as many of the countries lacked the technical capacity, analytical tools, and statistical data. Moreover, within partner governments there were inadequate incentives to follow a results-oriented approach, which in almost all cases is more demanding than a focus on outputs. Also, within countries there was not enough demand for monitoring and evaluation results. The evaluation concluded that donors were too demanding of existing institutions and structures that monitor projects and programs. Proposed approaches were found to be complex, with unwieldy indicators. Finally, the specific aid projects and programs rather than the requirements of the regular functions and service delivery of the governments continued to drive monitoring.

Fourth, public consultation about activities had expanded. Donors and government involved civil society and business more intensively in strategy formulation. In the view of the evaluating team, this did increase the ownership of reforms. However, the consultations were found to be limited, and as a result ownership remained narrow. Consultations were often confined to the executive branch of government, and some ad hoc discussions with organizations chosen by donors and government. In Uganda and Burkina Faso, for example, civil society and private-sector organizations as well as parliamentarians who were not consulted expressed dissatisfaction.

Poverty Reduction Strategy Papers

Two main developments informed the PRSP approach that emerged at the end of the 1990s.[4] First, partly facilitated by Wolfensohn's approach and the changes in government in Europe, NGOs became an important influence on the World Bank. Responding to pressure, in the spring of 1996 the World Bank and the IMF launched the heavily indebted poor countries scheme to reduce the external debt of eligible countries and achieve debt sustainability. This was not the first effort to reschedule debt, but it was the first involving the IFIs. A broad movement, encapsulated in Jubilee 2000, argued for further debt relief, particularly but not only by the IFIs. It also increased pressure to make this debt relief pro-poor and to address the negative consequences of structural adjustment. The international financial crisis in East Asia also increased pressure on the IFIs to review policies and their effects on poverty. During the 1990s the IFIs did indeed become more responsive to a broad range of international actors, and a much more open debate emerged, highlighted by the increased number of IFI documents published and the wide range and regularity of NGO publications.

Second, the changes happened against the background of an intensive debate about the effectiveness of aid. The World Bank's 1998 *Assessing Aid* report highlighted the problems with conditionalities that we discussed earlier. But it also stressed that aid could be effective only if recipient countries had sound economic management. Changes in the IMF included a response to the critique of inflexibility in its macroeconomic and fiscal options and also of the way conditionality had evolved over time and the need for better prioritization of policy measures (as well as division of labor among international institutions). In its new approach it increasingly looked at the quality of budgets and sectoral spending, including how additional funding through debt relief was to be used for spending in health and education, among other areas.

In 1999 the World Bank and the IMF endorsed the framework of PRSPs. Over time, the model was broadened to policy dialogue in all countries receiving concessional funding from the IFIs, with significant implications for national poverty reduction strategy formulation and the way donors engage with this. By 2005 about forty countries had a poverty reduction strategy, and a few had progressed to a second-generation strategy (Driscoll with Evans 2005). Initially, the PRSP was an instrument for borrower countries seeking to benefit from HIPC-II (the second heavily indebted poor countries program), which tried to make debt relief integral to broader efforts to implement poverty reduction strategies. Countries qualified for HIPC assistance if they faced an unsustainable debt burden beyond available debt relief mechanisms, established a track record of reform and sound policies through IFI-supported programs, and produced a full or interim PRSP. Qualifying for debt relief involved two stages: first, the country needed to demonstrate its ability to use assistance prudently; and second, the country had to establish a track record of good performance on agreed-upon structural policy reforms, maintenance of macroeconomic stability, and adoption and implementation of the PRSP. Very similar to the CDF approach, the PRSP approach was based on the following principles:

- an emphasis on country ownership and partnership between donors and recipient;
- formulation of a PRSP through national-level participation;
- a results-oriented approach, including establishing a link between debt relief and its impact on poverty; and
- comprehensive and long-term commitment.

Financial support for PRSP implementation was to be provided through a World Bank's poverty reduction support credit (as in the case of Uganda described in Box 6–3) and an IMF poverty reduction growth facility, the successor of the extended structural adjustment facility, itself a successor

---

Box 6–3. Uganda—Leading the Donors?

Much of the inspiration in the thinking on the new approaches at the end of the 1990s came from donors' experience in Uganda. In the eyes of many donors, Uganda during the 1990s had undergone successful stabilization and adjustment, and in the middle of the 1990s was seen as a model of success in development. Thus Uganda became to be seen as a model for effective aid relationships. Keys to its success included its strong leadership and the government's close relationship with donors, who in turn greatly encouraged the leaders to show they and not donors owned the development agenda. This did not mean the donors left the country; in fact, they went so far as to second economic experts to the finance ministry.

Since 1997 the government of Uganda and donors have actively coordinated attempts to improve aid effectiveness. The core of this is the government's Poverty Eradication Action Plan, an overarching strategy for poverty eradication that includes a commitment that donors will only support, not control, programs. It also describes preferred aid modalities. The implementation of the plan and donor coordination has been facilitated through the Poverty Reduction Support Credit (PRSC). Agencies providing budget support use the policy matrix as a framework for funding, and the medium-term expenditure framework for monitoring and implementation. Progress is assessed through one annual government-donor review.

of the traditional adjustment packages (described in Chapter 5). Targets and policies in PRGF programs would emerge directly from PRSP or similar frameworks. This was meant to integrate poverty reduction with macroeconomic policies. Moreover, discussions on the macroeconomic framework were made subjects for public consultation. Key programs and structural reforms for poverty reduction and growth had to be identified, prioritized, and budgeted in the PRSP. Within two years, over twenty countries reached the decision point, when debt relief was approved and interim relief began. Over time these countries would receive $36 billion in HIPC relief, reducing their debt by half. In 2006 the initiative had reduced $19 billion of debt in eighteen countries, and net transfers to HIPC countries had doubled (to $17.5 billion in 2004).

Much material has been generated reviewing the experience. There are few doubts that the debate has brought about a much stronger focus on poverty reduction, even though initial time pressure negatively influenced early experiences, focusing too much on the strategy paper. As with the CDF, there was much diversity in country experiences. Preparation of PRSPs involved clearer costing, linking the PRSP to the medium-term expenditure framework, the key instrument for policy dialogue between borrowers and lenders. It led to discussion of poverty issues across government ministries and enhanced the position of poverty analyses that had developed during the 1990s. Pressure on IFIs and other donors forced them to review the impact of aid on poverty much more carefully. The institution of the Poverty and Social Impact Analysis (PSIA), which we describe in some detail in Chapter 8, was a clear example of how innovative instruments were introduced under civil society pressure.

At the same time, observers like Stewart and Wang have emphasized that "there is no fundamental departure from the kind of policy advice provided under earlier structural adjustment programmes," for example, related to the role of the market, fiscal and monetary matters, inflation, and privatization (2003, 19).[5] Gaps between poverty profiles and proposed policies remained, and it has been noted that the poverty analysis in some cases insufficiently informed the development strategy—even if incorporated in the same document. Some observers have questioned whether donor lending sufficiently followed priorities in PRSPs, though it has to be acknowledged that PRSPs often included mere wish lists without prioritization and clear budgets.

The PRSP approach made a difference in the way donors approach the aid relationship. The challenges in leaving countries in the "driver's seat" remain substantial. The experiences indicate a tendency to continue to deal with the aid relationship in a bureaucratic manner. Regular emphases that the approach "is no panacea" in fact highlight that there were strong expectations—arguably too strong—that the approach would resolve problems in the aid relationship. Reviews such as that by Booth, Grigsby, and Toranzo (2006) on Latin America indicate that donors tend to get closely tied to paths set out through the PRSP process, and that disarray sets in when the partner government's policies do not follow plans set out earlier and do not (continue to) show commitment to the PRSP.

Further, the PRSP approach was radical in the promotion of participation in the formulation of national plans for poverty reduction. A great amount of technical work emerged to support this, building on, for example, poverty assessments and community participation, trying to move this "upstream" to influence the macro-policy discussions. A wide range of civil society organizations engaged in the donor dialogue and saw the process as an opportunity to open up space for political engagement. But there has also been much critique of the practices in participation.[6] The term *participation*—in the context of PRSPs, as elsewhere—has been used to mean different things. Some believe participation has remained ritualistic and that the macroeconomic framework has not changed following even good processes of participation; NGOs have often felt the economic model was a given. Sometimes, processes of participation remained outside the area of mainstream politics, excluding parliaments, trade unions, the private sector, women, and marginalized groups. Participation was not institutionalized but remained restricted to the processes related to aid disbursement. Where the donors did intensively engage with political leaders, as in Bolivia, subsequent political dynamics imposed great difficulties for the donors in implementing PRSPs (Booth, Grigsby, and Toranzo 2006).

Finally, there is the question of whether the objective of comprehensive and long-term plans—with which, in principle, hardly anybody disagrees—can be realized through this aid modality. PRSPs indeed cover most if not all areas or sectors relevant to development, even though a number of reviews, often sponsored by specialized agencies or departments in agencies, have questioned whether particular sectors or issues received sufficient attention. The 2005 IMF and World Bank review of PRSP progress highlighted that "comprehensiveness is important in order to capture the complementary nature of public actions across sectors" and quoted evidence from a review in Tanzania that "a comprehensive strategy does not mean sacrificing priority setting. In fact, the more comprehensive the strategy, the more important it is to identify its main priorities" (IMF and World Bank 2005, 16). The approach broadened the policy dialogue with donors beyond finance ministries, including a larger number of sectoral organizations and line ministries.

But there are questions about whether PRSPs have contributed to comprehensive and cross-sectoral policymaking. There are clear potential tradeoffs, which some of the writings on PRSPs have tended to ignore. One side of the critique has stressed the gaps in comprehensiveness in the development plans, the limited capacity for comprehensive planning, and the time that such planning requires.[7] Continuing differences over where aid efforts should focus are reflected in the discussion on PRSPs too. While some NGOs have seen this as a venue to argue for more emphasis on social sectors, others have argued that the big gap is in focus on other, so-called productive sectors. Yet others, in line with the Easterly critique of the "planners" have noted that insistence on comprehensive plans may be counter-productive. For example, Booth, Grigsby, and Toranzo (2006), reviewing the PRSP in Bolivia, Honduras and Nicaragua, conclude that comprehensiveness can conflict with ownership. They found leaders often do not feel committed to such comprehensive plans, and they argued that donors should be more pragmatic and flexible in supporting initiatives that arise from the leaders of the day (2006).[8]

Again, these critiques show that there is no magic bullet to solve the challenges of relationships between donors and recipients. Also, views on these new approaches—as with all approaches—continue to differ, among the official donors, NGOs, and Southern voices. Perhaps most problematic is the fact that new approaches often come with such high expectations. Moreover, the aid industry often quickly moves on to a next approach, partly because of frustrations about the lack of success, partly because home constituencies drive it to continue to find new ways of highlighting progress.

The Paris Consensus—Can Donors Let Go ?

Since the broad and often heated discussions about the PRSP approach that emerged from the debt-relief campaign, the idea of coordinating aid agencies has generated an enormous amount of attention. To a certain extent, this was a logical follow-up, as the amount of aid and the number of agencies have been increasing, and, as we highlighted above, the need for donors to coordinate development approaches led by recipient countries came out as one of the main challenges. Increasingly, also, the debate on aid effectiveness focused on the need for donors to harmonize their procedures with recipient country's priorities.

The OECD DAC is the main forum for this focus on aid effectiveness, leading to the drafting of guidelines on harmonization. Following the lead of the Monterrey Declaration on financing, in 2003 a "Rome Declaration on Harmonisation" was endorsed by ministers and top officials of aid recipient countries, and multilateral as well as bilateral aid agencies,[9] a declaration that was reaffirmed at the High Level Forum in Accra in September 2008.[10] Recipient countries had clearly expressed their concerns about donor practices, through a survey commissioned by the OECD DAC in 2003. Their main requests to the donors included simplifying donor procedures, and thus reducing transactions costs; donors agreeing among themselves on common sets of procedures and working more closely together; donors synchronizing their procedures with those of recipient countries, and increasingly relying on recipient countries' systems, for example, relating to budget cycles; and becoming more transparent, sharing more information between donors and recipients.

The Rome Declaration was followed by the Paris Declaration on aid effectiveness, which similarly focused on reducing the fragmentation in the aid industry and on finding ways to ensure that aid supports country-led development. This declaration was agreed to by sixty-one bilateral and multilateral donors and fifty-six aid recipient countries; fourteen civil society organizations acted as observers. Specific indicators for progress were agreed upon, and the DAC-OECD Working Party on Aid Effectiveness was made responsible for monitoring the declaration. The elements of this approach are set out in a triangle (see Figure 6–1).

The overarching goal is to increase aid effectiveness, combined with results-based management and increased spending. The Paris Declaration highlights the need for mutual accountability, for performance assessment frameworks to be shared between donors and recipients, and for assurance that incentive systems are in line.

Within the framework, *ownership* is seen as the first key ingredient for success. Following the development of PRSPs and national plans like the one in Uganda, many countries have now developed frameworks that

Figure 6–1. The Aid Effectiveness Pyramid

Managing for Results			4

Ownership *Partner countries*	Partners Set the Agenda		Mutual Accountability
Alignment *Donors-partners*	Aligning with Partners' Agenda	Using Partners' Systems	
Harmonization *Donors-donors*	Establishing Common Arrangements	Simplifying Procedures · Sharing Information	

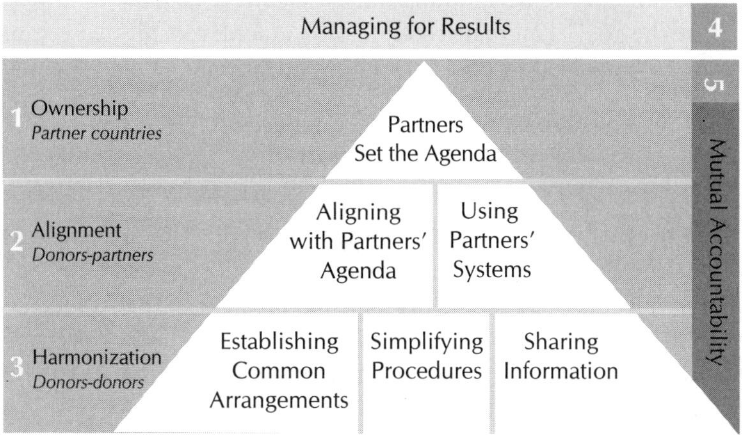

Source: The aid effectiveness pyramid, *OECD Development Co-operation Report 2005: Efforts and Policies of the Members of the Development Assistance Committee*, OECD 2005.

set out plans that allow donors and recipient countries to work together, with the countries "owning" the agenda.

Alignment refers to the way donors should engage with national plans and priorities. It calls for improving consistency between the priorities of donors and those of recipients. But it also implies consistency between donors' procedures and practices, on the one hand, and national institutions and processes, on the other. For example, aid instruments like sector approaches and budget support should become better at relying on national budgetary systems, and aid should complement existing systems and strengthen good practice.

Harmonization forms the base of the approach, focusing mostly on how donors work together. This calls for donors to establish common arrangements, share information, and simplify their procedures.

A survey carried out by the DAC in 2006—with data from thirty-four recipient countries and sixty donors—clearly highlights that there are still many challenges.[11] It notes that there are too many actors with competing objectives, especially in the poorest and most aid-dependent countries, leading to high transaction costs. Technical cooperation is still too donor driven. In-country practices do not always reflect agency commitment made at headquarters. It also mentions that donors should provide more assistance to develop the capacity that is required for taking ownership of the development agenda. There is still a long way to go before the goal of mutual accountability is achieved. Similar critiques continue to be voiced by civil society organizations.

Conclusion

Looking back at the enthusiasm for these new approaches at the end of the 1990s—driven by concerns about effectiveness internal to the aid industry, as well as external pressure as manifested in the Jubilee 2000 campaign—it is not easy to judge how much the aid industry has changed its behavior. Emphasis on country ownership is indicative of the difficulties that the aid industry has in "letting go." Forces are pushing in different directions.

Early in its history the aid industry felt forced to become deeply involved in the design and appraisal of projects. Many staff members spent considerable time working directly to promote these projects. The relationship was transformed with structural adjustment. Whether by choice or not, donors—the World Bank and the IMF, particularly—became deeply involved in the heart of their recipients' economic and financial decision making. And this happened at the time that government budgets were being cut, so their influence also became deeply unpopular. As a result, the IMF and the World Bank became many people's scapegoats.

Close involvement in itself is not problematic, but the balance of power between donor and recipient is. In the extreme case of China, which receives very little aid, project staff have very close relationships with the projects funded. Chinese government officials usually show appreciation of that engagement, and the technical expertise brought in, but the collaboration fits within a strategy that the government sets out. In the case of aid-dependent countries this is very different, and experience shows that it is very hard to create ownership where this does not exist, or where it is disputed. Approaches like CDF, UNDAF, and PRSPs probably have not changed the aid relationships as much as was hoped or expected. From the start the approaches were partly competitive, already indicating that they remained donor driven rather than fundamentally changing these relationships. The aid industry's urge to show results has continued, and in many cases intensified, which does not make leaving ownership to recipients any easier.

Approaches like PRSPs and CDF quickly became as controversial as anything in the aid industry or in public policy in general. For some, these approaches manifest the domination of global institutions; for others, agencies simply failed to implement the approach they advocated. Some have advocated deepening the approaches, particularly around the Paris Declaration, while others want to abandon approaches like PRSPs. The focus on aid coordination by some has been regarded as key to the survival of the industry, while others feel that it puts "Paris before poverty" and has started to neglect what aid can achieve on the ground. Finally, the approaches are caught in a "chicken or egg" situation, where capacity and political will need to be strengthened in countries that are dependent on aid, but building up capacity and will is also most difficult in those countries.

Further Readings

The DAC survey on progress in the aid effectiveness agenda and other documents are available at www.oecd.org.

Another excellent source of information on aid instruments is the Resource Centre website, www.gsdrc.org.

Civil society perspectives on the subject can be found at www.eurodad.org.

7

Development's Poor Cousins: Environment, Gender, Participation, and Rights

The aid industry's lexicon includes *cross-cutting* and *mainstreaming*, which, though jargon, highlight important aspects of the working of the industry. This chapter focuses on four of these aspects: environment, gender, participation, and rights. Each has a substantial literature of its own, and this chapter places these in the context of wider development debates and practices, how approaches have or have not influenced general debates, and areas of contestation and institutional constraints.

Mainstreaming has been most explicitly defined with respect to gender, often associated with the call of the Beijing Platform for Action that "governments and other actors should promote an active and visible policy of mainstreaming a gender perspective in all policies and programmes." Mainstreaming a gender perspective means assessing the implications for women and men of any planned action, including legislation, policies, and programs, at all levels and in all areas. It has also been associated with an organizational strategy to bring a gender perspective into all aspects of an institution's workings, including strengthening capacity and accountability.

The question of mainstreaming is relevant for the four issues described in this chapter, as they can be described as separate themes, or as relevant for all aspects of the aid industry. Often, consideration of these objectives leads the industry to look outside its own organizations, particularly bilateral agencies, and work with other government departments on issues such as climate change and human rights. At the same time, the four themes are the subject of strong advocacy by people within and outside the aid industry. Some of the advocates have come to doubt whether mainstreaming is the right way to promote goals, as they now believe that integration of radical objectives in the practices of the industry leads to a loss of transformative potential and that the industry's interest in these objectives is too much subject to fashion to be sustainable.

Development and Environment

By 2007 it was hard to imagine that environment ever was not central to the concerns of the aid industry: Al Gore's *Inconvenient Truth* had captured the attention of global audiences, receiving the Nobel Peace Prize jointly with the Intergovernmental Panel on Climate Change; the Stern Report in the UK, which looked at the economic impact of climate change, had mobilized political action at the highest level (including the prime minister calling for the World Bank to become a bank for the environment as well as development); and thousands of people had gathered in December 2007 on Bali for the UN Climate Change Conference. The aid industry, among other global and national institutions, had become keenly aware that environmental changes were posing great risks for future and even present generations.[1]

The Bali Conference—which focused on working out an agreement for a process to follow up on the 1997 Kyoto protocol, which was signed by OECD countries that committed themselves to reducing greenhouse gases—succeeded a series of international conference on the environment. In 1972, in Stockholm, the United Nations Conference on the Human Environment focused on the preservation and enhancement of the human environment. The declaration highlighted the need for protection and improvement of the environment as it affects the well-being of peoples and economic development throughout the world. It noted the link between environmental problems and underdevelopment, pressure caused by population growth, and noted, "A point has been reached in history when we must shape our actions throughout the world with a more prudent care for their environmental consequences." The UN's World Commission on Environment and Development, better known as the Brundtland Commission, in 1987 provided a common definition of sustainable development: "meeting the needs of the present without compromising the ability of future generations to meet their own needs."

The 1992 Earth Summit in Rio de Janeiro indicated the increased public attention to UN conferences. The summit stressed that "nothing less than a transformation of our attitudes and behaviour would bring about the necessary changes." At the conference governments recognized the need to take into account the environmental impact of any policy decisions and empowered the United Nations to monitor production of toxic components, use of fossil fuels, and promotion of public transport, among other things. This resulted in Agenda 21, according to the United Nations itself, "the most comprehensive and, if implemented, effective programme of action ever sanctioned by the international community." The summit commitments, reviewed in 1997, showed more disappointment than progress, and a strong North-South divide. The Bali conference ten years later comprised 187 countries that agreed to begin talks on climate change.

Can environment be integrated into development goals, analyses, and aid modalities? Ensuring environmental sustainability is part of the MDG framework. It commits the international community to integrating the principles of sustainable development into country policies and programs, and reversing loss of environmental resources; reducing the proportion of people without sustainable access to safe drinking water; and improving the lives of slum dwellers.[2] Following the Rio conference, many countries developed Agenda 21 plans. But the existence of goals and plans is not sufficient to guarantee that the issue is adequately addressed, and there is in the view of its supporters evidence that in PRSPs environment and sustainability often were insufficiently incorporated, and that not all MDGs have received equal attention.

At the conceptual level, whether environmental concerns are seen as part of the overarching poverty concern depends, of course, very much on how *poverty* or *development* are defined. As we discussed in Chapter 3, much and perhaps most attention has been to monetary dimensions, in headcounts of people under the poverty line, or in GDP. These definitions are inadequate to capture environmental issues, and they require extension in at least two ways. First, they need to view poverty as a multidimensional phenomenon and include people's interaction with their environment and access or entitlement to (natural) resources as elements of well-being and deprivation. Second, they need to incorporate a temporal dimension and look at the sustainability of the ways in which the environment is used and how existing production patterns maintain or diminish environmental resources in the long run.

How have environmental concerns been integrated into aid practices? First, the aid industry has made significant investment in environmental conservation, as shown, for example, in the ten cases put together by a number of researchers from IIED (Bass et al. 2005). This includes

---

Box 7–1. Poverty-Environment Links Are Contested

Links between poverty and environment are not straightforward. Poor people and poor nations use far less energy than rich ones. Even China will be a much smaller polluter per capita long after it becomes the world's largest emitter of greenhouse gases, and the poorest people in China will continue to use very little energy in the near future. Demographic changes also play an important role, and China has argued that its one-child policy has greatly reduced the country's environmental impacts.

Poor people are often *victims* of environmental degradation; they often live in the most vulnerable areas and have the least capacity to protect themselves. Poor people can *contribute* to environmental degradation; they often have no options or alternatives, and variability in income, for example, may lead to environmentally degrading practices. But poor people's practices or livelihoods can contribute to *conservation* of the environment, and degradation such as deforestation often follows poorer groups' loss of access to such resources. Environmental stress also can have an impact on *conflict,* for example, competition for land resources, affecting poor people as well as those who are better off. Links between environment and poverty are not merely an issue of resource availability, but depend on entitlements and power relations in access to resources and technologies. Advocates argue that policymakers, including donors, need to understand these complexities and to ensure that the voices of beneficiaries are adequately heard and understood.

---

long-term engagement of NGOs like the Aga Khan Rural Support Programme in Pakistan's northern areas, which started with social organization and leadership development and subsequently took up support to communities for livelihood development, and addressing environmental conservation through, for example, joint forestry projects (Zehra 2005). In China, the World Bank has supported a range of projects, sometimes integrating reforestation and soil improvement into projects (as in the Yangtze Basin project), or with a central focus on sustainable land use (as in the Loess Plateau Project) (Taylor 2005). Following the

Stern Report, the UK announced funding of £800 million, through the International Environmental Transformation Fund, for reducing poverty through environmental management and helping developing countries respond to climate change. It also announced funding of £50 million for tackling deforestation in the Congo Basin.

Second, environmental concerns are usually considered in projects through environmental appraisals or assessments. For the World Bank, the environmental assessment is one of the ten so-called safeguard policies that cover social and legal areas as well as environmental issues. These assessments intend to identify, avoid, and mitigate potential negative environmental impacts associated with any of the lending operations, and to ensure that project options under consideration are sound and sustainable. Use of the assessments is intended to ensure that the people who potentially will be affected have been properly consulted.[3]

In the case of the Poor Rural Communities Development Project in southern China (see Box 4–2), the World Bank environmental assessment concluded that the overall environmental impact of the project was likely to be positive.[4] The participatory approach is likely to contribute to reducing environmental degradation. Specific environmental benefits would include improved soil and water management, increase of permanent vegetation cover, improved agricultural and animal husbandry practices, and training in environmental better practices. While negative environmental effects could occur, these were likely to be modest and localized, such as degradation from improved road access, increased grazing exceeding the land's carrying capacity and causing soil erosion, increased waste disposal, and higher use of fertilizer and pesticides. It was expected that these negative consequences would be outweighed by positive environmental impacts achieved through the project, and that more negative development could be expected if the project did not take place. Finally, the project put in place an environmental management plan with measures to mitigate negative impacts and ways to monitor these measures.

To conclude, because of the recent interest in and the evidence on climate change, environmental concerns now are at the heart of the practices of the aid industry. Many of the recent efforts also involve more agencies and ministries outside the traditional aid industry. Environmental assessments are now well integrated into the daily operation of aid agencies. But interest in the environment has come in waves, and only the future will tell whether the current interest will be sustained.

Gender and Development: Advocacy and Mainstreaming

Like the environment, gender and development have never had an easy relationship. Much of the progress in bringing gender to the development agenda, as has been the case in other spheres of public policy, has been the result of sustained advocacy. As in the previous section we discuss this relationship in terms of development goals, analysis, mainstreaming in aid practices, and a critique of the results of a mainstreaming approach.

In discussing gender we use a definition that clearly delineates gender from sex: *sex* refers to the biological and physiological characteristics that define men and women; *gender* refers to the socially constructed roles, behaviors, activities, and relationship between the sexes that a particular society considers appropriate. For example, gender differences are women earning less than men for the same jobs, or women doing more housework than men. While all societies differ in the way they assign roles to men and women, gender differences and discrimination exist in all societies. Gender equality, therefore, means equal treatment of women and men in terms of access to resources, services, laws, policies and participation in decision making.

It is common to distinguish between two ways in which gender can be addressed. A Women in Development (WID) approach "calls for greater attention to women in development policy and practice, and emphasises the need to integrate them into the development process." The Gender and Development (GAD) approach "focuses on the socially constructed basis of differences between men and women and emphasizes the need to challenge existing gender roles and relations" (Reeves and Baden 2000, 3). Over time, emphasis has shifted from WID to GAD, though in practice the differences between the two approaches are not clear cut.

The third MDG focuses on the promotion of gender equality and the empowerment of women. The target associated with measuring progress is to eliminate gender disparity in primary and secondary education by 2015, and the four indicators used are the ratio of girls to boys in education, the ratio of literate females to males, the share of women in non-agricultural wage employment, and the proportion of seats held by women in national parliaments. Other MDGs also directly relate to the well-being of women, particularly to women's health. Moreover, it is commonly pointed out that gender equality is important for achieving the other MDGs, a so-called instrumental case for reducing gender inequalities. Two measures of gender inequality are summarized in the 1997 *Human Development Report:*

- The Gender Development Index or GDI is an indicator of gender inequality in basic capabilities. It is based on the Human Development Index, focusing on the three basic capabilities included in this (life expectancy, educational attainment, and income), and adjusts these for gender inequality. As with the HDI, this shows that higher GDP does not directly translate into better GDI, while there seems to be a closer relation between HDI and GDI.
- The Gender Empowerment Measure or GEM measures gender inequality in key areas of economic and political participation and decision making, such as seats held in parliament and percentage of managerial positions held by women.

A recent innovation in measuring gender inequality has come from the World Economic Forum. It is similar to a GDI and a GEM, assessing countries on how well they divide resources and opportunities among their male and female populations, regardless of the overall levels of these resources and opportunities. It focuses on four critical areas of inequality between men and women: economic participation and opportunity; educational attainment; political empowerment; and health and survival. It is worth noting that none of these measures cover people's attitudes to women or gender equality, though data for this are available through the World Value Survey.[5]

In the aid industry, and for advocates influencing it, the Convention on the Elimination of All Forms of Discrimination against Women (CEDAW), adopted in 1979 by the UN General Assembly, is the most important international framework.[6] The idea of mainstreaming gender—bringing gender issues into the mainstream of society and ensuring that gender equality is a primary goal in all areas of development—was emphasized as an international strategy for promoting gender equality by the Platform for Action adopted at the UN Fourth World Conference on Women, held in Beijing in 1995. In 1997 the United Nations defined the concept of gender mainstreaming as follows:

> Mainstreaming a gender perspective is the process of assessing the implications for women and men of any planned action, including legislation, policies or programmes, in any area and at all levels. It is a strategy for making the concerns and

experiences of women as well as of men an integral part of the design, implementation, monitoring and evaluation of policies and programmes in all political, economic and societal spheres so that women and men benefit equally, and inequality is not perpetuated. The ultimate goal is to achieve gender equality.[7]

A focus on mainstreaming means that adding a "women's component" is not sufficient, though there may be a need for activities that target women specifically or for affirmative action. It includes but goes beyond increasing women's participation through quotas for women in schools or watershed management committees, for example, or ensuring that women have equal access to training in development projects. Mainstreaming gender means bringing the experience, knowledge, and interests of women and men to bear on the development agenda. The goal of mainstreaming gender is to transform unequal social structures into equal and just structures for both men and women. To ensure this, it is advocated that development agencies have an institution-wide mechanism for ensuring gender equality, with high-level support, monitoring of progress, and recognition that all actions and programs *can* have a gender aspect and gender analysis should always be carried out. A specific example is the introduction of "gender champions," senior managers who ensure that gender is addressed in all parts of the organizations through regular reporting and inclusion of discussion in meetings. Some organizations use financial initiatives for its senior managers to promote addressing gender. Finally, a gender mainstreaming approach focuses on the intrinsic value of gender equality; while much research focuses on the instrumental value of addressing gender—showing that women's empowerment is good for other goals, such as child health, repaying micro-credit, or economic growth—a gender mainstreaming approach highlights that gender equality is a value in itself.

What does a GAD approach in development projects look like? Let's go back to the example of Poor Rural Communities Development Project in southern China (see Box 4–2)—not because this contained the best approach to gender, but because it helps to provide insight into how projects try to mainstream gender. First, the analysis in preparation for the project highlighted the strong gender differences in project areas, directly linked to levels of poverty. Despite official commitments to gender equality, some gender disparities were growing or remained large, for example, the ratio of newborn boys to girls (as an indicator of discrimination), maternal mortality in poorer regions, increasing ratios of women infected by HIV, higher levels of illiteracy among women, and lower levels of medical care or school attendance of girls compared to boys. The project proposed to mainstream gender equity and to address discrimination. It chose to use the participatory approach as the main vehicle to support the participation of women throughout the project cycle. Second, it was proposed that each of the three participating provinces produce its own gender mainstreaming strategy. This strategy was to include gender training for building management capacity, disaggregating data and monitoring project benefits for and impacts on men and women, and supporting specific initiatives to meet the particular needs of women, like maternal health.

While mainstreaming gender in projects remains demanding, the challenges become larger as we move up to aid modalities like sector approaches and PRSPs.[8] The first step in a sector approach to mainstreaming gender is analysis of gender issues and discrimination in the relevant sector, such as legal and regulatory framework, budgets, service delivery aspects, wage differentials, women's time availability, and so on. Gender budgets are a way to enhance a gender focus and participation within budget-making processes (see Box 7–2). This approach arose outside the industry, but many agencies have come to support it. As we noted above, preparations of sector approaches are time consuming and need the involvement of large numbers of stakeholders; a gender approach highlights this need to ensure women and representative groups are sufficiently consulted and are consulted in an appropriate way. To sustain gender mainstreaming the appropriate structures need to be in place. This may include attention to the gender balance within institutions and addressing existing gender stereotypes. Finally, the gender mainstreaming approach needs to be reflected in monitoring.

Gender Equality in Sector Wide Approaches highlighted the challenges for gender mainstreaming in sector approaches (OECD DAC 2002). It found that the approach to gender focused on narrowly defined investments in women or girls and did not address the underlying conditions that produce unequal opportunities for men and women. It found that organizing consultations in a gender sensitive way was challenging in many cases, that limited progress was made in addressing gender imbalances within the institutions responsible for implementing the sector approaches, and that gender-sensitive monitoring was weakly developed.

Similarly, gender mainstreaming was found to remain a big challenge in PRSP approaches, despite explicit guidance through the PRSP

Box 7–2. Gender Budget Initiatives

A gender budget initiative analyzes public expenditure or taxation from a gender perspective, identifying the implications and impact for women and girls. It may be located inside government departments, organized by officials and ministers, or established by researchers and civil society. It can cover the whole budget or selected departments or programs, and it can focus on different stages of the budget cycle. Perhaps fifty gender budget initiatives now exist around the world. The idea emerged in Australia in 1984 and inspired initiatives around the world.

The South African initiative was a collaboration among NGOs, research and policy institutions, and parliamentarians. In 1997 the South African government initiated a gender budget initiative, coordinated by the Ministry of Finance, involving citizens in the policy area of budgets. This initiative analyzed various years of national ministries and provincial budgets with respect to (1) the positions of women and men and girls and boys within each sector, (2) whether government policies adequately address problems, (3) resources allocated to implement gender-sensitive policies, and (4) how well resources reach intended goals.

The Tanzanian Gender Budget Initiative was started in 1997 by civil society and also works closely with government. It focused first on ministries of education and health, and then agriculture, trade and industry. Research findings are shared when the budget is being debated in Parliament. Women's organizations have been invited to participate in other government processes, such as the public expenditure review and the PRSPs.

The Ugandan gender budget initiative was started after the Forum for Women in Democracy, a women's rights group formed around female MPs. It commissioned national level and district level research on gender and budget issues and provided support to local level initiatives. Research has been carried out by university researchers along with parliamentarians and civil servants, journalists, and civil society activists. Some of the findings have been reflected in parliamentary budget reports. The popular report *Sharing the National Cake* helped to spread gender analysis ideas.

Sources: Commonwealth Secretariat 1999; Judd 2002; and Budlender 2003. A joint initiative led by UNIFEM brings together gender initiatives (www.gender-budgets.org). The International Budget project (www.internationalbudget.org) provides a broad overview of participatory budgeting initiatives.

sourcebook (Kabeer 2003; World Bank 2001; Klugman 2002). Reviews showed that only in half of the PRSPs was there a detailed discussion of gender issues. Poverty analyses often did not highlight different ways in which women and men experience poverty, and gender priorities were not fully or systematically reflected in discussions of policy priorities, budgets, and monitoring. It was noted that people responsible for drafting PRSPs often lacked knowledge of gender issues, while gender advocates often lacked the technical expertise to engage effectively in discussions on budgets.

A more radical critique has emerged from feminists and activists. According to Ines Smyth, former Oxfam GB gender adviser, "Terms such as 'empowerment,' 'gender,' and 'gender mainstreaming' which originated in feminist thinking and activism have lost their moorings and become depoliticized" (Smyth 2007, 582). The way gender is mainstreamed often draws heavily on instrumental arguments, for example, about the beneficial impact of gender equality on other MDGs. When mainstreamed, a focus on gender equality can lose the emphasis on the need to transform institutional rules, as they become absorbed in regular management structures of organizations without further reflection on the structures themselves (the idea of "gender champions" may be an example). As gender is mainstreamed, fewer resources may be made available for addressing women's needs explicitly.

Thus, whether progress has been made in mainstreaming gender is and will remain contested.[9] Alongside continued advocacy, analytical work and tools like gender budgets have made gender concerns more central to development thinking and national policies, even though the capacity of international agencies is not always matched at national levels. Observers of Latin America have noted that the record of gender inclusion in the region has been impressive and that gender has been addressed more effectively than other elements of social exclusion and race discrimination (Buvinić and Mazza 2008). Agreement on any single assessment should not be expected; advocacy for and debate around gender mainstreaming indicates that the development agenda remains complex with multiple tradeoffs, that there are different ways of measuring progress, and that there are differing objectives and expectations among the advocates of gender equality.

Participation

The aid industry's emphasis on participation, community organization, or development has moved in waves. While the basic idea that participation by beneficiaries is important is barely disputed any more, there is much debate over how important participation should be in project and program design and how many resources should be devoted to the process; whether it is a value in itself or merely of instrumental importance; and what can be expected from processes of participation. Participation can be defined as the process through which primary stakeholders influence and share control of development initiatives, decisions, and resources. It is based on a belief that individuals—poor or rich, man or woman—have the capacity to analyze their own reality and take action based on their analysis, given the opportunity. Mainstreaming participation is about the full and systematic incorporation of participatory methodologies into the work of institutions, which, according to advocates like Robert Chambers implies drastic changes in the attitudes of aid officials.

David Korten described the early waves in participatory (or participative) approaches (Korten 1980). The community development movement started in the 1920s, and the Ford Foundation funded a pilot project in Uttar Pradesh, India, in 1948—in a context where Gandhian principles favored community-based approaches even though Nehruvian-style modernization was proceeding simultaneously.[10] Indian community-development efforts inspired programs in over sixty nations during the 1950s, often described as the community development's decade of prominence. However, within a decade or so the optimism had already disappeared, partly because of the growing popularity of central planning, and partly because the experiments showed a series of weaknesses:

- community development experiments did not try to change existing power structures, which contributed to capture of benefits by local elites;
- there was limited attention to building up local organizations and capacity to solve problems and deal with broader administrative systems;
- agencies were set up separate from regular line departments, which caused coordination problems and bureaucratic conflict;
- when conventional bureaucracy was involved, project implementation was not very responsive to people's willingness and capability to participate. (see Korten 1980, 482)

But advocacy for strengthening participatory processes in development practices continued, as it did in other parts of public policy. For example, in 1974 Michael Cernea joined the World Bank as its first sociologist, in the newly established Rural Development Division. From the late 1970s he worked on guidelines for resettlement that became World Bank policy in 1980, and in the mid-1980s he organized an influential seminar series that resulted in the publication *Putting People First* (a title later used by Bill Clinton for a book in 1992). Around the same time Robert Chambers, another of the "fifty key thinkers in development" (Simon 2006), became influential through his idea of "reversals" of development reality, the need for "putting the last first," and "farmer first."[11] In Latin America ideas based on "participatory democracy" emerged in the second half of the 1980s (see Box 7–3), and, like other initiatives that emerged elsewhere, became popular within the aid industry.[12]

Despite the difficult years of adjustment—and sometimes because of it, as enhanced participation was often seen as an alternative while the state was rolled back, and instruments like social funds became popular initially as ways to ameliorate the effects of crisis and adjustment—a series of initiatives continued to emphasize the need for participation, and a wide range of instruments and resources has been developed, often drawing on initiatives like the one in Porto Alegre. Within the World Bank, Community Driven Development (CDD) emerged, drawing on participatory approaches in projects, building on the thinking about social capital, and incorporating the social fund approaches. According to the World Bank website, CDD "is an approach that gives control over planning decisions and investment resources to community groups and local governments." The CDD portfolio in the World Bank is approximately $2 billion a year. It operates in many areas of development, including disaster relief and preparedness, supporting livelihoods more generally, and so on. Support focuses on building the capacity of communities and enhancing their access to information, based on the assumption that with support they can become their "own agent of development"; on promoting reforms in the institutions that have an impact on the well-being of these communities; and on strengthening relations among communities and particularly between countries and local government.

The participatory approach came to influence the analyses that inform the practices of the aid industry. Participatory rural appraisal (commonly known as PRA) evolved from rapid rural appraisals that were basically a set of informal techniques used to collect essential data quickly. PRA is a set of methods that emphasize local knowledge and enable local people to make their own appraisal, analysis, and plans for

---

Box 7–3. Pro-poor Participatory Budgeting: Porto Alegre, Brazil

Decentralization in Brazil resulted in a three-tiered public budget: federal, state, and municipal. Changes in the 1988 Constitution allowed for some autonomy at the municipal level in determining revenues and expenditures in investment decisions. The decentralization of budgetary decisions and the long history of democratic civil society action contributed to the establishment of participatory budget making in Porto Alegre in 1989.

The creation of this new democratic institution enabled the participation of citizens in discussions of budgetary issues. The main institutions are regional and thematic plenary assemblies, which hold two rounds annually. All citizens are entitled and encouraged to participate in discussions about transportation, education, leisure, health, social welfare, and economic development. The assemblies and preparatory meetings define and rank regional or thematic demands and priorities. They elect delegates and councilors and carry out an evaluation of the executive's performance. The councilors then use general criteria to rank the demands of the assemblies to determine the allocation of funds and vote on the investment proposals of the executive. Although conflicts have arisen, most citizens believe that the participatory budget has resulted in improved services, for example, in water services and school enrollment.

---

development projects. Methods often involve group discussions and semi-structured interviews. Materials and visual aids and tools are used to help groups analyze development problems (through mapping and seasonal diagrams), prioritize solutions (through preference ranking), and facilitate joint action.[13] In the 1990s participatory approaches also started to influence poverty analysis, which had a predominantly quantitative focus. Participatory poverty analysis (PPA) became a central feature of the development of many of the PRSPs.[14] One of the most successful examples of this was in Vietnam. International NGOs had started with small-scale PPAs at local levels to guide projects. The 2000 *World Development Report* and World Bank support helped to start PPAs (which complemented quantitative poverty analysis) on a much broader scale.

Later, village consultations were used to get feedback from villagers on the draft of the PRSP; in the end twelve provinces were covered. These consultations are thought to have had a significant influence on the PRSP by highlighting the high costs of basic services in health and education, the importance of exclusion of migrants, the need to enhance community participation in infrastructure projects, and the need for better communication about and transparency in government projects, among other issues.[15]

Two examples illustrate participatory approaches in aid projects.[16] The first, the Rural Integrated Project Support program in Tanzania, started in 1988, is a district-level project including water, health care, education, agriculture, local government, savings and credit, transport and marketing, and natural-resource management. After an evaluation of phase one in 1993 showed weaknesses in program delivery at the community level, a participatory planning process was introduced, with a commitment to long-term support for strengthening participation. The program supported local communities and government authorities in the identification of priorities and action. According to reviews, this led to improvements in all aspects of the program with fairly limited resources (Blackburn, Chambers, and Gaventa 2000, 9). The second example, the Poor Rural Communities Development Project in China, emphasized an approach to inclusive and transparent project planning, implementation, and monitoring at the community level, building capacities for participation within the project-management system. It also tried to link village-level planning to county-level planning and implementation. The project developed specific participatory methods of poverty analysis, planning, implementation, and monitoring; trained facilitators at the county and township levels; and developed a pilot to maximize community participation.[17]

The extent to which participation has now been mainstreamed is subject to debate. The importance of participation is recognized in most aid agencies and in most sectors. Robert Chambers (2005) notes that participation finally has been mainstreamed. Data show the impact of participation on improving project quality and sustainability, on the extent of targeting and capture by elites, and on possibilities for scaling up (Mansuri and Rao 2004). There is also recognition that participation is no panacea, that time and resources need to be invested to make participation effective and meaningful, and that participation at local levels needs to be accompanied by changes in mainstream policymaking and implementation. Nonetheless, resistance to participation is common too, in part because of doubts about what it can achieve, and in part because of resistance of traditional top-down planners and aid agency staff.

In fact, the use of participatory approaches in development practice has come under fierce criticism.[18] In particular, it has been argued that the use of participatory methods by large aid agencies has been used more to legitimize their actions than to give people the power to make their own decisions, or that it was more about solving the delivery problems of aid agencies than empowering its beneficiaries. The latter was a main motivation for Wolfensohn's interest in community development, for example, in Indonesia. For some, mainstreaming participation has resulted in a loss of critical and political content. One key question is whether participation is a right, which we address in the next section.

Rights-based Approaches to Development

Among the four cross-cutting issues discussed in this chapter, approaches to rights probably have found least currency and have been least mainstreamed. On the one hand, like environment and gender, international conferences have emphasized development as a human right. Human rights, central to the US and French constitutions since the late eighteenth century, became part of global governance frameworks with the Universal Declaration of Human Rights and subsequent human rights treaties and bodies.

Human rights started to become integrated into the development discourse during the early 1970s, and the Declaration on the Right to Development was adopted by the UN General Assembly in 1986. The World Conference on Human Rights, held in Vienna in June 1993, re-affirmed the right to development, as established in the Declaration on the Right to Development . . . "as an integral part of human rights." Kofi Annan tried to move human rights to the core of the UN agenda. A number of NGOs, bilateral agencies, and UN agencies have developed policy papers and courses on mainstreaming rights, or rights-based approaches to development (see Box 7–4).

Mainstreaming rights, or making rights central to aid practices, faces large challenges. In the international arena, debates about human rights often become debates between North and South, and there are concerns that the concepts of rights reflect Western norms and do not allow for different or culturally specific manifestations. Moreover, the United States usually has refused to ratify international conventions that

---

Box 7–4. Human Rights Principles

The UNDP, stressing that human rights and development are two sides of the same coin, proposes four main human rights principles:

- *Universality and indivisibility:* Every woman, man and child is entitled to enjoy her or his human rights simply by virtue of being human. . . . Enjoyment of one right is indivisibly inter-related to the enjoyment of other rights.
- *Equality and non-discrimination:* Human rights are for everyone, as much for people living in poverty and social isolation as for the rich and educated. . . . Equality also requires that all persons within a society enjoy equal access to the available goods and services that are necessary to fulfil basic human needs.
- *Participation and inclusion:* Every person and all peoples are entitled to participate in, contribute to, and enjoy civil, economic, social, cultural and political development.
- *Accountability and rule of law:* States have the primary responsibility to create the enabling environment in which all people can enjoy their human rights, and have the obligation to ensure that respect for human rights norms and principles is integrated into all levels of governance and policy-making. (UNDP 2003, 7–8)

---

define rights, partly because of ideological objections, partly because of the potential implications of justiciable rights. Economic thinking has an almost natural aversion to debates on rights. Advocates of rights-based approaches have been criticized for overstating the potential of aid agencies (often the smaller ones), for politicizing development projects, and for creating false hope (Gready and Ensor 2005, 28–40). Most important for our discussion here is why and when rights approaches entered the approaches of the aid industry.

Peter Uvin (2004) emphasizes that human rights are poorly integrated into development approaches, and that this needs to be improved, as donors can do harm. He describes four ways in which human rights and development can be brought together. First, there is what he calls "rhetorical repackaging," which has been popular among aid agencies that need to maintain the moral high ground. This can be a first step to change but may also be a smoke screen. It can obscure the important difference between service-based and rights-based approaches to development. A focus on the distribution of goods and services to recipients is not incompatible but also not identical with those recipients having entitlements to these services.

Second, there is the possibility of donor conditionality that can make donor behavior more principled, for example, if the principles of the Paris Consensus were actually binding. Rights-related conditionality might ensure that aid agencies impose less self-censorship. However, Uvin agrees with the findings that conditionality is unlikely to be successful and never fully implemented. Moreover, conditionality is currently situated in contracts between governments, and does not necessarily—and in practice usually does not—translate into relationships of rights between governments and citizens.

Third, instead of conditionality, aid agencies can provide positive and constructive support. Aid agencies can support strengthening the institutions that promote human rights, though in practice rights projects suffer from the typical problems of project aid, such as being short term and fixed on disbursement. In fact, many agencies, including the World Bank, have supported projects related to legal and judiciary reform,[19] and advocacy for rights, such as ActionAid Brazil's support to achieving rights to food and sustainable nutrition (Antunes and Romano 2005) and a DFID-funded project helping poor communities in Bolivia gain identity cards, enabling them to vote for the first time, and to access social and health services.

Fourth, rights and development can be brought together through a rights-based approach to development. This provides a normative framework for achieving development priorities, redefines the nature of the aid relationship, and moves aid from being a charitable activity to one that is based on claims and justiciability. It sees beneficiaries as rights holders and project staff and policymakers as duty bearers.

Examples of moves toward rights-based approaches can be found among organizations that support children. Child welfare agencies have usually treated children as passive, seldom involving them in project or policy development. Under the influence of the UN Convention on the Rights of the Child, agencies have started to see children as holders of rights to express their views, have access to information, and participate in policy development (Theis and O'Kane 2005).

A right-based approach takes approaches to participation a step further. For CARE International, a human rights approach to its work implies that "we view people we assist as rights-holders and not simply beneficiaries or participants," and the overarching aim is to facilitate marginalized and vulnerable people to achieve their rights.[20] In the case of CARE's work in a pilot project in Rwanda, adopting a rights-based approach implied an internal transformation of the organization and construction of a culture of rights within the organization. Second, it carried out a participatory analysis of the causes of poverty in Rwanda, highlighting the rights issues underlying poverty (such as discrimination and unaccountable governance) and based choices for programming on this analysis. Third, it introduced rights-based monitoring ("bottom-up accountability") into its programs as a way to ensure that the children it supports, for example, hold CARE to account.

The UNDP Human Rights Principles (see Box 7–4) use the language of mainstreaming rights, illustrating a combination of the third and fourth approach. UNDP emphasizes that values, principles, and standards of human rights must guide and permeate the entire development programming process, adding that such an approach presupposes that human rights are reflected in a country's norms and institutions. In the view of UNDP this usually implies investing in advocacy and sensitizing partners on human rights, support for a sustainable system of legal and non-legal forms of enforcement, application of human rights in law and reality, and effective systems for societal monitoring of human rights enforcement.

A rights-based approach to development—in the fourth meaning as defined above—poses significant challenges to the aid industry. According to Peter Uvin, one of its main advocates, "the track record of the rights to development is catastrophic" (Uvin 2007, 598). Support for strengthening legal institutions and awareness of rights is undertaken only by a few agencies, and often in contexts that are not controversial. NGOs have developed various ways to strengthen advocacy for rights in many countries but are mostly still far removed from being "duty bearers" themselves. Moving from current aid practices to a rights-based approach is thus a deeply political process. The transformation from the current way in which the aid industry works, where it is largely accountable to its taxpayers and stakeholders, to one where beneficiaries become participants, and where aid agencies are accountable as duty bearers to rights holders, is still a long way ahead.

Conclusion

These four cross-cutting themes illustrate the complexity that the aid industry addresses. The industry has moved a long way from its 1950s and 1960s focus on technical projects and financing of countries' savings gaps. That narrow focus has been successfully challenged by advocates within and outside aid organizations who have placed issues of participation and gender firmly "on the agenda." The brief descriptions in this chapter show that the importance given to these issues moves in waves, with environment as a recent example of sudden increased interest.

The questions that these cross-cutting issues pose are not unique to the aid industry. Most public and private institutions have been or are perennially challenged to address questions of gender and rights more forcefully. What makes the aid industry different is that it is challenged mostly by its funders, and its main challenge lies in the translation of these pressures from taxpayers to the realities in which it works. Such influences are wide ranging; they can consist of changes with long-term implications, like the introduction of new acts, to short-term ones relating to politicians' need to show results. This highlights one of the key challenges to a rights-based approach to international development, even though expanding international frameworks increasingly provide the space for moving from a charitable approach to one where rights and duties drive the way the industry operates.

Within the aid industry the emphasis on mainstreaming continues. Different parts of the industry and different people within agencies continue to define main objectives in different ways—and continue to differ about whether they can focus on issues of gender and rights. Mainstreaming remains a strategy for people within agencies in which they continue to argue for the importance of addressing gender and rights because they are values in themselves and because they have an instrumental value in helping to address other goals (such as addressing gender inequality because it is good for growth, or enhancing participation because it improves project efficiency).

At the same time, the emphasis on mainstreaming itself is contested. Feminist advocates in particular have concluded that the gains in terms of integrating women's issues into existing policy have been modest and not transformative. They believe that political commitment and civil society mobilization remain essential to ensure such progress, and that mainstreaming may contribute to an instrumental approach to gender equality.

Further Readings

One of the most extensive sources on gender is the Sussex-based website http://www.bridge.ids.ac.uk/bridge/.

A wide range of sources on participation can be found at the website of the IDS participation team (www.ids.ac.uk) and the participatory learning and action resources at IIED (www.iied.org).

Bass et al. (2005) give an excellent introduction to poverty-environment links and offers a series of case studies on how environment has been incorporated into aid projects.

One of the most quoted sources on environment, based on Amartya Sen's entitlement framework, is Leach, Mearns, and Scoones (1997).

Gready and Ensor (2005) give a good overview of the history of rights approaches and a dozen case studies.

The World Bank's *Social Analysis Sourcebook* (2003) focuses on how social dimensions can be incorporated into the design of projects.

8

What Works in the Aid Industry? What Doesn't? How Do We Know?

The performance of aid is enormously contested. There is widespread critique of the practices of development aid, but as we saw, that critique is diverse, with different analysts seeing different problems with aid. Moreover, in the preceding chapters we saw that development approaches have evolved, often very quickly, making assessments of performance difficult. Some of the changes are political—for example, when new development departments get new ministers—but some are a direct reaction to problems identified in earlier approaches.

As a result of the increasing internal and external critique, and a growing need to show results for taxpayers' money, analyzing the impact of aid has become more important. Questions asked and methodologies used vary a great deal. At one end of the spectrum, studies have used cross-country statistical analysis to look at the impact of aid on economic growth, and this has become a large and contested field of enquiry. At the other end, receiving far less public attention, there are hundreds of studies on the results of development projects (most development agencies do evaluations of their projects). In between, new program or sector-wide approaches have developed their own forms of evaluation and monitoring. This chapter discusses these different approaches. (For definitions of terms used in evaluation, see Box 8–1 and Table 8–1).

It is important to emphasize that different agencies have different approaches to monitoring and evaluation. Many of the bilateral agencies have good systems for monitoring programs—as a form of regular supervision and feedback during the project cycle. But evaluation—the assessment of impact after the project has finished—is often less well developed.[1] The World Bank and the IMF have relatively strong systems of peer review at the design stage of projects, monitoring or supervision, and post-project evaluation by a relatively independent evaluation

---

Box 8–1. Preliminary Evaluation Definitions

In the science of assessment of the aid industry, and of public policy more generally, the following terms are of importance.

- Program *monitoring* helps to assess whether a program is implemented according to plan, enabling feedback and highlighting implementation problems. For example, are the steps implemented on schedule?
- *Cost-benefit analysis* assesses whether money is spent in the right way, compared to other possible uses, and is related to benefits created. For example, what is the realized return on investment in primary education?
- *Impact evaluation* determines whether the program has the desired effects on its beneficiaries. For example, have incomes increased as a result of a specific project or a policy change promoted by an international agency?
- Impact evaluation is normally *ex-post*, that is, after a project or program has been completed, but it is also possible to make *ex-ante* assessment to ensure that best knowledge is made available about the likelihood of impacts.
- *Causality* and *attribution* highlight that observed changes do not merely coincide with inputs from donor agencies but are the direct result of these actions. Proving causality is generally considered among the most difficult technical issues.

---

department; this may be because they provide loans, not grants, and are accountable to their members. New agencies like the Gates Foundation, the Clinton Foundation, the William and Flora Hewlett Foundation, and the Millennium Challenge Corporation all emphasize the need for better determination of whether their investments are well spent. But in all agencies, pressure may influence evaluation results and conclusions drawn.[2]

The following text first describes principles and practices of assessing whether projects have worked. It then moves to more recent discussions about the ways in which programs can be evaluated. Third, it highlights the controversial area of the impact of aid on economic growth.

Table 8–1. Evaluation and Indicators: From Input to Impact

	Input	Output	Outcome	Impact
Definition	Financial, human, and material resources used for project	The products, capital goods and services that result from the project (also the changes resulting from the project)	The short- and medium-term effects of an intervention'so utputs	Positive and negative, primary and secondary long-term effects, directly or indirectly, intended or unintended
Project Examples	Total project investment, and personnel working on the project	Number of loans disbursed

Repayment rates | Poor households have access to loans

Increase incomes

Poverty reduction | Dependence on informal lenders

Inequality between poor and not-so-poor |
| **Examples Sector-Wide Approach** | External resources coordinated with national policies | Strengthened government policies and plans

Improved measurement of policies | Implementation of policies

Greater efficiency in use of resources | Better use of resources lead to better development outcomes |

Sources: www.oecd.org; Walford 2003.

Measuring the Impact of Projects

In evaluating the impact of development projects, Judy Baker states:

> Despite the billions of dollars spent on development assis-
> tance each year, there is very little known about the actual
> impact of projects on the poor. . . . Many governments, insti-
> tutions, and project managers are reluctant to carry out im-
> pact evaluation because they are deemed to be expensive, time
> consuming, and technically complex, and because the find-
> ings can be politically sensitive, particularly if they are nega-
> tive. (Baker 2000, vi)

Often the most difficult issue that project evaluation has to deal with
is the question of impact; for example, whether changes in income in a
project area are due to the project or to other factors (such as private
investment in agricultural products or expansion of road networks). Ideally, an evaluation should compare the changes in the project area with
the changes in an area that is comparable in all aspects except for the
development project. This is called the *counter-factual*: what would have
happened if the project had not existed, or, for example, if patients with
the symptoms and personal characteristics had not been administered
medicines. However, such assessments are time consuming and expensive, making them particularly difficult for smaller organizations. Project
evaluation can address this through the use of comparisons, studying
beneficiaries as well as non-beneficiaries with similar socioeconomic status (for example, villagers in a nearby, non-project village).

There are two main ways to assess impact. First, experimental design
(or randomization) involves allocation of project benefits randomly
among eligible beneficiaries. While often seen as technically the best
way—Banerjee, for example, sees this as a key element to "making aid
work" (2007)—this method has at least two sets of problems. First, there
is the ethical question of denying benefits to eligible groups. While this
may be justifiable if full coverage is not achievable in any way, or if the
benefits from the experiment are so large that they outweigh ethical
objections, it may not be justifiable if it is essentially for a donor purpose. Second, there are practical questions about the cost of random
design, because the coverage need to be large enough to establish statistical validity. Moreover, there are many types of purposes, projects, and

certainly programs that do not allow for the creation of random experiments.

The quasi-experimental (or non-random) method is the second-best method, but it is usually the more practical alternative, and there is a large and often very technical literature on different approaches. The comparison uses statistical techniques rather than actual comparison, with comparison groups selected after project implementation. It uses existing data of comparable groups rather than randomly selected eligible groups.

A quantitative evaluation by IFPRI of the Red de Protección Social, a conditional cash transfer program in Nicaragua—which supplemented income to increase household expenditures on food, reducing primary-school desertion and improving the health and nutrition of young children—involved the first type, a randomized experiment; half of the communities received the benefits, while the other half did not. The moral justification for this was twofold: first, there was not enough evidence that this kind of intervention would be effective, and second, there was limited capacity to implement the project in all communities (Maluccio and Flores 2004). And as an example of the non-random approach, a World Bank evaluation of a Japan-supported secondary school scholarship program in Cambodia—which found improvements in retention and completion—was based on comparisons between recipients and non-recipients using samples of application forms and unannounced visits to the schools during which enrollment and attendance were recorded (Filmer and Schady 2006).

Further, the impacts of social funds in different countries have been compared, assessing success in reaching the poor, effect on living standards, quality of the infrastructure created in the context of social funds, and the costs of social funds as compared to institutions undertaking similar investments (Rawlings, Sherburne-Benz, and Van Dommelen 2004). The methods used for these comparisons tend to be qualitative and descriptive; advanced statistical techniques are of little use in carrying out such assessments.

Various methods of data collection can be used in evaluation. Forms of impact assessment usually rely on sources of quantitative data, often generated by the project itself, combined with data sources surveys on income, health, education, and so on. For example, the World Bank evaluation of social funds benefited from the baseline data created in each social fund but also the ability to compare different funds with similar design, in different countries (Rawlings, Sherburne-Benz, and

Van Dommelen 2004). Qualitative techniques—case studies, focus groups, interviews—are used, usually to understand changes in processes or the beneficiaries' perceptions of changes. The participatory methods described in Chapter 7 typically include ways of reporting that are driven by communities and facilitated by outsiders from the aid industry. As illustrated in an example from the Philippines, there has been a growing literature on how qualitative and quantitative methods can be combined (see Box 8–2).[3]

In the measurement of impact the following issues thus are important. First, the choice of indicator is crucial. Even if measurement is limited to an income poverty indicator, it is important whether one looks only at the number of people in poverty (head count) or also at the extent of their poverty (poverty gap). Much research on microfinance—like the evaluation in the Philippines—shows that poor households benefit, but not the poorest. Further, impact can be measured by wealth or assets, food security, child nutrition, quality of life, gender relations, or beneficiary satisfaction. But information for evaluation is often not readily available, and few projects invest heavily upfront in establishing baselines, thus restricting the choice of indicators.

Many of the outcome or output indicators may provide only part of the picture. Repayment rates may be a sign of improved income, but they also may be the result of pressure to repay (common in group-based lending, for example). Impacts can be different for different groups—the poorest may not be able to use micro-credit effectively, for example—and can be measured at different levels (individual, household, village, and so on). Within households, men and women are likely to be affected differently, and access to credit may change the relationships among household members. There may be effects on people not directly included in the project, positive or negative.

Projects that are targeted to poor people are usually assessed on errors of inclusion and exclusion. Inclusion errors describe whether (and, if so, how many) people benefit from the project even though they were not eligible. In the literature this is also known as leakage. Exclusion errors describe how many people who were eligible did not get project benefits. This can occur for a number of reasons, not all due to the project, but a measurement of these errors does give an important indication of how well projects perform. For example, incentives to project staff for increasing lending may lead to exclusion of the poorest borrowers, a finding in much of the analysis of microfinance projects, including the example from the Philippines (described in Box 8–2).

Box 8–2. Project Evaluation:
Asian Development Bank's Microfinance in the Philippines

A special evaluation study assessed whether microfinance projects—including the Rural Microenterprise Finance Project in the Philippines—reduced the poverty of rural poor households and improved the socioeconomic status of women in developing member countries. The study used quantitative tools on data from a nationwide survey conducted among 2,274 households in 116 villages, and 28 microfinance institutions. Qualitative tools such as focus group discussions were used to gather information on intra-household dynamics in order to assess the effects of microfinance on the status of women. Sample surveys covered 566 women and were designed to complement and validate the focus-group discussions.

The impact study used a quasi-experimental design that required treatment and comparison areas for each of the twenty-eight microfinance institutions. These areas were geographically different. Two types of household respondents were surveyed: households that received micro-credit loans, and households that did not receive loans but qualified to join the program. Statistical (econometric) techniques were used to estimate impact and showed the following:

- Micro-credit loans had positive (and "mildly significant") impacts on beneficiaries' income, overall expenditures, and food expenditures.
- The impact on per capita income and expenditures was regressive. The project reached poor households, but not in significant numbers. The impact was negative for households with lower incomes. The study concluded that targeting microfinance on the poorest households may not be the most appropriate way to help them escape poverty. The household survey found that only 10 percent of the respondents were classified as poor and 4 percent as subsistence poor (using the official Philippine poverty line).
- The evaluation showed that the project helped to reduce the dependence of participating households on other loans such as those from informal moneylenders and more expensive loans from financial institutions. The proportion of participating households with savings accounts increased, as did the saved amounts. The program increased the number of micro-enterprises and the number of persons employed in them, reflecting that the program was designed to cater to the entrepreneurial poor.

Source: ADB 2007.

A particularly difficult question refers to longer-term changes and impacts, a question seldom addressed in aid projects because of the short-term and project-centered engagement of agencies. The Southwest Poverty Project, one of the earlier World Bank poverty programs in China, is an example of a project based on a long-term evaluation. The World Bank lent $400 million in the second half of the 1990s based on an evaluation that focused on the long term. The project worked closely with the National Bureau of Statistics, carrying out surveys every year during the project, in both project and non-project villages, with a follow-up survey four years after the end of the project. The evaluation found that the project had been well targeted in terms of having selected poorer villages, and that during the project the project villages improved compared to the non-project villages. The follow-up survey showed that the positive impact could still be found after four years, but that the impacts were much smaller (Ravallion 2008).

Impact assessment can vary a great deal. Some agencies are more concerned than others about scientific evidence to show how well projects work. There are various methods to do assessments, and data availability and quantity are serious constraints. Assessments become more difficult—or at least methods need to differ—if the project is complex.

Evaluating Program Approaches

The evaluations described above focus on project approaches with clearly identifiable inputs, even though the outcomes and impacts are difficult to identify. With program approaches (described in Chapter 5), monitoring and evaluation change drastically. With social funds, as already described, which are funding mechanisms for different projects, organizational forms are different in each country and different methods need to be applied to make comparisons. Thus, comparisons usually rely more on descriptions and qualitative assessments than on statistical techniques.

Evaluations of sector-wide approaches (SWAps) often emphasize that the approach is primarily about changing the way that aid is delivered, particularly the way donors work with governments (Walford 2003). They are not just a program or set of activities, but rather are a way to coordinate and support sector activities; their aim is to improve policies and resource allocation. The evaluation methods described above do not identify effects of policy, or whether they have contributed to increase resource allocation to particular priority sectors; that is, attribution of change to donor programs is very difficult. Policy changes are very complex and often difficult to trace. For example, improvements in health-service delivery may be as much the result of leadership of policymakers or administrators as the result of existing donor programs—or it may result from both. It is equally difficult to assess whether the absence of policy change implies the failure of a program. Making comparisons with other countries is virtually impossible, because conditions tend to be too different to make such comparisons meaningful.

So, different kinds of indicators are proposed—though ones with much less application and experience than in the evaluations described above. For health-sector programs, according to Walford, the purpose of a SWAp is usually about better use of resources, both private and public, and better results in the health sector; thus monitoring indicators ought to reflect results in terms of health and poverty-reduction objectives. Indicators based on policy implementation include, for example, that implementation reflects the agreed expenditure patterns, or that expenditures focus on the key objectives, such as increased spending in rural areas and for primary care. Greater efficiency in the use of resources may involve improvement in administrative capacity, for example, by reducing duplication, and enhancement of technical efficiency in areas like equipment provision.

The measurement of these objectives often requires qualitative assessment. For example, donors do not find it easy to measure the extent to which government feels ownership and accepts agreed-upon priorities, the extent to which other stakeholders feel they have an influence on sector policy and plans, and the extent of participation in development of the policy. To measure improved resource allocation, aid agencies have used indicators regarding efforts to reach the poor, measures to address maternal mortality or family planning, mechanisms to reduce inappropriate investments in hardware and training, drug quality control, and public knowledge about appropriate treatments. Strengthening national systems of planning also requires indicators that are often not easy to capture: procurement, the role of the private sector, the extent to which the budget reflects available domestic and aid resources, improvements in the capacity to monitor quality and uptake of services, and others. Finally, because the objectives of sector approaches often involve improved working with donors, assessment may include, for example, measures on the reduction of time spent by top health officials meeting donors and attending project reviews.

In a similar vein, the monitoring of PRSPs focuses on processes, combined with using a wide range of monitoring systems for various elements of public policy. In a World Bank PRSP sourcebook, a range of components of a monitoring system is described, indicating that in many countries capacities for monitoring and dissemination of evaluation need strengthening. A poverty monitoring system is needed to track key indicators over time, including the tracking of public expenditures and outputs and quick monitoring of household well-being. The World Bank document further highlights the need for rigorous assessment of the impact on poverty of interventions that are key components of the strategy (World Bank website). Box 8–3 discusses a new instrument that donors have proposed in this context in order to assess impact "ex-ante," before decisions on policy directions were taken, and to assess the most likely outcomes of different scenarios. Because a PRSP is a strategy involving multiple sectors and ministries, the evaluation of impact—as opposed to the impact of a specific component of a strategy—is especially challenging.

Moreover, other types of evaluation, such as assessing the process of formulating a poverty reduction strategy, are important, but experience in this has developed only recently. The PRSP process is seen as an agreement between a government and its citizens about what the government will be accountable for in delivery of services; donors assess the credibility of governments' commitments. Some of the key indicators, besides those related to MDGs, that might need monitoring include accountability to parliaments/legislatures on PRSP implementation (while providing an adequate basis for external accountability to donors), coherence across government departments, and coordination of project-driven reporting and monitoring requirements. The coordination of reporting requirement—and the integration of this in the country's budget cycles—was seen as a key element of the implementation of program approaches, though there have been doubts whether reporting requirements have been reduced, whether donors can reduce their requirements, and about national capacity to produce the necessary data and analysis.

Similarly, budget support—as the instrument behind sectoral or national development plans—would require a mix of indicators relating to policy processes and to ones that refer to the aid relationship. A DFID report on the "evaluability" of budget support lists the following:

Box 8–3. Poverty and Social Impact Analysis

Poverty and Social Impact Analysis was developed in the context of PRSPs, after the IMF and the World Bank agreed in 2000 to consider the poverty and social impact of major reforms in their lending programs. PSIA is an ex-ante analysis of intended and unintended consequences of policy interventions on the well-being or welfare of different groups, particularly the poor and those at risk of falling into poverty. PSIA intends to promote debate on evidence-based policy choices, to create an understanding of the poverty and the social impacts of policy reforms, and to determine the tradeoffs among policy choices.

In Mozambique a PSIA was organized during the process of developing its PRSP (the Action Plan for the Reduction of Absolute Poverty) covering the years 2000 to 2005. The PSIA focused on the impact of a possible rise in fuel tax, which was then under debate, because the price of fuel had not changed in five years, despite inflation. The revenue raised from an increased tax would be used to support development priorities, such as road maintenance. But many people in Mozambique argued that increasing the fuel tax would increase poverty, even though the share of fuel in the economy was small.

To analyze the potential impacts, researchers undertook the following activities:

- interviews and discussions with key decision makers in the government and the private sector to explain the existing assumptions about the fuel tax;
- review of the existing literature to identify assumptions about the nature of poverty in Mozambique;
- household surveys to prepare a poverty profile;
- limited qualitative field research in Zambezia about the use of fuel and transport, including use among vulnerable groups;
- a quantitative analysis of the way in which fuel prices would be transmitted through the economy using a social accounting matrix; and
- a calculation of the impact of price rises on households and the way in which demand would fall.

Continued on page 184

This analysis concluded that the short-term impact of a rise in fuel tax on poverty would be modest. And while the analysis did not look at the potential use of the additional government revenue, it did highlight that it was possible that more people would be lifted out of poverty through more pro-poor spending than would fall into poverty due to the increased fuel tax.

Sources: www.prspsynthesis.org; OECD DAC 2003b.

- a single multi-donor process should allow senior government officials to devote time to policy making, instead of dealing with a large number of individual project missions;
- predictability of aid flows;
- improvement in the overall direction and consistency of budget allocations;
- effectiveness of the state and public administration, and use of government systems and work to strengthen them;
- stronger domestic accountability, improvement in transparency and accountability to the country's parliamentary institutions and electorate;
- and government capacity to reduce poverty. (Lawson et al. 2003)

Experience in the monitoring and assessment of program approaches is recent. But it is evident that the requirements for monitoring are expanding and becoming more complex. The methods of monitoring also are different, as many of the indicators do not allow for quantification or for creating control cases or experiments. This in itself is not problematic, but qualitative information ought to have equal power. The expanding lists of indicators, however, may stretch the capacity of systems carrying out the monitoring and may lead to an increasing role for the donors.

Aid and Economic Growth—Will We Ever Know?

Since the late 1980s there has been an ever-growing literature in the aid industry—now amounting to over a hundred papers—looking at the impact of aid at the macro level, in particular at economic growth. This followed the unearthing by Paul Mosley of a micro-macro paradox that stated that aid, while efficient at the project level, had no clear effect on the overall economy (Mosley 1987). This paradox greatly influenced subsequent work on aid effectiveness, which we described in earlier parts of this book; in this section we focus on the way this impact has been assessed and the debates that have arisen around the question.

The key question that these analyses have asked is about the correlation between amounts of aid and the way it is provided (such as project or program aid, on the one hand), and economic growth shown by economic indicators such as savings, on the other. Economists have been particularly concerned about this question, not only because of the question of whether aid has a positive impact, but also because large-scale funding can have negative effects; for example, it may lead to appreciation of the exchange rates and decreasing competitiveness of the economy (the Dutch disease), and it may have a negative impact on government budgeting processes (rent seeking). Research has also started to look at impacts at the sector level, for example, whether higher levels of aid result in increased school enrollment or improved health indicators.

The research on the effects of aid at the macro level is older, beginning in the 1960s (Roodman 2007). Over time, not only has interest in whether aid works increased, but data have become more widely available and of better quality, and computers have made it possible to establish links among different factors. Controversy already existed in the 1970s; some concluded that aid did well, others said it did no harm, while still others could not see any positive impact of aid. After Mosley produced his findings showing that there was no effect of projects at the micro level on macro-level indicators, a paper from the London School of Economics showed there was no significant effect of aid on savings or growth, which in turn "launched a thousand regressions of growth" (Roodman 2007, 5).

One of the main responses to this, a rebuttal according to some, came from the World Bank. Craig Burnside and David Dollar (the latter also one of the main authors emphasizing how important economic growth is for poverty reduction) argued that aid *did* work, but in good policy environments, consisting of openness to trade, low inflation, and balanced government budgets (Burnside and Dollar 2000). Subsequently a whole series of analyses have added to this argument, each looking at slightly different conditions that makes aid effective: stronger government institutions and economic policies, democracy, countries emerging from civil war, and so on. This type of analysis also became the basis of aid allocations models used by donors, including in the design of the Millennium Challenge Account, to decide in which countries to provide more aid—the countries with large numbers of poor people *and* the kind of policies that makes that aid effective.

But even this apparently straightforward finding—that aid works in the right environment—has been criticized, even though this has not diminished its influence on policy. The independent evaluation of World Bank research stated: "Bank reports prepared for Monterrey did not present a balanced picture of the research, with appropriate reservations and skepticism, but used it [World Bank research on aid effectiveness] selectively to support an advocacy position" (Banerjee et al. 2006, 56). And, using data sets on aid flows, policies, and economic growth, authors like Easterly, Levine, and Roodman found that adding countries and years of observation to the data led to a different conclusion: there was no evidence that aid was effective, and that more research was needed (Easterly, Levine, and Roodman 2003). Others were particularly concerned with the question of causality, and it remains difficult to decide when and where providing aid causes economic growth, and when and where that economic growth leads to receiving more aid. From my own experience in India observing the provision of aid to Andra Pradesh, which received more aid than any other state, I conclude that the latter *can* be the case.

Many other variants of the argument and the identified problems with analysis exist. Some show that aid works in some countries and not others; some focus on short-term versus long-term aid and impacts; others address the question of declining marginal returns. Statistical techniques continue to improve, but these usually lead to more questions being asked. Obviously, whether the aid industry contributes to economic growth will remain an important question, but perhaps the issues involved are too complex to be summarized in the simple indicators used in the regressions.

Conclusion

There are good reasons why it will remain very difficult to assess whether aid has worked or not. First, the objectives of aid have and continue to vary, for a range of reasons. Of course, it would be of limited value to hold all forms of aid or all aid providers to the same measurement stick. Given the diversity of motivations and perspectives, and the diversity of agencies, all of which have their own rules of reporting, accountability, stakeholders, and procedures for using evaluations, it should come as no surprise that measurement is and probably will remain rather imprecise.

Second, generalized conclusions about the impact of aid on global poverty are extremely misleading. For example, in the second half of the twentieth century more people than ever before were lifted out of poverty. Is that a sign that the global aid architecture that developed during the same period was working? Or is the failure to meet some of the MDGs agreed upon in 2000, or the failure to meet them in some regions, or meeting some but not others, proofs of the industry's failure? Put simply, the aid industry, unlike other types of industries, does not have a simple bottom line meansuring success or failure. Nor should one try to push this question too far, because the need to show results may drive agencies away from longer-term projects of capacity building into areas where results are more immediate and easier to achieve.

Does aid works? If asked in this simple fashion, the question is perhaps too difficult to answer. Abhijit Banerjee asserts that aid institutions are lazy and resist knowledge, because they do not use randomized trials enough (2007, 7, 16). This is simplistic and neglects the diverse nature of the aid industry. The proposed outcomes of international development are multiple and frequently changing. Put in technical terms, the question suffers from a dependent variable problem—what is being measured is not defined clearly enough, or in different ways. And even if the focus is on a single variable—such as economic growth—the technical complexities for answering the question remain. However, there are good instruments—quantitative as well as qualitative—that allow insight into whether certain forms of support have worked and whether some have worked better than others. In the end, the important issue may not be to find the perfect science but to improve the ways in which the industry can be held accountable. While more needs to be done to strengthen accountability, progress is being made.

Further Readings

Many of the aid agencies have good websites that show methods and results
    of evaluation, including the World Bank (including the new evalua-
    tion initiative at website www.worldbank.org/dime) and OECD.
Baker 2000 is a classic regarding project evaluation.
Roodman 2007 may be the most accessible description of the debate on aid
    and growth; other evaluation studies by CGD staff and descriptions of
    successful cases in health support can both be found at www.cgdev.org.

9

Challenges for the Aid Industry in the Twenty-first Century

This book has described how development aid works, or, to put it simply, what happens with the $150 billion or so of funds disbursed annually for aid. It has discussed the numerous institutions involved and their histories, the rapidly changing trends in international development, and the most important instruments that are available to the aid industry. The book's objective was not to decide whether aid works or fails, but rather to inform its readers about how the aid industry works. Moreover, as we have seen in this book, the aid industry is incredibly and increasingly diverse. During these first years of the twenty-first century, aid flows have been increasing, a growing number of players have become involved, and there has been agreement to focus on the MDGs.

Is it possible to clearly assess how aid works? There are certainly many instruments and measurements through which assessments can be made; indeed, the assessment of aid has become a cottage industry of its own. Each of these has its own merits, and as aid has come under increased scrutiny—and rightly so—the assessments have received increased attention. But there is no one way of assessing whether aid works. Many technical and perhaps unresolvable questions remain. And, at least as important, each organization has its own mandate, politics, institutional settings, and incentives. There may even be negative side effects in focusing on results, particularly if these need to be shown quickly. Finally, as the number of donors is increasing it is becoming even less likely that measures of success will be agreed upon.

There has been much effort toward aid harmonization (described in Chapter 5), and the MDGs form the most unified framework since aid as we know it began, just after the Second World War. The first has done much to enable more efficient partnerships, and the second to help enhance global support for international development and provide overall indicators for progress in development. But the future of these efforts is not as clear-cut as some of the more optimistic writings on the Paris Consensus (see Chapter 6) suggest. I hope that readers understand the challenges that exist and have obtained insight into the variety of aid agencies and approaches. In conclusion, this chapter describes major challenges the aid industry will face over the coming years.

Will Aid Become Irrelevant?

As discussed in Chapter 1, some people have questioned the relevance of aid. In the context of globalization, particularly increases in international trade and migration, will aid still provide added value? Are the postwar institutions, perhaps, unable to adapt to the new global environments? As countries like China and India are doing so well, with very little aid, what rationale exists for the large and still growing aid programs? Even these countries are rapidly expanding their aid programs. Should aid focus on the "bottom billion"—the forty or so countries where aid is arguably crucial to escape the poverty trap? It is possible that the kind of aid might need to be very different from what it currently is (Collier 2007).

The current wave of interest in international development aid and the way it has passed the "time of crisis for international development cooperation" (Degnbol-Martinussen and Engberg-Pedersen 2005, xiii) are no reason for complacency regarding the relevance of aid. It is quite possible that another period of "aid fatigue" such as that in the early 1990s, will arrive. The US interest in aid since 9/11 is very welcome, but it may prove transitory as the role of aid in the security and reconstruction agenda comes under increased scrutiny or interest simply wanes, as it has before. National domestic interest in aid is deeply political and hence subject to change. The impact of the current economic depressions on commitments to aid is yet unknown. While there is strong and continued interest in the consensus-democracies of Nordic countries, French and UK systems may be more volatile, although in the UK there is a reasonable expectation that even with a change in government, aid will retain the important position that it has held since 1997.

There is no evidence that the aid industry will become redundant in the foreseeable future, and under President Obama the United States may also become a stronger supporter of international aid efforts and institutions. National politics are increasingly interdependent on the global scale and ascribing an increasingly important role to the aid industry. At present, the amounts of money involved, the number of players (including those who move from being recipients to being donors), public interest, and the number of students of international development are continuing to grow. In fact, the increased number of agents in the industry is one of its main challenges.

Increasing Amounts of Aid and Number of Donors

There are currently two trends in the industry. First, there are strong voices for the harmonization of aid, which have resulted in what is known as the Paris Consensus, and for more multilateral approaches to aid. This trend makes the entirely credible argument that donors need to work together to support plans for development that are formulated by the recipient government in consultation with its citizens. The fact that these ideas have been agreed upon—it might be too optimistic to state this represents a consensus—is a sign that the aid industry is concerned about its outcomes, prepared to take lessons from the past seriously, and is willing to take significant steps to change its way of operating.

Second, the number of donors is increasing, and so are total financial aid flows (even though few countries are achieving the commitment of 0.7 percent of GNI), both because the old players are increasing funding and because newcomers like China and the various foundations are putting in significant amounts. These newcomers do not immediately join the old clubs, and they may not want to, partly for technical and partly for political reasons. When they do, they will change the club rules, but, as with all existing clubs, there will be resistance to this. The approaches of the newer donors may be complementary to those of the older ones, but they may also conflict; for example, the focus of China's aid on infrastructure is generally regarded as very welcome, because this has been an area that the old donors have tended to neglect, but China's insistence on noninterference can be at odds with the old donors' emphasis on promoting good governance as a precondition for development.

Perhaps the main challenge to the industry is not the trends themselves, but the need to recognize that they exist. Insisting on donor coordination if only some of the donors are joining the debate may not be very fruitful. It may hamper redefining the process in terms of the ways in which aid is provided and even in terms of the way the international community understands how development and poverty reduction happen. While many recipient countries are committed to the processes of harmonization, donors need to be aware of its political nature and the likelihood that national and international changes will redefine the conditions in which these debates happen. Perhaps surprisingly, the World Bank may have been among the first to recognize this by realizing that it needs China more than China needs the World Bank, and by appointing a Chinese scholar as its chief economist in early 2008. Recent discussions about the G20 and reform of IFIs suggest the changes are taking place ever more rapidly.

Need versus Capacity

Though there are some questions about how much additional aid has been provided since the commitments for debt relief were articulated, and history has shown that it is not very likely that many countries will provide 0.7 percent of their GNI, there is little doubt that total amounts of aid were increasing, at least till the start of the 2008–9 economic crisis. Even at stagnant percentages the total amounts were increasing, while the number of recipients have been declining as major countries like India and China move from being recipients to donors.

One of the big debates in the industry is and will probably remain whether this additional aid could be spent in ways that remain or become increasingly accountable. Views on this are diametrically opposed. On the one hand, there are groups of economists looking at macro indicators of aid and economic growth showing that aid works. Advocates—like Jeffrey Sachs, who stresses how hugely under-funded health systems are in countries like Kenya—reject arguments that increases should be conditional on improved governance. But events in Kenya in late 2007 and early 2008 showed how difficult it is to sustain such arguments and that the aid agencies are not neutral to national politics. There are the many new initiatives that cover new niches—for example, the Global Fund and the Millennium Challenge Account—and put significant money behind countries' good or improved conditions of governance. Arguments like Collier's (2007) about the way aid needs to be restructured are of interest but do not give guidance on how additional aid can be spent.

On the other hand, there are those who argue that one cannot prove aid causes growth rather than the other way around, or that macro analyses cannot be relied on. Potentially influential people like Easterly have provided a convincing though also debatable argument that grand planning is misguided. He argues for smaller and more experimental approaches, which probably do not allow for the large increases in amounts of aid. The growing literature on new aid modalities like budget support is not unequivocally proving that the right approach has been found. And if there is increasing pressure for showing that aid works, in a technical or more populist sense, this is also likely to push the industry to smaller projects and programs.

Probably the biggest challenge in this debate is focused on what has been called absorptive capacity, which summarizes a complexity of both technical and political preconditions for aid to be effective in reducing poverty. The main dilemma was already implicit in the aid effectiveness debate and research, which showed that aid worked where good policies exist. Of course, many of the countries with many poor people do not have those good policies. Though the aid industry now has a much better understanding of the importance of good policies, or governance, for development and poverty reduction, it has—at the same time—learned that it is extremely difficult to change policies. And while there are some cases where large amounts of funding have been put behind supporting governments—for example, those emerging from war—it is not clear that there are enough such cases to warrant large increases of aid. The different modalities of new donors will only complicate this equation.

Is Aid about Poverty or Development?

With the simultaneous changes in the World Bank and bilateral organizations during the 1990s, the aid industry has become firmly focused on poverty reduction, so much so that newcomers to aid organizations now find it hard to imagine the situation in which poverty reduction was only one of a handful of objectives, as it was in the UK before the change in government in 1997. With the agreements on the MDGs and increasing pressure to show that aid is or can be effective, the aid industry is increasingly measured against specific and increasingly well-marked trends in well-being.

This is mostly good news, and for most in the aid industry the main challenge is to defend this against other motives. But there are also challenges about the focus itself. First, a focus on reaching the poorest may skew aid support to directly identifiable outcomes rather than to the broader institutions that are required for a country's development, and on effectiveness rather than human rights, or on mainstreaming gender at the risk of losing sight of the need to transform institutional rules. The focus on primary education has been a clear example. Based on thinking and research that showed primary education had high rates of return, and that primary education would benefit the poor, a strong focus on primary education has dominated since the 1990s. This has tended to ignore higher education, and it has become increasingly clear that higher education systems—which often suffered during the 1980s period of adjustment—are also a central element for a country's development. The key roles donors have played in social-sector debates, moreover, have limited the ability of countries to develop their own traditions of and approaches to social policies (de Haan 2007).

Second, the focus on poverty can lead to a focus on *targeted* poverty interventions, the kinds of projects that we described in Chapter 4. Most aid agencies recognize that this needs to be balanced by support for broader institutions and conditions that enable sustained poverty reduction, such as economic growth, investment climate, and so on. But some observers have argued that this focus on poverty also narrows down a development agenda, at the cost of support to more inclusive institutions, or of a rights-based approach that emphasizes access to services and policy processes for the entire population. The focus on MDGs has given a clearer direction to the aid industry in terms of where to aim its efforts, but to some this also has led to a loss of emphasis on global social justice, which was equally important in the summit from which the MDGs emerged.

Aid Is and Always Has Been Political

The role of politics is raised here merely as an observation; the main challenge is in realizing its reality. The aid industry is not only about funding for development or poverty reduction, but also part of the international politics between North and South, and South and South. As described in this book, while part of aid is allocated based on ideas about aid effectiveness—variously defined—part of it is politically determined, and some agencies are very explicit about the need for aid departments to be close to foreign-policy objectives in order to maintain political support. The role of politics also implies that directions in the industry will continue to follow immediate interests and the beliefs of individual politicians, making the path of the aid industry at times feel like a roller-coaster ride.

What this implies is that to assess aid purely on its technical impact is important, particularly to increase its accountability, but provides insufficient insight into the aid industry. Because the aid industry has had and will continue to have multiple objectives, it is important to continue to see technical assessments in the political context. This makes an informed advocacy by external agencies ever more important, to help lend force to the aim to ensure that the aid industry—within its political margins—continues to be steered in the direction of global justice and becomes a stronger part of an international framework for promoting this. It is a very imperfect instrument, but one of the best available.

The average voter knows very little about what aid does and has little base to judge claims made by either official aid agencies or those who criticize them. Even students in international development know little about the political parties' policies and manifestos on aid. This is all the more important because the aid industry is almost unaccountable to its beneficiaries—unlike, say, a national ministry that provides health services. A better informed public debate is essential to keep pushing the industry in the right direction.

In Conclusion

In 1998, in a confession that started much of the work on aid effectiveness that we discussed in the Chapter 8, the World Bank stated:

> Foreign aid has at times been a spectacular success. . . . Foreign aid played a significant role . . . contributing ideas about development policy, training for public policymakers, and finance to support reform and an expansion of public services. Foreign aid has also transformed entire sectors. . . . On the flip side, foreign aid has also been, at times, an unmitigated failure. . . . Consider Tanzania, where donors poured a colossal $2 billion into building roads over 20 years. Did the road network improve? No. For lack of maintenance, roads often deteriorated faster than they were built. . . . Foreign

> aid in different times and different places has thus been highly
> effective, totally ineffective, and everything in between.
> (World Bank 1998)

Since that report was written, much discussion has taken place about aid effectiveness and serious attempts have been made to reduce the numbers of failures, but the statement is still a candid assessment of what the industry has achieved. This book has tried to show why the aid industry does what it does and to provide a basis for understanding the reasons for both failures and successes, and why success has not been more commonplace. The book has given examples of things that have worked and perhaps convinced readers that some aid money has been well spent, that it has improved things that would not have improved in the absence of aid. I think we can be optimistic about a continued interest in the aid industry and increasing technical capacity to contribute to solving problems. But there are also many doubts about what the industry has done. This is due to several factors: overall assessment of such a complex venture is difficult; idealism can get ahead of good policy; the political nature of development is often neglected; and foreign policy and commercial motives can get the upper hand. This book does not provide a final assessment, but it is to be hoped that it has given its readers grounds for making their own assessments.

Notes

1. Why Is Aid Contested?

1. As an illustration, in October 2007 the John Templeton Foundation hosted an electronic exchange of ideas on the question of whether money will solve African problems, highlighting such divergent views. Similar differences in views on what the Word Bank should, can, and cannot achieve are described in Mallaby 2005.

2. In Easterly's words, Sachs "thinks aid can end poverty and I think it cannot. . . . The end of poverty comes about for home-grown reasons, as domestic reformers grope their way towards more democracy, cleaner and more accountable government, and free markets" (quoted in Harman 2007).

3. ODA dropped from $35.8 billion in 2005 to $35.1 billion in 2006. The DAC and World Bank recognized that 2005 had been a peak year, following large-scale civil society advocacy and governments' attention.

4. OECD aid for the least developed countries fell by 20 percent in the 1990s, more than the overall aid decline (Browne 2007, 2). This percentage had increased significantly since the 1960s (Lancaster 2007, 39).

5. The formation of the Commission for Africa contributed to putting developing nations and particularly Africa on the map, as Thabo Mbeki stressed during Tony Blair's last official visit to the continent. Gordon Brown remained a strong advocate before he took over from Tony Blair, and he continued his advocacy, including advocacy at the World Economic Forum annual meeting in Davos in January 2008, and following the 2008 financial crisis.

6. UN Millennium Development Project 2005. Jeffrey Sachs, adviser to the UN secretary general—accompanied by rock star Bob Geldof and featured in a 2005 MTV special *The Diary of Angelina Jolie and Dr. Jeffrey Sachs in Africa*—published his call to increasing commitment to aid in order to eradicate illnesses and promote agriculture particularly in Africa (Sachs 2005).

7. On the other hand, Tony Killick (2005), in the same *IDS Bulletin*, whose title is "Increased Aid: Minimizing Problems, Maximizing Gains," argues that additional aid will divert attention from improving the quality and the effectiveness of aid. James Manor in that issue sums up the arguments for and against increasing aid: views continue to differ around questions of absorptive capacity, possibilities for governance reform, likelihood that aid will be delivered in coordinated manner, donors' "unhelpful habits," and continued questions around aid dependency, issues we come back to later.

8. Opinion polls show that US citizens overestimate the amount of aid given by their government by as much as 15 times according to one and 40 times according to another poll (quoted in Bolton 2007, 154–55).

9. See Riddell 2007: Chapter 7; and www.oecd.org on Public Opinion and Engagement for Development.

10. Arvind Subramanian, with Raghuram G. Rajan, also wrote a 2005 IMF working paper titled "What Undermined Aid's Impact on Growth."

11. The reference to buzzwords in development practices is from an article by Cornwall and Brock (2005) and is a theme subsequently taken up in a special issue of *Development in Practice* (Cornwall 2007).

12. Many of the authors in this strand of "deconstructive" commentary are anthropologists. A related anthropological approach focuses on describing "the interaction of ideas and relationships in development arena" (Lewis and Mosse 2006, 5). Uma Kothari and Martin Minogue, quoting Ignacy Sachs, argue "there has been a failure of the postwar development project" (2002, 2).

13. Interviews at the Swedish development agency found two-thirds of staff felt that disbursement rates were actively monitored in the day-to-day business (Ostrom et al. 2002); this study is an explicit attempt to document the agency's internal incentives and how this affects aid effectiveness and particularly sustainability (see also Ebrahim and Herz 2007, 6).

14. For example, in May 2008 DAC expanded to thirty-nine the list of countries that will receive untied aid; See "DAC Chair Announces Agreement to Untie Aid to More Countries," May 22. Available at www.oecd.org.

15. The OECD DAC statistics provide information about the status of tying aid, with Greece and Canada having the highest levels of tied aid among countries that provided information (DAC 2007, Table 23 and Table 24 of the Statistical Annex). But other examples of tied aid remain. The ORET/MILIEV Programme, a combination of grants and loans, development, and environment objectives in partner countries, helps Dutch companies find access; and Swedish contractors tend to benefit from Swedish aid (Ostrom et al. 2002).

16. John Degnbol-Martinussen and Poul Engberg-Pedersen (2005, 10–11) describe moral and humanitarian motives, and critique of the moral obligation, in more detail.

2. The Aid Industry Defined

1. Online at the oecd.org website. DAC is the OECD's specialized committee that handles development cooperation. Data on aid flows of its more than twenty members are available online and in the annual *Development Cooperation Report*. Members also periodically review the amount and quality of aid programs.

2. Mary Anderson (1999) discusses whether aid can support peace, or war; she describes a number of case studies of aid projects in conflict situations.

3. This is so even though in many organizations the implementation of emergency or humanitarian aid is institutionally separated from that of development aid.

It is now often argued that preparedness for disasters should be part of all development efforts. Good sources of information are the ALNAP (www.alnap.org) and ProVention Consortium (www.proventionconsortium.org) websites.

4. Different practices are described in OECD DAC (2007), and Brainard (2007a, 54). In each country these organizational models are constantly evolving, resulting in, for example, the creation of a separate ministry in the UK in 1997 and the decision in the United States in 2006 to bring the director of foreign assistance formally within the State Department structure.

5. Amounts of aid from China are unclear. China does not provide these figures to OECD; the aid program used to be considered a state secret; and possibly even the ministry that has the main responsibility for aid does not know the total figures, because aid is provided by various ministries and agreed upon through Chinese embassies abroad. As of 2008, the direction of organization of the Chinese aid program was unclear, and political considerations appeared to leave it in a relatively uncoordinated state. According to Kurlantzick (2007, 202), Beijing officials had expressed an interest in building a Chinese version of a permanent aid bureaucracy like USAID; Chinese officials also visited the UK and Canada to study its agencies.

6. The 2008 US presidential election gave rise to a lively debate to try to inform future policies (Lancaster 2008), and the debates have continued since.

7. Natsios's article describes the Congressional restrictions on aid and provides a number of recommendations to improve the partnership with Congress. Judith Tendler described the working of USAID, also highlighting the many restrictions on and unpopularity of aid (Tender 1975).

8. Amsden adds that its negative impact was limited because "developing countries never got hooked on it and . . . could go their own way," referring to relatively open-ended US trade policies from 1950 through the 1980s.

9. In August 2007 the US NGO CARE decided to forego $45 million a year in federal financing for food aid, as it believed the system was inefficient and possibly harmful to the people it aims to support.

10. President Bush, speech at the Inter-American Development Bank (IADB), March 14, 2002. Available at http://www.whitehouse.gov. See also http://www.mcc.gov and http://www.cgdev.org.

11. Swedish approaches to international development, including the implications of the political move toward the center-right in 2006, are discussed in the first of a series on development issues in European countries by *The Broker* (Lammers 2008).

12. Sweden has passed a bill that commits all government departments to contribute to development in eleven policy areas. According to a coalition of NGOs, which has composed a "coherence barometer," the record so far is mixed (Lammers 2008).

13. The evaluation department of the ministry, for example, carried out a major evaluation of policies in Africa (Ministerie van Buitenlandse Zaken, 2008).

14. Recent changes in Canadian aid have been discussed in the special November 2007 issue of the *Canadian Journal of Development Studies*. The classic on Canadian aid is D. R. Morrison 1998.

15. Villageization was a regional targeted anti-poverty intervention, providing inputs, education, and health to the remote rural poor, but in badly understood contexts. Uma Kothari (2006) describes the continuity between colonial and post-colonial institutions.

16. The three main developing regions all have institutions similar to the World Bank. The IADB was established first, in 1959, to provide loans and technical cooperation to development projects (to "contribute to the acceleration of the process of economic and social development of the regional developing member countries, individually and collectively") and became a model for the other regional institutions. The IADB is owned by forty-seven member countries; it is governed by boards of governors and of executive directors. As in the World Bank, voting power is based on financial contributions, but the charter ensures the position of majority stockholder for the borrowing member countries as a group.

17. In 2006 loans outstanding amounted to $28 billion to seventy-four countries, of which $6 billion to fifty-six were on concessional terms. Concessional lending consists of the Poverty Reduction and Growth Facility, the Exogenous Shocks Facility, the Heavily Indebted Poor Countries Initiative, and the Multilateral Debt Relief Initiative, often linked to PRSPs.

18. This includes the nomination of candidates for the Bank's president, which, with the appointment of Wolfowitz in 2005, became highly controversial. Like decisions at the IMF, Bank decisions are in the form of informal agreements rather than written in the constitution, and thus are dominated by the main economic powers.

19. According to Mark Malloch Brown, the UN "was not corrupt but incompetent. Its failures were supervisory and operational. There was inadequate auditing and in many cases little-to-no attempt to rectify the faults that were found in audit" (2007, 2).

20. The new secretary-general, Ban Ki-moon, has been credited with playing an important role in the Darfur crisis, in climate-change agreements, and in helping to convince the government of Myanmar to open its door to international assistance and personnel.

21. Bolton, a strong opponent of multilateralism, wanted the UN to switch to voluntary contributions and to make voting dependent on a country's financial contribution to the UN. More recently, US policy has became more supportive of the UN, a trend reinforced under President Obama.

22. While this study is presented as independent, it seems to contain little critical reflection on the UNDP.

23. The International Committee of the Red Cross (ICRC) is a neutral organization, set up in 1863, dedicated to protect the lives and dignity and to support victims of war and internal violence.

24. The first annual International Labour Conference adopted the first six Conventions, and in less than two years, sixteen Conventions and eighteen Recommendations were adopted. Convention No. 87 on the freedom of association and the right to organize was adopted in 1948.

25. DFID started a new civil society program in Orissa, managed by a Delhi-based NGO. DFID found hundreds of NGOs in Orissa bidding for funds and rumors that individuals were offering services to write proposals.

26. These are data from Giving USA, which monitors US donations (cited in *The Guardian*, September 28, 2007).

27. "Philanthropy Oscars," *The Economist* (September 22, 2007), 69.

28. There are cases where aid flows seem to be determined by the low-income status of the recipient but are also the result of historical links, such as Belgian aid to the Congo.

3. The Evolution in Thinking about Aid and International Development

1. This anthropologist was Gloria Davis, who described the history of social development in a 2004 World Bank paper; a few years before Davis was appointed, the first sociologist, Michael Cernea, was hired by the World Bank (Davis 2004).

2. Amsden describes the period 1950–1980 as the "First American Empire," which favored "trade, not aid," with much flexibility in allowing deviations from free trade and in the promotion of alternative development models (2007, chap. 3).

3. The right to development was finally adopted as a UN General Assembly resolution in 1986 (Uvin 2007, 598).

4. See, for example, Lin 2007. Lin became the World Bank chief economist in 2008.

5. The affordability and also the potential impact of education on economic growth rather than the intrinsic value of education became a central concern.

6. For example, Ha-Joon Chang claims that Northern "bad Samaritans" continue to provide simplistic and ideological advice that often serves the donor countries' interests (Chang 2007).

7. For a description of the use of the concept of social capital in the World Bank and how this helped to form a bridge for its social scientists with other bank staff, see Bebbington et al. 2006. Many critiques of the concept and its use have been written, for example, Harriss 2002.

8. The international comparison is far from easy. A critical factor in this international comparison is the availability of comparable price data, which recently has undergone major revisions, leading to big changes in estimates of numbers of poor people. For a discussion of this in the context of China, see Ravallion et al. 2008.

9. Eyoh and Sandbrook label the new approach a "pragmatic neo-liberal development model" and highlight the similarities with the "Third Way" promoted by Tony Blair and Bill Clinton (2003, 228). The approach found expression in the CDF promoted by World Bank President Wolfensohn.

10. Lynn Squire was among the people who had helped to bring these data sets together. He later set up the Global Development Network.

11. For a quantitative analysis of key words used in UK white papers between 1960 and 2006, see Alfini and Chambers 2007.

12. Edward Anderson, personal communication. This finding came out of work within a short-lived initiative (2004 to 2006) called the Inter-Regional Inequality Facility, which aimed to fund activities to strengthen South-South dialogue on inequality. For more information on this initiative, see its website.

4. Development Projects

1. Tendler quotes Mason and Asher's *World Bank since Bretton Woods* and an article by Baum in *Finance and Development* in 1970 (Tendler 1975, 87).

2. Grove and Zwi (2008) propose an additional tool to address these concerns: a Health and Peace Building Filter for health programs in settings of conflict.

3. A short summary of the World Bank's evaluation of the Fourth Project on Rural Roads is available at www.worldbank.org.

4. The success of rural roads in contributing to poverty reduction is described in the 2004 World Bank document entitled "Reducing Poverty, Sustaining Growth: Scaling Up Poverty Reduction."

5. IDA 2007. During the 1990s the World Bank's infrastructure investment lending declined by 50 percent. The decline in lending by international institutions was matched by a decline in government spending; public investment in Latin America's three largest countries, for example, fell from 10 percent of GDP in the mid-1970s, to around 2 percent by 2000 (Kessler 2005).

6. The Green Revolution had less impact in Africa than elsewhere. The Gates and Rockefeller Alliance for Green Revolution in Africa aims to address this; here the lead is taken by the private sector rather than the public sector, which led the 1960s Green Revolution.

7. An enormous amount of literature is available on the Grameen Bank. For a good introduction, see World Neighbors, 1994.

8. See, for example, these World Bank documents: De Silva and Sum 2008, World Bank 2002, and Rawlings et al. 2004. External and critical studies include Cornia 1999 and Tendler 2000.

9. An IMF paper by Cordella and Dell'Ariccia (2003) uses an econometric model to show that program aid is more effective than project aid, because governments can reallocate money when receiving support, for example, specifically to build schools.

10. See, for example, World Bank 2007, which documents partnership for innovation in China. Available at www.worldbank.org.

5. Hard-nosed Development

1. The literature on structural adjustment is huge. For a short overview, see David Simon 2002.

2. Tony Killick, one of the main authorities in this field, writes: "Generally, conditionality has not been effective in improving economic policies. . . . It has failed to achieve its objectives and therefore lacks practical justification. . . . Over-reliance on conditionality wasted much public money [and] the obstacles to adequate improvement are probably intractable" (Killick 2002, 483). International civil society organizations continue to criticize IFIs approaches to conditionalities (see www.eurodad.org).

3. An exception to this was funding for education. Increased funding for primary education was seen as desirable, but in addition to improving efficiency this was

because increased state funding would leverage additional funding from the central government.

4. For a range of "African voices" on adjustment, see Mkandawire and Soludo 2002.

5. Subsequent key World Bank documents include *Governance: The World Bank's Experience* (World Bank 1994) and research papers such as "Governance Matters" (Kaufman et al. 1999). In the UK, Foreign Secretary Douglas Hurd in a 1990 speech launched the idea that governance was central for development cooperation (Jenkins 2002, 486), and its status was elevated by DFID's third white paper since 1997 (DFID 2006).

6. In providing grants or loans, donors are also concerned about fiduciary risk, that is, whether donor funds are properly accounted for, are used for the intended purposes, and represent value for the money.

7. See IDA Resource Allocation Index 2007, available at www.worldbank.org.

8. This report stressed that technical efforts needed to be accompanied by a strong and persistent political will in both developed and developing countries. The head of the IMF added a note of caution, observing that slow progress in reforms often reflects lack of institutional capacity rather than lack of political will.

9. Concerns about the need for better understanding of politics had also emerged in PRSPs (see Chapter 6), which some saw as depoliticized documents, and the extensive processes of consultation that often increased the space of civil society tended to neglect the legislature.

10. *Budget support* can be defined as a form of program aid to support a plan or policy program developed by the recipient government. Budget support is channeled directly into the financial management, accountability, and procurement system of the recipient country. *General budget support* is financial support to the budget as a whole, and *sector budget support* implies support to a particular sector, typically a sector-wide program.

11. An exception is the Agriculture Investment Programme in Kenya.

12. A number of agencies have argued for a dramatic increase in aid efforts in social protection, too, though this has not as yet resulted in sector initiatives on the scale of those in the health and education sectors.

6. Country-led Approaches and Donor Coordination

1. James D. Wolfensohn and Stanley Fischer, joint note, April 5, 2000.

2. Kofi Annan, letter to James Wolfensohn, May 11, 2001. The World Bank and the IMF also were quick to emphasize the complementarity between CDF and PRSP approaches, though institutionally there was some competition between the initiatives.

3. World Bank, Operations Evaluation Department, 2003. The management response was also published and supported many of the conclusions and recommendations made. Available worldbank.org.

4. The PRSP approach gave rise to large number of publications, including an ODI monitoring web page on behalf of donors (http://www.prspsynthesis.org/), and many from NGOs. Interest started to wane somewhat after 2003.

5. A similar critique has been expressed regarding the CDF. Owusu (2003) argues that this approach settled a longstanding debate over development strategies in favor of neo-liberalism and global integration.

6. For a good discussion that emphasizes that the process of participation was strongly led by government, see Stewart and Wang 2003.

7. Cheru, for example, emphasizes the weak state capacity in Africa as a hindrance for poverty analysis, implementation of programs, monitoring, and "co-ordination of economic policy formulation and implementation [which have] been hampered by constant inter-ministerial infighting, as well as by the disconnect between key sector ministries and ministries of finance" (Cheru 2006, 369).

8. Some observers of Latin America (see Dijkstra 2005) have argued that the PRSP approach should be abandoned; in the view of Booth, Grigsby, and Toranzo, emphasis should be put on donors' alignment and harmonization, a central part of a PRSP approach, in a way that allows strategic support to specific initiatives (2006).

9. OECD DAC 2003a. These guidelines, approved in the Rome Declaration, offer a set of "good practices" for donor-government engagement, inter-donor co-ordination, and intra-donor reform. The goal is to simplify and harmonize procedures, reducing costs and enhancing efficiency.

10. Third High Level Forum on Aid Effectiveness, Accra Agenda for Action, endorsed 4 September 2008, to accelerate and deepen implementation of the Paris Declaration on Aid Effectiveness. Available on the oecd.org website.

11. OECD DAC 2007. See also the Eurodad report *Turning the Tables*, which emphasizes similar points and highlights the common critique that support still comes with too many conditionalities.

7. Development's Poor Cousins

1. According to its website, the United Nations Environment Programme (UNEP) is mandated to "provide leadership and encourage partnership in caring for the environment by inspiring, informing, and enabling nations and peoples to improve their quality of life without compromising that of future generations."

2. I believe there is no clear argument for including improvements for poor urban (and not rural) inhabitants under the environment MDG. This seems largely the result of a desire to limit the number of MDGs and difficulty in including urban poverty under other MDGs.

3. The policy and processes are described in Operational Policy (OP)/Bank Procedure (BP) 4.01: Environmental Assessment, an umbrella policy for the environmental safeguard policies that include, among others, natural habitats, forests, and dam safety. Available at http://web.worldbank.org.

4. Full project documents and assessments are available at www.worldbank.org.

5. Seguino (2006) has used this survey to analyze global trends in gender norms, and how they relate to other gender indicators. Survey available at http://www.worldvaluessurvey.org.

6. The 1945 UN Charter recognized equality between men and women as a global goal.

7. Quoted in the *Report of the Economic and Social Council for 1997*, A/52/3, 18 September 1997, IV/I/A, 2.

8. The following material is based on OECD DAC 2002.

9. Seguino, on the basis of the World Values Survey, highlights global progress toward valuation of gender equality, hypothesizing economic growth does contribute to this. On the other hand, MDGs that are closely related to gender equality, such as women's health, tend to be the ones where progress is slowest (Seguino 2006).

10. Albert Mayer was the key pioneer behind the Uttar Pradesh project, which became a model for other community development projects in India. More information is available at www.lib.uchicago.edu.

11. For a brief descirption of Cernea's and Chambers's contributions to development, see Simon 2006, 66–78; a 2007 conference at IDS Sussex celebrated twenty years of "Farmer First."

12. Research at IDS Sussex focuses on this new wave of participation, which it sees to be "deepening" democracy (see IDS *Policy Briefing* 34 [March 2007], available at www.oecd.org).

13. See, for example, the FAO website on participation at www.fao.org.

14. Robb (2001) describes a series of arguments for civic engagement in PRSPs, including enhancing ownership, accountability, and civil society capacity building.

15. See the short note by Thanh (2005, 78), who led community consultations in two provinces; the experience in Vietnam is described in some detail in Shanks and Turk 2003.

16. Participatory approaches are also central to much of the literature on approaches to reconstruction after disasters and disaster risk reduction (see www.alnap.org; www.proventionconsortium.org).

17. The UK-based organization ITAD was responsible for working with three provinces to develop and implement the participatory approach (see www.itad.com/PRCDP/).

18. For a collection of essays on the downside of participatory approaches, see Cooke and Kothari 2001. For an optimistic assessment of participatory approaches, see Chambers 2005.

19. Such projects are usually part of the governance agenda. For a discussion of approaches to strengthen justice systems in order to reduce poverty, see Sage and Woolcock 2007.

20. CARE International, quoted in Amnesty International, *Our Rights, Our Future* (4 September 2005), 11.

8. What Works in the Aid Industry? What Doesn't? How Do We Know?

1. An interesting exception is a study by the UK National Audit Office (NAO). The NAO focuses on auditing government offices' accounts, but also reports on the

efficiency with which taxpayers' money is spent. Reports are available at www.nao.org.uk.

2. It is not uncommon for agencies to look for "friendly" evaluations and to influence studies by the choice of consultants.

3. The best resource for this is the Q2 website at http://www.q-squared.ca/.

Reference List

ADB (Asian Development Bank). 2007. *Effect of Microfinance Operations on Poor Rural Households and the Status of Women.* Special Evaluation Study. Operations Evaluation Department. Manila: ADB. Available at www.adb.org.

Adelman, Irma. The Role of Government in Economic Development. In Tarp 2000, 48-79.

Alesina, Alberto, and David Dollar. 2000. Who Gives Foreign Aid to Whom and Why? *Journal of Economic Growth* 5, no. 1: 33-63.

Alfini, Naomi, and Robert Chambers. 2007. Words Count: Taking a Count of the Changing Language of British Aid. *Development in Practice* 17, no. 4-5 (2007): 492-504.

Amsden, Alice H. 2007. *Escape From Empire: The Developing World's Journey through Heaven and Hell.* Cambridge, Mass: The MIT Press.

Anderson, Mary. 1999. *Do No Harm: How Aid Can Support Peace—or War.* London: Lynne Rienner Publishers.

Antunes, Marta, and Jorge O. Romano. Combating Infant Malnutrition— An Experience of Networking in the Social Struggle for the Human Right to Food and Sustainable Nutrition. In Gready and Ensor 2005, 131-43.

Aslam, Abid. 2008 (January). Watchdog Faults IMF Loan Conditionalities. Available at www.globalpolicy.org.

Baker, Judy L. 2000. *Evaluating the Impact of Development Projects on Poverty: A Handbook for Practitioners.* Series Directions in Development. Washington DC: World Bank.

Banerjee, Abhijit Vinayak. 2007. *Making Aid Work.* A Boston Review Book. Cambridge, MA: The MIT Press.

Banerjee, Abhijit, Angus Deaton, Nora Lustig, and Ken Rogoff. 2006. An Evaluation of World Bank Research, 1998–2005. Washington DC: World Bank. Available at worldbank.org.

Barder, Owen. Reforming Development Assistance: Lessons from the UK Experience. In Brainard 2007b, 277-320.

Bass, Stephen, Hannah Reid, David Satterthwaite, and Paul Steele, eds. 2005. *Reducing Poverty and Sustaining the Environment: The Politics of Local Engagement.* London: Earthscan.

Batliwala, Srilatha, and David Brown. 2006. *Transnational Civil Society: An Introduction*. Bloomfield, CT: Kumarian Press.

Bebbington, Anthony J., Michael Woolcock, Scott Guggenheim, and Elizabeth A. Olson. 2006. *The Search for Empowerment: Social Capital as Idea and Practice at the World Bank*. Bloomfield CT: Kumarian Press.

Berkman, Steve. *The World Bank and the Gods of Lending*. Sterling, VA: Kumarian Press, 2008.

Binnendijk, Annette. 2001 (May). Results-based Management in Donor Agencies. DAC Working Party on Evaluation. Available at www.oecd.org.

Blackburn, James, Robert Chambers, and John Gaventa. 2000. *Mainstreaming Participation in Development*. OED Working Paper Series No. 10. Washington DC: World Bank, Operations Evaluation Department.

Bolton, Giles. 2007. *Poor Story: An Insider Uncovers How Globalisation and Good Intentions Have Failed the World's Poor*. London: Ebury Press.

Booth, David, A. Grigsby, and C. Toranzo. 2006. Politics and Poverty Reduction Strategies: Lessons from Latin American HIPCs. ODI Working Paper No. 262. London: ODI.

Brainard, Lael. 2007a. Organizing U.S. Foreign Assistance to Meet Twenty-First Century Challenges. In Brainard 2007b, 233-66.

———, ed. 2007b. *Security by Other Means: Foreign Assistance, Global Poverty, and American Leadership*. Washington DC: Center for Strategic and International Studies, Brookings Institution Press.

Brandt, Willy. 1980. *North-South: A Programme for Survival*. London: Pan Books.

Brown, Mark Malloch. 2007. Holmes Lecture: Can the U.N. Be Reformed? Annual Meeting of the Academic Council on the UN System (ACUNS), June 7.

Brown, A., M. Foster, A. Norton, and F. Naschold. 2001. The Status of Sector Wide Approaches. ODI Working Paper 142, London: ODI.

Browne, Stephen. 2007. *Aid to Fragile States: Do Donors Help Or Hinder?* Discussion Paper No. 2007/01. Helsinki: UNU-WIDER.

Budlender, Debbie. 2000. The Political Economy of Women's Budgets in the South. *World Development* 28, no. 7: 1365-78.

———. 2003. Gender Budgets and Beyond: Feminist Fiscal Policy in the Context of Globalisation. *Gender and Development* 11, no. 1: 15-24.

Burnside, Craig, and David Dollar. 2000. Aid, Policies, and Growth. *American Economic Review* 90, no. 4 (September): 847-68.

Buvini, Mayra, and Jacqueline Mazza. 2008. Addressing Exclusion: Social Policy Perspectives from Latin America and the Caribbean. In Dani and de Haan 2008, 123-44.

CAFOD, Christian Aid, Trócaire. No date. Monitoring Government Policies: A Toolkit for Civil Society Organisations in Africa. London: CAFOD. Available at www.internationalbudget.org.

Cassen, Robert, et al. 1986. *Does Aid Work?* Oxford: Clarendon.

Cedergren, Jan. 2007. We're Working on It: Development Partners' Efforts for Effective Aid. *Poverty in Focus* (October): 26-27. Brasilia: International Poverty Centre. Available online.

Chambers, Robert. 2005. *Ideas for Development.* London: Earthscan.

Chambers, Robert, and Gordon Conway. 1992. Sustainable Rural Livelihoods: Practical Concepts for the Twenty-first Century. Discussion Paper 296. Brighton: IDS.

Chang, Ha-Joon. 2007. *Bad Samaritans: Rich Nations, Poor Policies, and the Threat to the Developing World.* London: Random House.

Chen, Martha, Renana Jhabvala, Ravi Kanbur, and Carol Richards, eds. 2007. *Membership-Based Organizations of the Poor.* London: Routledge.

Cheru, F. 2006. Building and Supporting PRSPs in Africa: What Has Worked Well So Far? What Needs Changing? *Third World Quarterly* 27, no. 2: 355-76.

Collier, Paul. 2007. *The Bottom Billion: Why the Poorest Countries Are Failing and What Can Be Done about It.* Oxford: Oxford University Press.

Collier, Paul, and David Dollar. 1999. Aid Allocation and Poverty Reduction. World Bank Policy Research Working Paper No. 2041. Washington DC: World Bank.

Collier, Paul, and N. Okonjo-Iweala (World Bank Task Force Leaders). 2002. World Bank Group Work in Low-Income Countries under Stress: A Task Force Report. Washington DC: World Bank.

Commission for Africa. 2005. *Our Common Interest: Report of the Commission for Africa.* London: Penguin Books. Available at www.commissionforafrica.org.

Commonwealth Secretariat. 1999. *Gender Budget Initiative.* London: Commonwealth Secretariat.

Cooke, Bill, and Uma. 2001. *Participation: The New Tyranny?* London: Zed Books.

Cordella, Tito, and Giovanni Dell'Ariccia. 2003. Budget Support Versus Project Aid. IMF Working Paper No. 03/88. Washington DC: IMF. Available at www.imf.org.

Cornia, Giovanni Andrea, Richard Jolly, and Frances Stewart. 1987. *Adjustment with a Human Face.* Oxford: Clarendon Press.

Cornwall, Andrea. 2007. Buzzwords and Fuzzwords: Deconstructing Development Discourse. *Development in Practice* 17, no. 4-5: 471-84.

Cornwall, Andrea, and Karen Brock. 2005. What Do Buzzwords Do for Development Policy? A Critical Look at "Participation," "Empowerment," and "Poverty Reduction." *Third World Quarterly* 26, no. 7: 1043-60.

DAC. 2006. The Netherlands: DAC Peer Review: Main Findings and Recommendations. Available at www.oecd.org.

————. 2007. Development Cooperation Report. Paris. Available at www.oecd.org.

Dani, Anis A., and A. de Haan. 2008. *Inclusive States: Social Policy and Structural Inequalities.* Washington DC: World Bank.

Das, Vidya. 2003. Kashipur: The Politics of Underdevelopment. *Economic and Political Weekly*, 4 January.

Davis, Gloria. 2004. A History of the Social Development Network in the World Bank. Social Development Paper No. 56. Washington DC: World Bank.

Degnbol-Martinussen, John, and Poul Engberg-Pedersen. 2005. *Aid: Understanding International Development Cooperation.* London: Zed Books.

De Haan, Arjan. 2007. *Reclaiming Social Policy: Globalization, Social Exclusion, and New Poverty Reduction Strategies.* Basingstoke: Palgrave Macmillan.

————. 2008. Disparities within India's Poorest Region: Why Do the Same Institutions Work Differently in Different Places? In *Institutional Pathways to Equity: Addressing Inequality Traps*, ed. Anthony Bebbington, Anis Dani, Arjan de Haan, and Michael Walton, 103-36. Washington DC: World Bank.

De Haan, Arjan, and Max Everest-Phillips. 2006. Can New Aid Modalities Handle Politics? Paper presented at WIDER Annual Conference, Helsinki, June.

Delgado, Christopher L. 1997. *Africa's Changing Agricultural Development Strategies.* IFPRI 2020 Brief 42. Washington DC: IFPRI. Available at www.ifpri.org.

Desai, Vandana. 2002. Role of Non-Governmental Organizations. In Desai and Potter 2002, 495-99.

Desai, Vandana, and Robert B. Potter, eds. 2002. *The Companion to Development Studies.* London: Hodder Arnold.

De Silva, S. and J-W. Sum. 2008. Social Funds as an Instrument of Social Protection: An Analysis of Lending Trends: FY 2000-2007. Social Protection Discussion Paper. Human Development Network Social Protection. Washington DC: World Bank.

De Soto, Hernando. 1986. *El Otro Sendero: La Revolución Informal.* Lima: Instituto Libertad y Democracia.

DFID. Annual. *Annual Report.* London: The Stationary Office.

————. 2000. Realising Human Rights for Poor People: Strategies for Achieving the International Development Targets. London: DFID.

————. 2006. *Eliminating World Poverty: Making Governance Work for the Poor*, London: The Stationary Office, 2006. Available at www.dfid.gov.uk.

Dijkstra, G. 2005. The PRSP Approach and the Illusion of Improved Aid Effectiveness: Lessons from Bolivia, Honduras and Nicaragua. *Development Policy Review* 23, no. 4: 443-64.

Dollar, David, and Aart Kraay. 2002. Growth *Is* Good for the Poor. *Journal of Economic Growth* 7, no. 3: 195-225.

Doriye, Joshua. 1992. Public Office and Private Gain: An Interpretation of the Tanzanian Experience. In Wuyts, Mackintosh, and Hewitt, 91-113.

Driscoll, R., with Alison Evans. 2005. Second-Generation Poverty Reduction Strategies: New Opportunities and Emerging Issues. *Development Policy Review* 23, no. 1: 5-25.

Easterly, William. 2006. *The White Man's Burden: Why the West's Efforts to Aid the Rest Have Done So Much Ill and So Little Good.* New York: Penguin Press.

Easterly, William, Ross Levine, and David Roodman. 2003. New Data. New Doubts: A Comment on Burnside and Dollar's "Aid, Policies, and Growth (2000)." Available at www.nyu.edu.

Ebrahim, Alnoor, and Steve Herz. 2007. Accountability in Complex Organizations: World Bank Responses to Civil Society. World Bank Working Paper 08/27. Available at www.globalpolicy.org.

Eurodad. 2008. Turning the Tables: Aid and Accountability under the Paris Framework. A Civil Society Report. Brussels: European Network on Debt and Development.

Eyben, Rosalind. 2008. Power, Mutual Accountability, and Responsibility in the Practice of International Aid: A Relational Approach. IDS Working Paper 305. Brighton: IDS.

Eyoh, Dickson, and Richard Sandbrook. 2003. Pragmatic Neo-liberalism and Just Development in Africa. In *States, Markets, and Just Growth: Development in the Twenty-first Century*, ed. A. Kohli, C. Moon, and G. Sörensen, 227-57. Tokyo: United Nations University Press.

Fasulo, Linda. 2003. *An Insider's Guide to the UN.* New Haven, CT: Yale University Press.

Filmer, Deon, and Norbert Schady. 2006. *Getting Girls into School: Evidence from a Scholarship Program in Cambodia.* Policy Research Working Paper 3910. Washington DC: World Bank.

Flickner, Charles. 2007. Removing Impediments to an Effective Partnership with Congress. In Brainard 2007b, 225-53.

Foster, Mike. 2000. New Approaches to Development Co-operation: What Can We Learn from Experiences with Implementing Sector Wide Approaches. ODI Working Paper 14. London: ODI.

Foster, Mike, and Jennifer Leavy. 2001. The Choice of Financial Aid Instruments. ODI Working Paper 158. London: ODI.

Fritz, Verena, and Alina Rocha Menocal. 2007. Development States in the New Millennium: Concepts and Challenges for a New Aid Agenda. *Development Policy Review* 25, no. 5: 531-52.

Gaspart, F., and J-P. Platteau. 2006. The Perverse Effect of Cheap Aid Money. Paper presented at the WIDER Conference, Helsinki, June.

Gready, Paul, and Jonathan Ensor, eds. 2005. *Reinventing Development? Translating Rights-Based Approaches from Theory into Practice.* London: Zed Books.

Grillo, Ralph. 2002. Anthropologists and Development. In Desai and Potter 2002, 54-60.

Grindle, Merilee. 2002. Good Enough Governance: Poverty Reduction and Reform in Developing Countries. Mimeo. Cambridge, MA: Kennedy School of Government, Harvard University.

———. 2007. Good Enough Governance Revisited. *Development Policy Review* 25, no. 5: 533-74.

Grove, Natalie J., and Anthony B. Zwi. 2008. Beyond the Log Frame: A New Tool for Examining Health and Peacebuilding Initiatives. *Development in Practice* 18, no. 1: 66-81.

Hancock, Graham. 1989. *Lords of Poverty.* London: Macmillan.

Harman, Danna. 2007. Is Western Aid Making a Difference in Africa? Two US Economists Debate the Value of Antipoverty Efforts. In *The Christian Science Monitor* (August). Available online.

Harriss, John. 2002. De-politicizing Development: World Bank and Social Capital. London: Anthem Press.

Hart, Keith. 1973. Informal Income Opportunities and Urban Employment in Ghana. *Journal of Modern African Studies* 11, no. 1: 61-89.

Hatton, Michael J., and Kent Schroeder. 2007. Results-based Management: Friend or Foe? *Development in Practice* 17, no. 3: 426-32.

Hedger, Edward, and Zainab Kizilbash Agha. 2007. *Reforming Public Financial Management When the Politics Aren't Right: A Proposal.* ODI Opinion No. 89. London, ODI. Available at www.odi.org.uk.

Helleiner, Eric, and Bessma Momani. 2007. *Slipping into Obscurity? Crisis and Reform at the IMF.* Working Paper No. 16, Waterloo, Ont.: Centre for International Governance Innovation. Available at www.cigionline.org.

Hjertholm, Peter, and Howard White. 2000. Foreign Aid in Historical Perspective. In Tarp 2000, 80-102.

Hoebink, Paul, and Olav Stokke, eds. 2005. *Perspectives on European Development Co-operation: Policy and Performance of Individual Donor Countries and the EU.* Milton Park: Routledge.

Institute for Health Sector Development. 2003a. Mapping of Sector Wide Approaches in Health. Report for the Swedish International Development Cooperation Agency. London: Institute for Health Sector Development.

———. 2003b. Sector-Wide Approaches in Education. Background paper for UNICEF workshop. London: Institute for Health Sector Development.

IDA (International Development Association). 2007. Aid Architecture: An Overview of the Main Trends in Official Development Assistance Flows. February. Available at www.developmentgateway.com.au.

ILO. 1972. Employment, Income and Equality: A Strategy for Increasing Productive Employment in Kenya. Geneva: ILO.

IMF (Independent Evaluation Office). 2007. An IEO Evaluation of Structural Conditionality in IMF-Supported Programs. Washington DC: IMF. Available at www.imf.org.

IMF and World Bank. 2005. PRS Review: Balancing Accountabilities and Scaling Up Results. Washington DC: World Bank. Available at www.worldbank.org.

Isbister, John. 2003. *Promises Not Kept: Poverty and the Betrayal of Third World Development.* 5th ed. Bloomfield, CT: Kumarian Press.

Jenkins, Rob. 2002. The Emergence of the Governance Agenda: Sovereignty, Neo-Liberal Bias, and the Politics of International Development. In Desai and Potter 2002.

Judd. K., ed. 2002. *Gender Budget Initiatives.* New York: UNIFEM.

Kabeer, Naila. 2003. "Institutionalising Gender Equity Goals in the Policy Process." In *Gender Mainstreaming in Poverty Eradication and the MDGs: A Handbook for Policy-makers and Other Stakeholders, ed.* Naila Kabeer. London: Commonwealth Secretariat/IDRC/CIDA.

Kanbur, Ravi. 2001. Economic Policy, Distribution and Poverty: The Nature of Disagreements. Available at www.people.cornell.edu/pages/sk145/papers.htm.

Kanbur, Ravi, ed., Q-Squared. *Qualitative and Quantitative Methods of Poverty Appraisal.* Delhi: Permanent Black, 2005.

Kaufman, Daniel, Aart Kraay, and Pablo Zoida-Lobaton. 1999. Governance Matters. World Bank Policy Research Working Paper 2196. Washington DC: World Bank.

Kessler, Timothy. 2005. Social Policy Dimensions of Water and Energy Utilities: Knowledge Gaps and Research Opportunities. Paper presented at the Arusha Conference, New Frontiers of Social Policy. December 12-15. Available at www.worldbank.org/socialpolicy.

Kharas, Homi. 2007. The New Reality of Aid. Paper presented at the Brookings Blum Roundtable. Available at www. brookings.edu.

Killick, Tony. 1999. *Making Adjustment Work for the Poor.* ODI Poverty Briefing 5. London: ODI. Available at www.odi.org.uk.

———. 2002. Aid Conditionality. In Desai and Potter 2002, 480-84.

———. 2005. Don't Throw Money at Africa. *IDS Bulletin* 36, no. 3 (September): 14-19.

Klugman, J., ed. 2002. *A Sourcebook for Poverty Reduction Stategies.* 2 vols. Washington DC: World Bank.

Korten, David C. 1980. Community Organization and Rural Development: A Learning Process Approach. *Public Administration Review* (September/October): 480-511.

Kothari, Uma. 2006. From Colonialism to Development: Continuities and Divergences. *Journal of Commonwealth and Comparative Politics* 44, no. 1: 118–36.

Kothari, Uma, and Martin Minogue, eds. 2002. *Development Theory and Practice: Critical Perspectives.* Basingstoke: Palgrave.

Kurlantzick, Joshua. 2007. *Charm Offensive: How China's Soft Power Is Transforming the World.* New Haven, CT: Yale University Press.

Lammers, Ellen. 2008. Aiming Global: Swedish Debates on International Development. *The Broker* 9 (August). Available at www.thebrokeronline.eu.

Lancaster, Carol. 2007. *Foreign Aid: Diplomacy, Development, Domestic Politics.* Chicago: The University of Chicago Press.

Lancaster, Carol. 2008. *George Bush's Foreign Aid: Transformation or Chaos?* Washington DC: Center for Global Development.

Land, T., and V. Hauck. 2003. Building Coherence between Sector Reforms and Decentralization: Do SWAps Provide the Missing Link? Discussion Paper No. 49. Maastricht: European Centre for Development Policy Management, 2003. Available at www.ecdpm.org.

Lavergne, Réal, and Anneli Alba. 2003. CIDA Primer on Program-Based Approaches. Gatineau, Quebec: CIDA Policy Branch. Available at www.acdi-cida.gc.ca.

Lawson, Andrew, David Booth, A. Harding, and F. Naschold. 2003. General Budget Support Evaluability Study Phase 1: Synthesis Report. Evaluation Report EV643. East Kilbride: DFID. Available at www.dfid.gov.uk.

Leach, Melissa, Robin Mearns, and Ian Scoones. 1997. Environmental Entitlements: A Conceptual Framework for Understanding the Institutional Dynamics of Environmental Change. IDS Discussion Paper No. 359, Brighton: IDS.

Lewis, David, and David Mosse, eds. 2006. *Development Brokers and Translators: The Ethnography of Aid and Agencies.* Bloomfield, CT: Kumarian Press.

Lewis, Stephen. 2005. *Race against Time.* Toronto: House of Anansi Press.

Lewis, W. Arthur. 1954. Economic Development with Unlimited Supplies of Labour. *The Manchester School* 22, no. 2: 139-91.

Lin, Justin Yifu. 2007. Development and Transition: Idea, Strategy and Viability. Cambridge University Marshall Lectures. October 31–November 1.

Lipton, Michael. 1977. *Why Poor People Stay Poor: Urban Bias in World Development.* London: Temple Smith.

Lundberg, Matthias, and Lynn Squire. 1999. The Simultaneous Evolution of Growth and Inequality. Mimeo. Washington DC: World Bank.

Mallaby, Sebastian. 2005. *The World's Banker: A Story of Failed States, Financial Crises, and the Wealth and Poverty of Nations.* New Haven, CT: Yale University Press.

Maluccio, John, and Rafael Flores. 2004. *Impact Evaluation of a Conditional Cash Transfer Program: The Nicaraguan Red de Protección Social.* IFPRI Discussion Paper No. 184. Washington DC: IFPRI. Available at www.ifpri.org.

Manji, Firoze, and Carl O'Coill. 2002. The Missionary Position: NGOs and Development in Africa. Mimeo. Available at www.fahamu.org.

Manor, James. 2005. Introduction. *IDS Bulletin* 36, no. 3 (September): 1-7.

Manor, James, ed. 2007. *Aid That Works: Successful Development in Fragile States.* Washington DC: World Bank.

Mansuri, Ghazala, and Vijayendra Rao. 2004. Community–Based and –Driven Development: A Critical Review. *The World Bank Research Observer* 19, no. 1: 1-39.

Maxwell, Simon. 2006. What's Next in International Development? Perspectives from the 20% Club and the 0.2% Club. ODI Working Paper 270. London. Available at www.odi.org.uk.

Ministerie van Buitenlandse Zaken. *Het Nederlandse Afrikabeleid 1998-2006: Evaluatie van de Bilaterale Samenwerking.* No. 308. The Hague: IOB Evaluaties (February). Available at www.minbuza.nl.

Mkandawire, Thandika, and Charles C. Soludo, eds. 2002. *African Voices on Structural Adjustment: A Companion to Our Continent Our Future.* Dakar, Senegal: Council for the Development of Social Science Research in Africa; Africa World Press. Available at www.idrc.ca.

Morrison, D. R. 1998, *Aid and Ebb Tide: A History of CIDA and Canadian Development Assistance.* Waterloo, ON: Wilfrid Laurier University Press.

Mosley, Paul. 1987. *Overseas Aid: Its Defence and Reform.* Brighton: Wheatsheaf Books.

Mosley, Paul, and Marion J. Eeckhout. 2000. From Project Aid to Programme Assistance. In Tarp 2000, 131-53.

Mosse, David. 2005. Global Governance and the Ethnography of International Aid. In Mosse and Lewis 2005, 1-36.

Mosse, David, and David Lewis, eds. 2005. *The Aid Effect: Giving and Governing in International Development.* London: Pluto Press.

Mosse, David, and David Lewis. 2006. Theoretical Approaches to Brokerage and Translation in Development. In Lewis and Mosse 2006, 1-26.

Murphy, Craig N. 2006. *The United Nations Development Programme: A Better Way?* Cambridge: Cambridge University Press.

Narayan, Deepa. 1997. *Voices of the Poor: Poverty and Social Capital in Tanzania.* ESSD Studies and Monographs Series No. 20. Washington DC: World Bank.

Natsios, Andrew S. 2006. Five Debates on International Development: The US Perspective. *Development Policy Review* 24, no. 2: 131-39.

OECD DAC. Annual. *Development Co-operation Report.* Paris: OECD. Available at www.oecd.org.

———. 1995. Shaping the Twenty-first Century: The Contribution of Development Co-operation. Paris: OECD. Available at www.oecd.org.

———. 2002. *Gender Equality in Sector Wide Approaches: A Reference Guide.* Paris: OECD DAC. Available at www.oecd.org.

———. 2003a. Harmonising Donor Practices for Effective Aid Delivery: Good Practice Papers. Paris: OECD DAC. Available at www.oecd.org.

———. 2003b. *Promoting Pro-Poor Growth: Practical Guide to Ex Ante Poverty Impact Assessment.* DAC Guidelines and Reference Series. Available at www.oecd.org.

———. 2005. Lessons Learned in the Use of Power and Drivers of Change Analyses in Development Cooperation. Network on Governance. Available at www.gsdcr.org.

———. 2006. "The Challenge of Capacity Development: Working Towards Good Practice." Network on Governance. DCD/DAC/GOVNET (2005)5REV1. Paris: OECD. Available at www.oecd.org.

———. 2007. Aid Effectiveness: 2006 Survey on Monitoring the Paris Declaration. Overview of the Results. Paris: OECD. Available at www.oecd.org.

Ostrom, Elinor, Clark Gibson, Sujai Shivakumar, and Krister Andersson. 2002. Aid, Incentives, and Sustainability: An Analysis of Development Co-operation. Stockholm: Swedish International Development Co-operation Agency. Available at www.sti.ch.

Owusu, Francis. 2003. Pragmatism and the Gradual Shift from Dependency to Neoliberalism: World Bank, African Leaders, and Development Policy in Africa. *World Development* 31, no. 10: 1655-72.

Pearson, Lester. 1969. Partners in Development: Report of the Commission on International Development. New York: Praeger Publishers.

Poku, N. K., and A. Whiteside. 2002. Global Health and the Politics of Governance: An Introduction. *Third World Quarterly* 23, no. 2: 191-95.

Radelet, Steven. 2007. Strengthening U.S. Development Assistance. In Brainard 2007b, 93-119.

Rajan, Raghuram G., and Arvind Subramanian. 2005. *What Undermines Aid's Impact on Growth?* IMF Working Paper WP/05/126. Washington DC: IMF.

Ravallion, Martin. 2008. Are There Lasting Impacts of Aid to Poor Areas ? Evidence from Rural China. World Bank Working Paper No. 4084. Washington DC: World Bank.

Ravallion, Martin, et al. 2008. China Is Poorer Than We Thought, But No Less Successful in the Fight against Poverty. World Bank Working Paper 4621. Washington DC: World Bank.

Rawlings, L. B., L. Sherburne-Benz, and J. Van Dommelen. 2004. *Evaluating Social Funds: A Cross-Country Analysis of Community Investments.* Regional and Sectoral Studies. Washington DC: World Bank.

Reeves, Hazel, and Sally Baden. 2000. *Gender and Development: Concepts and Definitions.* Bridge Report No. 55, Brighton: IDS Sussex. Available at www.bridge.ids.ac.uk.

Rice, Condoleezza. 2008. Rethinking the National Interest: American Realism for a New World. *Foreign Affairs* (July/August): 2-26.

Riddell, Abby. 2002. Synthesis Report on Development Agency Policies and Perspectives on Programme-based Approaches. Paper prepared for the Forum on Accountability and Risk Management under Program-based Approaches, Ottawa, Canada, 19-21 June. Available at www.sti.ch.

Riddell, Roger C. 2007. *Does Foreign Aid Really Work?* Oxford: Oxford University Press.

Robb, C. 2001. Linking Participatory Poverty Assessments to Poverty Reduction Strategy Papers. Mimeo. Washington DC: World Bank.

Roodman, David. 2007. *Macro Aid Effectiveness Research: A Guide for the Perplexed.* Centre for Global Development Working Paper No. 135. Washington DC: Centre for Global Development. Available at www.cgdev.org.

Rostow, Walt Whitman. 1960. *The Stages of Economic Growth: A Non-communist Manifesto.* Cambridge: Cambridge University Press.

Sage, Caroline, and Michael Woolcock. 2007. Breaking Legal Inequality Traps: New Approaches to Building Justice Systems for the Poor in Developing Countries. BWPI Working Paper No. 17. Manchester: BWPI.

Salemink, Oscar. 2006. Translating, Interpreting, and Practicing Civil Society in Vietnam: A Tale of Calculated Misunderstandings. In Lewis and Mosse 2006, 101-26.

Sachs, Jeffrey. 2005. *The End of Poverty: Economic Possibilities For Our Times.* New York: Penguin Press.

Schulpen, Lau. 2005. All in the Name of Quality: Dutch Development Cooperation in the 1990s. In Hoebink and Stokke 2005, 406-47.

Scoones, Ian. 1998. Sustainable Rural Livelihoods: A Framework for Analysis, Working Paper 72. Brighton: IDS.

Seguino, Stephanie. Plus Ça Change? Evidence on Global Trends in Gender Norms and Stereotypes. *Feminist Economics* 13, no. 2 (2006): 1–28.

Sen, Amartya. 1981. *Poverty and Famines: An Essay on Entitlement and Deprivation.* Oxford: Oxford University Press.

———. 1999. *Development as Freedom.* New York: Alfred A. Knopf.

Shanks, Edwin, and Carrie Turk. 2003. Refining Policy with the Poor: Local Consultations on the Draft Poverty Reduction and Growth Strategy in Vietnam. Policy Research Working Paper No. 2968. Washington DC: World Bank.

Sida, Department for Democracy and Social Development. 2006. Power Analysis—Experience. Concept Note. Stockholm: Sida.

Simon, David. 2002. Neo-liberalism, Structural Adjustment and Poverty Reduction Strategies. In Desai and Potter 2002, 86-92.

———, ed. 2006. *Fifty Key Thinkers on Development.* London: Routledge.

Smyth, I. 2007. Talking of Gender: Words and Meanings in Development Organisations. *Development in Practice* 17, no. 4: 582–88.

Sserumaga, S. 2003. Sector-Wide Approaches in the Administration of Justice and Promoting the Rule of Law: The Ugandan Experience. Paper for the Seminar on the Rule of Law, European Initiative for Democracy and Human Rights, 3-4 July, Brussels.

Stern, Nick. 2002. Dynamic Development: Innovation and Inclusion. Munich Lectures in Economics. November 19.

Stewart, Frances, and Michael Wang. 2003. *Do PRSPs Empower Poor Countries and Disempower the World Bank, Or Is It the Other Way Around?* Working Papers Series, Queen Elizabeth House, University of Oxford. Available at www.qeh.ox.ac.uk.

Subramanian, Arvind. 2007. A Farewell to Arms. *The Wall Street Journal* (August 22). Available at www.cgdev.org.

Tarp, Finn, ed. (with Peter Hjertholm). 2000. *Foreign Aid and Development: Lessons Learnt and Directions for the Future.* Copenhagen: University of Copenhagen.

Taylor, John. Environment-Poverty Linkages: Managing Natural Resources in China. In Bass et al. 2005, 73-99.

Tendler, Judith. 1975. *Inside Foreign Aid.* Baltimore: Johns Hopkins University Press.

Thanh, Hoangh Xuan. 2005. *Participatory Poverty Research and Policy Influencing in PRSP Processes: The Vietnam Case.* Participatory Learning and Action No. 51, London: IIED. Available at www.iied.org.

Theis, Joachim, and Claire O'Kane. 2005. Children's Participation, Civil Rights and Power. In Gready and Ensor 2005, 156-70.

Thérien, Jean-Philippe. 2002. Debating Foreign Aid: Right Versus Left. *Third World Quarterly* 23, no. 3: 449-66.

Thobani, M. 1983. Charging User Fees for Social Services: The Case of Education in Malawi. World Bank Staff Working Paper 572. Washington DC: World Bank.

Thorbecke, Erik. 2000. The Evolution of the Development Doctrine and the Role of Foreign Aid. In Tarp 2000, 17-47.

Uvin, Peter. 2004. *Human Rights and Development*. Bloomfield, CT: Kumarian Press.

——. 2007. From the Right to Development to the Rights-based Approach: How "Human Rights" Entered Development. *Development in Practice* 17, no. 4: 597-606.

UN (United Nations). 2002. Report of the International Conference on Financing for Development, Monterrey, Mexico, 18-22 March. Available at www.un.org.

UNDP. Various years. *Human Development Report.* New York: Oxford University Press.

——. 2003. Poverty Reduction and Human Rights. A Practice Note. New York: UNDP. Available at www.undp.org.

UN Millennium Development Project. 2005. *Investing in Development: Millennium Development Goals*. London: Earthscan.

United Nations Uganda. 2005. United Nations Development Assistance Framework of Uganda, 2006-2010. Kampala: The United Nations System.

Wahlberg, Katarina. 2008. Food Aid for the Hungry? *Global Policy Forum* (January). Available at www.globalpolicy.org.

Walford, Veronica. 2003.Defining and Evaluating SWAps: A Paper for the Inter-Agency Group on SWAps and Development Cooperation. London: Institute for Health Sector Development.

White, Howard. 2005. The Case for Doubling Aid. *IDS Bulletin* 36, no. 3 (September): 8-13.

Wolfensohn, James, and Stanley Fischer. 2000. The Comprehensive Development Framework (CDF) and Poverty Reduction Strategy Papers. Washington DC: IMF, April 5. Available at www.imf.org.

Woolcock, Michael. 2007. Higher Education, Policy Schools, and Development Studies: What Should Masters Degree Students Be Taught? *Journal of International Development* 19: 55-73.

World Bank. Various years. *World Development Report*. New York: Oxford University Press.

——. 1989. *Sub-Saharan Africa: From Crisis to Sustainable Growth*. Washington DC: World Bank.

——. 1994. *Governance: The World Bank's Experience*. Washington DC: World Bank.

——. 1998. The Money—and Ideas—of Aid. *World Bank Policy and Research Bulletin* 9, no. 4 (October-December).

———. 2001. *PRSP Source Book, draft for comments.* Available at www .worldbank.org/poverty/strategies.

——— (Operations Evaluation Department). 2003. *Toward Country-led Development: a Multi-partner Evaluation of the Comprehensive Development Framework.* Washington DC: World Bank, Operations Evaluation Department. Available at www.worldbank.org.

——— (Social Development Department). 2003. *Social Analysis Sourcebook: Incorporating Social Dimensions into Bank-Supported Projects.* Washington DC: World Bank, Social Development Department.

———. 2004. *Reducing Poverty Sustaining Growth: Scaling Up Poverty Reduction.* A Global Learning Process and Conference in Shanghai. Washington DC: World Bank. Available at www.worldbank.org.

———. 2007. *China and the World Bank: A Partnership for Innovation.* Washington DC: World Bank.

World Neighbors. 1994. Bangladesh: Microcredit. The Quiet Revolution series. Documentary. World Neighbors, CASID.

Wuyts, Marc, Maureen Mackintosh, and Tom Hewitt. 1992. *Development Policy and Public Action.* Oxford: Oxford University Press/The Open University.

Zehra, Maheen. Creating Space for Civil Society in an Impoverished Environment in Pakistan. In Bass et al. 2005, 20-43.

About the Author

Arjan de Haan's career has straddled the practitioner and academic sides of international development. He joined the Institute of Social Studies in The Hague, the Netherlands, in April 2009, where his teaching and research focus on the role of social policy in development.

Before that, from 2006 to 2008, he worked for DFID in its office in China, where he managed rural development and knowledge programs, and contributed to the UK response to the Wenchuan earthquake in 2008. He developed support to South-South learning, research to articulate the lessons from China's development path, and an international workshop on international experience with policy responses to economic crises.

During 2005–6 he was visiting professor at the University of Guelph, Ontario, Canada, where he started to work on this book after teaching undergraduate courses on international development. He published *Reclaiming Social Policy* (Palgrave Macmillan, 2007) and has continued to work on this theme, including a focus on social policy experiences of the emerging economies of Asia (Sage India, forthcoming), and in the context of the 2008 financial meltdown.

During 1998–2005 he worked for DFID as well. During 2004–5 in DFID's Policy Division in London he initiated policy analysis on inequality and social exclusion for the Growth and Investment Group and in collaboration with the authors of the World Development Report on inequality. He was social development adviser in the Orissa program of the DFID India office during 2001–4, where he advised on the content of budget support, started a new civil society program, and supported work on gender budgeting and poverty analysis. From 1998 to 2001 he was social development adviser in London, where he managed programs of social-science research, worked with World Bank colleagues on strengthening processes of participation in PRSPs, and developed policy analysis for the emerging social protection agenda.

Before joining DFID, Arjan worked at and directed the Poverty Research Unit at the University of Sussex, where he led innovative analysis on social exclusion and poverty monitoring. He led the analysis of migration in the IDS program on sustainable livelihoods and published on the role of migration, including in an edited book with Ben Rogaly, *Labour Mobility and Rural Society* (Frank Cass, 2002).

His PhD at Erasmus University Rotterdam also focused on labor migration, particularly the rural-urban transition in Eastern India.

Arjan is a proud husband and father of two young children. He loves soccer and baseball, but not, it has to be admitted to the Canadian students who inspired this book, ice hockey.

Index

Also from Kumarian Press...

International Development

The World Bank and the Gods of Lending
Steve Berkman

Southern Exposure: International Development and the Global South in the Twenty-First Century
Barbara Thomas-Slayter

Players and Issues in International Aid
Paula Hoy

New and Forthcoming:

A Fragile Balance: Re-examining the History of Foreign Aid, Security and Diplomacy
Louis A. Picard and Terry Buss

Civil Society under Strain: Counter-Terrorism Policy, Civil Society, and Aid Post-9/11
Edited by Jude Howell and Jeremy Lind

Freedom from Want: The Remarkable Success Story of BRAC, the Global Grassroots Organization That's Winning the Fight against Poverty
Ian Smillie

Coping with Facts: A Skeptic's Guide to the Problem of Development
Adam Fforde

Visit Kumarian Press at **www.kpbooks.com** or call **toll-free 800.232.0223** for a complete catalog.

Kumarian Press, located in Sterling, Virginia, is a forward-looking, scholarly press that promotes active international engagement and an awareness of global connectedness.